# Praise for *Dealing with Feeling*

"*Dealing with Feeling* makes a big promise—and delivers. With warmth, wisdom, and utmost clarity, Marc Brackett explains where our emotions come from and how, specifically, we can manage and learn from them. I truly loved this brilliant book and will recommend it to anyone and everyone! It's that good." —Angela Duckworth, #1 *New York Times* bestselling author of *Grit* and professor of psychology at the University of Pennsylvania

"An insightful read about how to handle the space between stimulus and response. Marc Brackett is a widely respected expert on emotional intelligence, and his book offers a lucid look at practical ways to improve at managing feelings." —Adam Grant, #1 *New York Times* bestselling author of *Think Again* and *Hidden Potential* and host of the podcast *ReThinking*

"*Dealing with Feeling* takes us on a brilliant and heartfelt journey to master one of life's most essential skills: managing our emotions. At a time when stress and worry are dominating so many people's lives, Brackett's blend of personal story and science reminds us that a better path—with more peace, joy, and fulfillment—is indeed within our grasp."
—Vivek Murthy, former surgeon general of the United States and *New York Times* bestselling author of *Together*

"In *Dealing with Feeling*, Marc Brackett teaches readers how to master the life-changing skill of managing their reactions to life's inevitable challenges. In this transformative book, Brackett offers a comprehensive road map to emotional well-being. A must-read for anyone looking to thrive in today's emotionally charged world—which should be everyone!"
—Lisa Damour, *New York Times* bestselling author of *The Emotional Lives of Teenagers*, *Under Pressure*, and *Untangled*

"We've been taught to hustle, achieve, and move fast—but not to feel. I followed that path for years, until I realized something was missing.

*Dealing with Feeling* helped me understand that our emotions aren't detours—they're directions. When we learn to listen to them and use them wisely, they lead us to deeper relationships, more meaningful work, and a truer version of ourselves."

—Ben Silbermann, cofounder and executive chairman of Pinterest

"In this wonderfully written and lively book, Marc Brackett gives us the tools to understand and manage emotions with wisdom and skill. *Dealing with Feeling* is essential reading for anyone seeking a richer emotional life and a deeper understanding of the value of emotional intelligence."

—Peter Salovey, president emeritus and Sterling Professor of Psychology at Yale University

"In a world transformed by AI and constant change, *Dealing with Feeling* should be required reading for all leaders. Marc Brackett makes a compelling case that emotion regulation isn't a soft skill—it's a strategic advantage for leading teams, building ethical products, and thriving under pressure."

—Deborah Quazzo, managing partner of GSV Ventures and cofounder of the ASU+GSV Summit

"Life is tough, and now more than ever we need the skills to navigate our emotions with confidence. In this practical and compelling book, Brackett delivers science-backed strategies to help us manage our feelings with clarity, strength, and purpose—even in life's most challenging moments. This is the essential guide to thriving in an unpredictable world."

—Kenneth Cole, designer and founder of the Mental Health Coalition

"Marc Brackett's powerful and kaleidoscopic book *Dealing with Feeling* declares with grace and wit and style that emotion regulation is the single most important skill we can develop in today's world. We live in shattered times and Brackett wants to help us put the mosaic back together."

—Colum McCann, *New York Times* bestselling author and cofounder of Narrative 4

# DEALING
## WITH
## FEELING

Also by Marc Brackett
*Permission to Feel*

# DEALING WITH FEELING

## Use Your Emotions to Create the Life You Want

### Marc Brackett

FOUNDING DIRECTOR, YALE CENTER FOR EMOTIONAL INTELLIGENCE
PROFESSOR, YALE CHILD STUDY CENTER

CELADON
BOOKS
NEW YORK

The names and identifying characteristics of some persons described in this book have been changed, as have dates, places, and other details of events depicted in the book.

DEALING WITH FEELING. Copyright © 2025 by Marc Brackett. All rights reserved. Printed in the United States of America. For information, address Celadon Books, a division of Macmillan Publishers, 120 Broadway, New York, NY 10271. EU Representative: Macmillan Publishers Ireland Ltd., 1st Floor, The Liffey Trust Centre, 117–126 Sheriff Street Upper, Dublin 1, DO1 YC43.

www.celadonbooks.com

Charts courtesy of the author

The Library of Congress Cataloging-in-Publication Data is available upon request.

ISBN 978-1-250-32959-2 (hardcover)
ISBN 978-1-250-32960-8 (ebook)

The publisher of this book does not authorize the use or reproduction of any part of this book in any manner for the purpose of training artificial intelligence technologies or systems. The publisher of this book expressly reserves this book from the Text and Data Mining exception in accordance with Article 4(3) of the European Union Digital Single Market Directive 2019/790.

Our books may be purchased in bulk for specialty retail/wholesale, literacy, corporate/premium, educational, and subscription box use. Please contact MacmillanSpecialMarkets@macmillan.com.

First Edition: 2025

10 9 8 7 6 5 4 3 2 1

*To everyone striving for deeper connections, greater success,
and lasting well-being*

# Contents

Introduction: A Life-Changing Skill That Must Be Learned     1

## Part One: Where Are We Now?

1. Imagine a World     9
2. Seven Reasons We Can't Deal with Our Feelings     19

## Part Two: Definitions

3. What Is Emotion Regulation?     39
4. Emotion Regulation in Action     56
5. What Is Co-Regulation?     63
6. Co-Regulation in Action     78

## Part Three: Building Blocks

7. The Hidden Driver of Regulation: Rethinking Your Beliefs About Emotions     91

8. From Chaos to Clarity: Labeling Your
   Emotions Precisely                                        107

## Part Four: Strategies

9. Quieting Your Mind and Body                               127
10. Redirecting Your Thoughts                                147
11. Cultivating Your Emotional Strength Through
    Relationships                                            172
12. Optimizing Your Emotion Regulation Budget                195

## Part Five: Practice Makes Permanent

13. How Children Learn to Regulate Emotions                  223
14. Becoming the Best Version of Yourself                    239
Epilogue: A Vision Realized                                  257

*Your Practical Guide to Building Emotion*
   *Regulation Skills*                                       *265*
*Resources*                                                  *277*
*Acknowledgments*                                            *279*
*References*                                                 *283*

# Introduction

## A LIFE-CHANGING SKILL THAT MUST BE LEARNED

*Forces beyond your control can take away everything you possess except one thing, your freedom to choose how you will respond to the situation.*
—Viktor E. Frankl, *Man's Search for Meaning*

Think of a lens. Here, take it in your hand.

I want you to hold this lens up to your eye and look at your life—all of it, past and present.

Look at everything that's ever happened to you, every experience, then look at the emotions you felt—anger or sadness or stress or insecurity or any of those other feelings we all have from time to time. Look at the pleasant emotions, too, like joy and contentment and satisfaction and love and pride and hope.

Now, focus on the things you said or did or thought in response to those emotions.

Your kids misbehaved. Your boss asked questions about a project you managed. An old friend reminded you of something embarrassing you did long ago. You suddenly felt a weird pain in your chest.

In response to those things, what did you do? How did you react?

Maybe you screamed at your kids. Or you spent the rest of the week fearing you'd be fired. Or you got mad at your friend but didn't say a word. Or you spent a sleepless night scared you might be seriously ill.

When you experienced challenging moments, did you lose your cool or fly off the handle or freak out or melt down? Was your spirit crushed? Did you cower in fear? Were your hopes dashed? Did you give up on a dream?

Again, let's not examine unhappy emotions only. Look through the lens at the first time you fell in love, or when you got a promotion at work and couldn't wait to celebrate, or when you kicked your junk food habit and got healthy, or when someone praised you for being kind. How did you handle those feelings?

Keep using your lens to examine every time an emotion influenced you to act one way or another, and now ask yourself: *Did those actions help me, or did they hurt me? Did I deal with my feelings, especially the difficult ones, in ways that improved my life or made it worse? And how did my responses affect the people around me, the people I love? Was I my best possible self for them or some other version of me?*

Taken all together, these moments determined the course of your life. You felt an emotion, and you reacted by saying or thinking or doing something in response.

*But what about the things that were beyond my control?*, you could fairly ask. It's true, you can't be responsible for what other people do and say. But no matter how they behaved, you were the one who felt the emotion and reacted to it.

I'm going to say something that might strike you now as an exaggeration, but I'm hoping that by the time you finish this book, you'll agree: Virtually everything that has ever happened in your life—good, bad, happy, sad, frustrating, satisfying, joyous, discouraging, depressing—was influenced by how you responded to your emotions. How you dealt with your feelings.

I'll go even further: Pretty much everything that has gone right in your life was the result of you having an intelligent, helpful response to an emotion you experienced. And nearly every time something went wrong—meaning whenever an outcome was not the one you wished for and did not serve your goals—it was because you had an unwise reaction to what you felt. You did or said something you may even have regretted, something you wished you could take back and do over. Of course, there are times when illness or accidents affect us in ways beyond our control; even then, our responses to these situations make a difference. But there are no do-overs, only the future where we can do better. And so, from now on, beginning today, I want you to please keep this in mind: The degree to which you will get what you want out of life is equal to how well (or poorly) you deal with your feelings. That alone will make the difference between happiness and sadness, fulfillment and frustration, contentment and disappointment, success and failure.

You might possess extraordinary talents and valuable skills, but learning to regulate your emotions is essential to fully unlocking your potential. On the other hand, if you possess modest abilities but can deal wisely with your feelings, you will likely succeed in most aspects of your life.

Alas, many of us believe that the way we respond to our emotions is an intrinsic part of ourselves, a fixed aspect of our personalities—something at our very core, impossible to change.

Which is simply not true.

That's the message of this book: It's in our power to understand our emotions and decide how we'll respond to them, and there are mindsets, skills, and strategies for doing that which can be taught and must be learned. By learning them, then using them, we'll gain control over our lives and increase our chances of success—at home, at school, at work, and everywhere else.

This does *not* mean we'll try to control our emotions. Or that we'll suddenly be happy all the time. That's impossible. We feel what we feel.

But we *can* choose how we'll respond to those feelings—what we'll say and do and think. How we'll deal. And those choices will make all the difference in our lives.

The epigraph at the top of this introduction is a famous quote from Viktor E. Frankl, a psychologist who arrived at his wisdom when he was a prisoner in the Auschwitz concentration camp. It's impossible to imagine a situation where a human being's inability to control what happens to them could be more complete or more terrifying. Frankl accepted that, yet he also saw that there was one power, one form of control, that could never be taken from him: the ability to decide how he would respond to his fate, how he would deal with his feelings.

Hopefully none of us will live through what Frankl endured. But his truth is also ours: We all have the power to decide how we will respond to whatever life throws at us.

Think of the people we admire—the ones who face enormous challenges and don't give in to the emotional upheaval they experience. We use the expression "grace under pressure" to describe it. The *pressure* is all the intense, triggering emotions we'll ever face. The *grace* is the ability to stop ourselves from reacting in ways we later regret, and instead to deal with our feelings as we know we should—in ways that reflect our best selves.

I am the founding director of the Yale Center for Emotional Intelligence and a professor in the Child Study Center at Yale University. As a psychologist and scientist, I've been researching these issues and teaching these skills for decades.

But it was the arrival of the COVID-19 pandemic that opened my eyes to the profound, often unseen human truths embedded in what I had been studying. When we went into lockdown, the panic, the insecurity, the fear set in. I started receiving hundreds of emails from parents, schools, and corporations around the world trying to help children and adults who were struggling with the extreme emotions they were experiencing.

That made me want to investigate what the average person knows about how to manage their feelings—what they have been taught, how, and by whom. I surveyed thousands of people from all walks of life, and what did I find? That most of us haven't been taught very much about regulating the way we respond to our emotions. The adults I spoke with didn't even have vocabulary to describe their feelings with any precision.

And without that, I knew, they would be unable to identify what they felt or deal with it. Fewer than 10 percent of the people I surveyed said they had learned skills for managing their emotions while growing up at home. Even fewer said they were taught these skills in school or elsewhere.

This book is my attempt to help us all do better in this critical life skill. Based on my research and what other scientists have found, my aim here is to show how we can all learn to deal with our emotions in positive, intentional ways that serve our life goals.

There's no magic involved in dealing with feelings. No one was born knowing how to regulate their emotions. If you can't do it successfully, it's likely because no one ever showed you how. Everything this book teaches is a practical skill, like so much of what you've learned. With practice, we can all deal with our feelings as we've always wished we could.

We'll start with the first steps of the process—shifting our mindsets and cultivating emotional awareness. Next, we'll learn how to deactivate intense, unwanted feelings and find the mental space we need to think about how to respond *before* we react. After that, we'll cover all the strategies and skills that will allow us to respond calmly and wisely to our emotions, one by one.

There's a lot to learn. But it's worth it.

The terrible time of COVID also taught me a personal lesson I'll never forget.

My mother-in-law, who lives in Panama, visited us in the spring of 2020. She was supposed to leave after a few weeks, but then, suddenly, the entire world shut down. Her little visit lasted . . . eight months.

Life under quarantine already had my nerves on edge, and a new housemate added to the challenge. One night, when I was particularly exhausted from a day trying to cope, she said something that set me off. We went back and forth, and not in the nicest ways. Finally, I stopped trying to hide my irritation.

"Marc," she said, "aren't you supposed to be the director of a center for emotional intelligence?"

"Not tonight I'm not!" I snarled and stormed off to bed.

I've told that story many times, just to show that even I'm still learning to deal properly with my feelings, and it usually gets a laugh. But I don't always tell what happened next.

In bed that night, I reflected on my nasty little outburst. I realized that my mother-in-law was right—I actually *am* the director of a center for emotional intelligence, and if I can't handle my emotions any better than I did, what hope is there for everybody else?

Before I fell asleep, I resolved to show up as my best self when I saw my mother-in-law in the morning. When she came into the kitchen, I apologized and made her a cup of coffee.

In that spirit, I offer you a chance to do better, too, and a way to make it happen.

PART ONE

# WHERE ARE WE NOW?

# 1.

# Imagine a World

*Vision without action is merely a dream. Action without vision just passes the time. Vision with action can change the world.*

—Nelson Mandela

Here's what I'd like you to imagine: a world where every human being knows how to deal constructively with their feelings.

Go ahead, imagine it.

No rush, I'll give you another minute.

Okay, maybe another minute won't be enough. There's still a pretty enormous gap between that imaginary world of excellent emotion regulation and the often unhinged one we all inhabit today.

Still, we can dream, and maybe a dream can become a destination, and then a destination can become a reality. It happens.

If it were to happen, this is what we might find.

There's a new CEO, hired from outside the company, which is often a scary time for employees. But this is worse than usual. It's gone straight downhill from day one.

There's something clearly defensive about her vibe, especially when she introduces new ways of doing things. She seems to automatically suspect the team she inherited of resisting her changes. Often, what looks like resistance is just the employees not totally understanding what she wants them to do or why. But she doesn't seem to get that. And nobody wants to be the one to tell her.

You feel as though you're in a challenging spot. On the one hand, you've always been a model employee who receives great feedback and evaluations from your bosses. You know you're a valuable worker, and that means a great deal to you. You don't want to jeopardize that.

But you also can tell that this new boss doesn't see you that way. Maybe she thinks you're not anywhere near her wavelength when it comes to how things should be done. Or maybe she believes you're just not up to the job.

You're not the only one who feels this way—by now you and all your colleagues have shared stories about tense exchanges with the new boss. Gradually, it's turning into an "us against her" situation. A very unhealthy thing.

Here's your dilemma: You feel that as a good employee, you're responsible for trying to break down this wall that's forming and open a line of cooperation and communication. On the other hand, you fear that broaching the subject will make you seem openly resistant and cause the boss to hold it against you, and maybe even retaliate.

You could take the path of least resistance—the route all your co-workers are choosing—and say nothing. But that wouldn't feel right to you.

So, you decide to start the process gently by sending her a note. Something to allow her to consider the message and absorb it calmly without having to react on the spot to the bearer of uncomfortable news. Something that won't trigger her too much. It's risky, but if handled properly it will show your good faith.

Now, what do you say in your email? You can't sugarcoat the situation or sound as though you're trying to curry favor. You're actually a little scared, but you can't let that stop you from taking action. You need to state your case clearly. You have to assume that she, too, operates in good faith. Most of all, you need to sound cooperative and optimistic.

Maybe something like this:

Dear Janet,

It's been six months since you've come on as our CEO and I know we've hit some rough spots. I want to figure out how to work better with you, which is why I'm sending this note. I'd like very much to sit down with you to hear what this period has been like for you, and to find ways to make the future better than the past. I hope you realize we all want to succeed in our jobs and help the company succeed, too. We also want to do our best to help you do your best.

Sincerely,

Mike

You send that note and then you wait. Maybe a little longer than you'd like. You try not to read too much into what that delay might mean. Eventually, you get an email back:

Hi Mike,

I got your note and appreciate what you've shared. Let's find a time we can sit down together and talk through this. I look forward to it.

Best,

Janet

You're driving home from the office. That should make you happy. It used to. Now . . . not so much. It's a problem. But not an easy one to explain, not even to yourself. Definitely not to the person at home waiting for you.

Is it boredom? Maybe.

Is it minor irritations that have built up over the years? Maybe.

Is it something more serious? *Maybe.*

That's what makes it hard to talk about: so many maybes.

So you don't say anything. You learn to live with that sense of dread and anxiety that now comes every day while driving home from the office. Because even those emotions are preferable to what might replace them if you ever said how you honestly feel.

At work, it's totally different. There, the energy is positive. You know what to do to make good things happen. And you're surrounded by other people also working toward the same goals. You're part of a team. You're appreciated and admired. You're loved. It feels great.

It's hard to leave that at the end of every day knowing what awaits you.

So sometimes you and your colleagues extend the party over cocktails. Or you stop at the gym. Same great vibe there. You know what to do to get the feedback you desire. It's a high.

But at some point you have to head home. Where it's a low.

Perhaps other people—perhaps *most* people—accept that existence as a part of being an adult human being. You can't always get what you want. Things could always be worse. So, they abide. They settle. If necessary, they ignore their feelings and go a little numb.

Night after night, their dinner conversations are dull or nonexistent. Date night is a chore. Naturally, the sex suffers. It's difficult to hide your feelings there.

That's really a hazardous condition, because at a certain point you, like others in similar situations, might begin looking elsewhere for what you once got at home.

There's another popular alternative—half the couples you know are either divorced or on the way. Maybe they could have said or done something to avert that outcome, but they didn't have the nerve or the desire to try.

This is not how it will go for you.

Instead, tonight at dinner, you'll work up your courage, take a few deep breaths, look the person you love in the eye, and say what must be said, perhaps the scariest phrase in the English language, the short, simple statement that could lead to, well . . . who knows where?

To hurt feelings and tears and anger? To the admission that you both have work you need to do? That's a possibility.

To the discovery that your partner has been feeling those same awful things, and maybe even more deeply? That's another.

There, at the dinner table together, you will face a frightening moment of truth. You feel it in your gut. This could turn into something totally unexpected, something life-changing, and not in a pleasant way. We know all the metaphors—a snowball rolling downhill, picking up size and speed, gaining terrible momentum; or pulling a loose thread and watching the whole garment unravel.

Even knowing all this, and the awful fate you could be risking, you find the emotional courage to say the dangerous, necessary words:

"Honey, we need to talk."

Your sixteen-year-old sidles into the kitchen to gulp down the usual four-minute breakfast before school. You notice that something is a little off today. It's nothing obvious, just a weird energy. You've been observing this kid closely since birth. You can tell.

"Good morning," you say, a little louder than normal, just to gauge the response.

"Hi." A mumble. No eye contact. Body language signaling *Do not disturb. Keep your distance.* Because you're an emotionally intelligent parent, you do just the opposite.

"Hey," you say, "everything okay?"

A shrug. But a shrug that speaks volumes.

This is a pivot point for most interactions like this. For the parent, it can be easy to tell yourself, *Hey, I asked my kid what's the problem and they wouldn't tell me. I assume it's something they want to handle on their own, so I'm not going to insist and push my child further away. Better just to monitor the situation.* And there are times when that is the emotionally intelligent, truly sensitive way to respond. Depending on the moment, gentle prodding can come across as parental bullying.

Or, instead of with silence, your kid responds in a snarky way, which gets you off the hook since it's clear this child has zero intention of opening up or seeking your help. If they're honest, lots of parents will admit that they're a little scared to find out what's troubling their kids. Is it drugs? Sex? Self-harm? Maybe you're better off not knowing, because then you'd have to do something, but *what*?

For the kid—well, we've all been there back when we were young. Parents tend to be clueless at moments like this. It can be torture explaining whatever's going on in language that Mom or Dad can understand. Better to let it go.

Despite all that, you push on.

"Come on," you say. "Let's talk for a few minutes."

"I'll miss my bus."

"I'll drive you to school on my way to work. We can talk in the car."

"Dad, it's nothing. Everything's fine."

"I'm glad everything's fine. But tell me what's going on anyway."

"Nothing."

"Okay, you know that's not a real answer. Something is always going on."

"Just the usual stuff."

"Everything good with your friends?"

"Yeah."

"Everything good with basketball?'

"Yeah."

"You and your girlfriend are getting along?"

"Dad, she's fine."

"How are you doing with your grades?"

"Okay."

You heard something in that *okay*. It sounded different from all the other perfunctory answers.

"How's chemistry?"

"Same."

Same is not good. Same means there's still a problem.

"He still giving you a hard time?"

"Dad, he's that way with everybody."

What your child is telling you by trying not to tell you is that the class bully is still at it. You can hear it between the lines.

"Okay, but I'm not everybody's father; I'm yours. And your problem is my problem. So how are we going to handle this?"

Silence. But you see a tear beginning to form in the corner of your child's eye. Devastating.

"Tell me, does the teacher know?"

"No."

"Okay, so maybe that's where we should start."

"No! I'm not a baby. I'll handle it."

"I know you will," you say, "but let's discuss *how*. Let's have a talk about the best way forward."

"Can we talk about it later?"

"Let's talk about it now," you say.

At this point, the chances are decent that together you'll come up with a few possible solutions for the bully problem. More important, you've made it clear that it's okay to talk about difficult—in this case, even embarrassing—feelings. You've let your child know that you care, and that it's possible to find useful strategies for handling difficult situations, and that it's smart to get help finding them.

"Okay," your kid says, now looking you straight in the eye, "if it were you, how do you think you would've handled it?"

At the start of the school day, a little boy walks into his kindergarten classroom and goes straight to the Mood Meter.

It's a square bulletin board divided into quadrants: One is green, one yellow, one red, and one blue. Green signifies a mood that is pleasant and calm; yellow is also pleasant but more energized; red is energized but unpleasant; blue is low-key and also unpleasant.

To one side of the board, on a shelf, are small photos of each child in the class. Every morning when the children arrive, their first task is to pin their picture on the quadrant that matches how they feel.

There are pictures all over the board.

The boy takes his photo, places it in the blue quadrant, then goes to his seat.

A moment later a girl enters, puts her portrait in the green quadrant, then studies the rest of the board.

She walks over to the boy and says, "Hi."

"Hi," he says.

"Why are you in the blue?" she asks.

"My dog is sick."

"How are you feeling?" the girl asks.

"Sad," he says.

"Do you want to come with me to the strategy wheel?" she asks.

"Okay," he says, and rises, and they walk together to a carnival-type wheel of fortune next to the Mood Meter.

Taped all around the wheel are notes of the students' own ideas for good ways to deal with difficult feelings.

"Okay," the girl says, "spin it."

The boy gives it a whirl. It stops on a note, which he reads aloud.

"It says, 'Read a book you like.'"

"Do you want to try and read a book?" the girl asks.

"I don't know," he says. "Maybe."

"Spin it again," the girl says.

He gives it another whirl and reads the note where it lands.

"It says, 'Take a walk.'"

"Do you want to?" the girl asks him.

"Not really," he says.

"Okay," she says. "Spin again."

He gives it another try.

"It says, 'Draw a picture to make you feel calm.'"

"Can you do that?" the girl asks.

"I guess."

"Can you draw a picture of you playing with your dog?" she asks.

"I'll try."

They return to their seats. The boy takes out crayons and paper and draws a picture of himself and his dog, with a smile on its face, at the park. He stares at it awhile, then rises, goes back to the Mood Meter, and moves his photo into the green.

This final bit of imagining is the most challenging one.

Imagine a world where we all deal with our feelings in healthy, intelligent ways. Without letting our emotions control us or push us to say or do things that harm us and the people around us.

I don't mean that each of us would properly regulate how we respond to our feelings 100 percent of the time. What I mean is that we would always try and mostly succeed, and when we fell short, we would recognize where we went wrong and do better next time. I mean that the difficult emotions like rage, envy, resentment, anxiety, despair, and all the rest would no longer have the power to damage our relationships and destroy our well-being.

In that world, even the big picture would look different. We would choose only representatives who truly represent us—our best selves. The people we'd elect, the authorities we'd empower, the administrators who run our institutions would automatically consider how their decisions influence our ability to deal with our feelings.

Even on hot-button issues, they wouldn't act in anger or in haste. When they detected hostilities rising, they would defuse them and seek solutions. They would craft their public statements keeping in mind how everyone—even their opponents—would receive them. They would be honest about their own emotions and deal with them before their impulses hardened into battle lines. Those leaders would set an example for all the administrators and institutions that have enormous impacts on our daily lives. Educators would acknowledge the power of emotion in schools, for teachers and for students. They would set emotional health as *the* top priority, knowing that otherwise teachers can't teach, and students can't learn.

Today, policymakers often use checklists to measure the impact of their decisions on the environment, on corporate governance, on equity, and on other criteria. Imagine a world where public policies are judged by how they affect the ability of people—children included—to handle their emotions.

How would our lives be different in such a world? Many of the scourges of contemporary living—the violence, the mistrust, the division, the rage, the mental illnesses of depression and anxiety, and the burnout—would lose their influence over our society.

They'd be replaced with . . . what?

Something better, that's for sure.

So—how do we get there?

# 2.

# Seven Reasons We Can't Deal with Our Feelings

*Pain is inevitable. Suffering is optional.*
—Haruki Murakami

That chapter we just finished—it was a nice dream, wasn't it?

Unfortunately, it's not our reality, not yet at least.

There are many reasons we don't already deal with our feelings in positive, beneficial, healthy ways that produce desirable outcomes.

These are the big ones.

### 1. WE DON'T VALUE OUR EMOTIONS

We don't accept or pay attention to them, or understand them, so how *could* we value them?

Granted, we usually know in a general way what we're feeling at any given moment. I'm furious. I'm sad. I'm joyful. I'm anxious. I'm frustrated.

Sometimes (but not always) we even recognize *why* we feel what we feel. I'm fuming because that driver just stole my parking spot. I'm sad because my dog died. I'm joyful because I think I'm in love. I'm anxious because I found a lump on my neck. I'm frustrated because my husband or wife or partner or friend doesn't truly *get* me.

But we don't always give ourselves permission to honestly *feel* what we're feeling. Meaning to own it, admit it, acknowledge it, let it in, welcome it, live with it.

*Feel* it.

Why might this be?

Often, emotions are difficult—messy, challenging, unpleasant, embarrassing. When that's the case, we might prefer to deny their existence altogether. That can seem convenient in the short term. But emotions don't evaporate just because we wish they would. When we try to smother our feelings or pretend we don't feel them, we make it harder, not easier, to deal with them effectively.

Feelings can be troublemakers—they put us in awkward positions or make us face choices we'd rather not confront. They can force us to see truths—about ourselves, about other people—that we wish we hadn't seen. Our feelings can be scary—even to ourselves.

Many times, we take emotions as signs of weakness and vulnerability. They tell us that we're afraid, or insecure, or ashamed. Nobody wants to feel those things, even when feeling them is a way of discovering a truth about our lives.

And if we believe emotion equals weakness, we might mistake a lack of emotion for strength—although what it really might indicate is an inability to deal with feelings. It's dangerous to think that silent means strong, when it could just mean scared and shut down.

And if *we* have trouble dealing with our feelings, it will be just as tough for the people around us. This is a universal human experience—often, we'd rather not know when our loved ones, friends, and colleagues have difficult emotions of their own. It becomes an unspoken pact—you won't burden me with your honest feelings, and I won't burden you with mine.

There are even huge historical forces that come between us and our emotions—powerful cultural, racial, religious, gendered, and political influences that weigh on us, whether we realize it or not.

So—plenty of reasons we don't give ourselves (or one another) the relaxed, or optimistic, or even sad or afraid, sometimes you can just experience it without any further thought.

This reminds me of a first-grade class I visited. I asked the students how they were feeling, and one boy said he was frustrated. I quickly asked, "What do you need?" He responded, "Nothing, sir, I'm okay. It'll go away."

Of course, when we're feeling something that challenges our composure or is sending us down a path that might lead to a poor outcome, we need to do something more.

In those cases, we need to regulate.

How has this simple truth escaped us for so long? That brings us to number three on the list.

### 3. NOBODY TAUGHT US AT HOME

As parents and guardians, we see our main job as instructing our kids in the skills and habits necessary for successful living. Beginning soon after birth, we start to teach them a long list of things—how to brush their teeth and wipe their behinds, how to read and write and count, how to hold a fork and a spoon and a knife, how to bathe, dress, tie their shoes, shake hands, speak to adults, ride a bike, kick a soccer ball, save money, do long division, put the laundry in the hamper, say their prayers, et cetera. The lessons are constant. Aside from showering our children with love and kindness and support, teaching them life skills is our number-one priority.

But do we teach them *the* most important life skill—how to deal with their feelings in positive, non-harmful, non-self-defeating ways?

Take a guess. (Mostly, no.)

Maybe, if we ourselves have these skills, we will be admirable role models who set good examples, which is of course a powerful method of instruction. An invisible one, however—dealing with feelings is mostly an internal process, not like cooking an egg or driving a car. It happens mostly inside our heads. We're never sure when our children are paying attention to us or understanding what we're doing and why. So we can't tell if the kids are absorbing proper lessons about navigating emotions just by watching us do it. Even *if* we do it well.

So, in addition to being good role models, are we offering our children explicit and memorable lessons in how to handle life's challenging moments? Are we explaining to them precisely what goes through our own minds as we deal with strong feelings? Do we sit them down when they're struggling and talk it through, listening carefully without interrupting and offering constructive suggestions for how they might best proceed?

Probably not.

Which—assuming we believe that handling tough emotional moments is an important ability—is puzzling.

Why *don't* we teach them how to do it?

Maybe because when we were their age, no one taught us.

Maybe because nobody thought it could be taught.

When I give talks, I usually ask people whether they received any instruction in dealing with their feelings when they were growing up. A few say they got some. More than three-quarters say they got none.

Then I ask, "How much of your education in healthy emotion regulation came from your parents?"

The most common answer: "Almost none."

Once this sobering truth sinks in, I ask the room, "How do you think your own children would answer that question today?"

Instant discomfort all around. You can tell exactly what they're thinking: *Am I messing my kids up the same way my parents did to me?*

Sometimes I'll lighten the mood by asking, "If you had to make a movie of your emotion education, what would the title be?"

Here are some of the good ones:

"Alien."

"The Cover Up."

"I'll Give You Something to Cry About."

"The Pressure Cooker."

"Brave Face."

"Home Alone."

"Don't Ask, Don't Tell."

"Invisible Pain."

And my current favorite:

"Emotional Constipation."

When I ask those audiences what emotion lessons they *did* absorb as children, here's what they say:

"Don't talk about it."

"Smile and pretend everything is all right."

"Get over it."

"Suck it up."

"Let it go."

"Focus on the good things."

"Don't dwell on the negatives."

"Toughen up."

"Get angry, yell, get it out of your system."

"Don't burden everyone else with your problems."

"Go to your room."

"Stop sulking."

As children, we were mostly left to sink or swim, which is exactly what we did—we sank *and* we swam, depending on the force of the emotion and a long list of other factors. The key thing is that we were on our own to figure it out.

No wonder, then, so many of us feel ill-equipped to teach these critical skills to our children. We still don't know them.

In fact, we often find ourselves teaching lessons on how *not* to handle emotional responses in healthy ways. For instance, if unmanageable feelings lead our kids to yell and cry and stomp their feet and behave in other unpleasant ways that children tend to do, chances are that we'll immediately shift into "cut it out" or disciplinarian mode. We'll tell our child to stop crying or we'll yell right back and threaten or punish or berate or even worse. The issue is no longer how they feel and why, but how poorly they're (and you're) dealing with it.

That might be effective in squelching a tantrum today, but it's useless in showing a child how to avert one in the future. We've let that kid down by not looking past the "bad" behavior to examine the emotions causing it and discuss how to handle them better.

Or we go to the other extreme—we become "snowplow parents" who try to clear a child's path of all challenges and difficulties. When we succeed at that task, our kids gain zero experience at dealing with reality and the unhappy emotions that sometimes result. We steal from these children the chance to learn how to deal with life's ups and downs.

Again, we do this mainly because we ourselves have no practical philosophy for how to deal with our own emotional lives. So how could we teach our kids to deal with theirs?

All the research backs me up on this. Authoritarian parenting—setting harsh rules without any explanation, expecting obedience or punishment—when a child is two frequently results in poor emotional and behavioral regulation at age five. Conversely, the greater a child's emotion regulation skills are at age five, the less likely they will be to have emotional problems, and the more likely to be productive in school, at age ten.

In my own research, I ask parents what they want for their children. The first thing they say is happiness and well-being. Second is persistence and resilience. Third is purposeful work and career satisfaction. Then comes kindness, compassion, and responsible decision-making. Next is meaningful relationships and love. After that, civic-mindedness and financial security.

But nearly all of these depend on a single skill *not* on that list: the ability to deal with feelings in healthy, beneficial ways. And this isn't just my opinion—it's backed by thousands of studies conducted by our team and other researchers across the globe.

Now take a moment to think back to your childhood. What lessons, if any, did you receive about how to deal with your feelings? What's the title of your movie? And how does what you learned influence how you deal with emotions today, in helpful or not-so-helpful ways?

## 4. NOBODY TAUGHT US AT SCHOOL EITHER

If we're not learning to deal with our feelings at home, then maybe these lessons should take place in the classroom. It makes sense when you consider how much time children spend in school and how important their mental state is for their ability to learn. If your kid isn't in a healthy frame of mind, and the other kids aren't either, they're not ready to absorb lessons in geography or algebra or anything else. Their classroom is not going to be conducive to learning.

There are schools where an emphasis on emotional well-being is working wonders. In Seattle, I visited a school that has an atypical way of dealing with kids who arrive late. Rather than being sent to a disciplinarian's office for a reprimand, they go to a person whose job it is to greet them and ease them into the flow of the school day. Often, kids are late due to circumstances beyond their control—their parents couldn't get them out of the house on time, or their transportation was undependable, or some other reason. It makes no sense to punish them. Instead, the aide who has been trained to handle these moments brings the child to what they call the "strategy wall"—a bulletin board describing various methods of calming strong emotions and handling them strategically and with positive goals. That may sound like a lot to ask of an elementary school student, but these kids have become adept in the language and skills of emotion regulation. They practice these strategies and techniques so often that by the time they get to class, they're ready to learn. And for kids who are chronically late, their families get additional support. That contrasts with the way many schools handle students who respond poorly to strong emotions. Two kids are caught fighting. Maybe one is bullying the other. Most often, the bully is punished with detention or suspension (or even worse—seventeen states in the United States still permit corporal punishment in schools). The bullied child becomes the object of scorn and shame.

Now both children are suffering. They are in highly activated emotional states, and neither one is getting any help with that from adults.

The bully is full of anger, most likely due to a situation at home, and has no strategy for how to handle it (besides beating up other kids). The child who was the victim in this case also is expected to deal with challenging, uncomfortable feelings alone.

In the past, we depended on families to prepare children to perform well in school—not just to learn but to conduct themselves politely away from their parents, in group settings where cooperation is key. It didn't always work flawlessly. But there was no sense of the widespread meltdown that we see in our schools today, the alarming incidence of emotional disorders requiring (but not always receiving) psychotherapy and medication.

Once it became clear what was happening, schools began to adapt to this new reality, creating programs to teach kids to recognize and express what they were feeling and then manage those emotions. Great strides were made, in my opinion, and are still being made in schools all around the world. There's a ton of research, including my own for the last two decades, showing how social and emotional learning, or SEL, is benefiting individual students and entire school systems.

But somewhere along the way, teaching emotion skills became—like so much of our lives lately—a political issue. According to a *New York Times* opinion column, "the reality [is] that schools are ground zero for the culture wars." There's a backlash of people insisting that lessons in emotion regulation should be taught in the home, by parents, and not by educators. It's hard to argue with that, in theory—except that so many teachers report how difficult it is for today's students to regulate their emotions, which impacts classroom climate, instruction, and learning. And let's not forget that the school day itself is saturated with emotions.

My point here is that very few of us were taught how to deal with our feelings, and despite the wealth of information we now possess, many kids who need this instruction still aren't getting it. Just one more reason we don't deal properly with our feelings: If we don't learn how at home *or* at school, where will this education take place?

There's an old saying among educators: "What gets tested gets taught." Policies prioritize standardized testing, which leads schools to focus almost exclusively on academic subjects even though the ability to deal with our feelings is a prerequisite for optimal learning. It's a fundamental misunderstanding of the power of emotions: They are inherent to the learning process. Emotions drive attention, and attention drives learning.

Our emotion regulation education has to begin early, continue in school, and go on forever.

### 5. WE LOVE THE QUICK FIX

All around, we see signs that we're having a hard time with modern living. The resulting attempts at "self-care" are everywhere—breathing exercises, tantric yoga, mindfulness training, guided meditation, self-help books, stress balls, forest bathing, detox cleanses, medi-spas—the list goes on and on. So too does the array of pharmaceutical products to ease our psychological and emotional difficulties.

There is something inherently human about the desire for instant gratification. If one quick fix doesn't work, there's always another just around the corner. Yet our endless search keeps us from confronting the truth: There are no quick fixes—only gradual ones. True progress comes from strategies that genuinely address our challenges and focus on finding the most practical solutions. Saying "I'm sorry" to a loved one after a fight might calm things down for the night, but it won't address unhealthy dynamics in your relationship. Eventually you'll have to take action, and there probably won't be anything quick about whatever follows.

We don't really *fix* feelings, anyway. We learn to understand what they can teach us and how to use them to achieve our goals.

Social media is full of attempts at quick fixes. As we listen to podcasts or scroll through Instagram, we kid ourselves that we're about to find the perfect cure for what ails us.

Can you remember the last five self-help tips you found on Instagram?

Everyone there seems to have the greatest idea ever to help people deal with their feelings. One influencer with fifteen million followers recently shared, "Just say bye-bye to your anxiety. Just say, 'I don't have space for you anymore in my life.'"

If only it were that easy. These "tips" do more harm than good, in my opinion. They're inundating us with advice that doesn't work for longer than a millisecond or convincing us that we've resolved an issue that hasn't been addressed at all. And then the problems persist—and our mental strength to perform the real work gets weaker (and that's supported by research!).

For adolescents, social media is the primary setting where emotional issues are discussed . . . and discussed . . . and discussed, to no avail. And yet kids keep on scrolling . . . and scrolling.

Technology is a blessing and a curse for young people. Social media exploits teens' vulnerabilities, leveraging social comparisons at a time when nature is remodeling their brains to be more sensitive to the influence of peers. The average teen spends five-plus hours a day on social media. Heavy use is associated with increased anxiety, depression, loneliness, low-quality interactions, and even impaired brain development. Of course, technology needs to be better evaluated and regulated; the surgeon general of the United States has called for labels on social media warning parents that the platforms might damage adolescents' mental health. But what if we provided adolescents with tools to monitor their fluctuating emotions while scrolling and taught them strategies to regulate those feelings? Maybe they'd take a tech break on their own.

Jonathan Haidt, in his book *The Anxious Generation*, offers the following recommendations to mitigate the negative impact of social media on young people's mental health:

- Raise the minimum age for social media apps from thirteen to sixteen to protect young users.
- Limit social media use to one to two hours per day to reduce anxiety and depression.

- Ban smartphones from schools to encourage face-to-face interactions and reduce distractions.
- Re-norm the peer landscape to reinforce healthier, safer online choices.
- Urge parents to engage their children in offline, play-based activities to develop problem-solving skills, social skills, autonomy, and resilience.

Haidt's suggestions appeal to many people because they are so clear-cut, but the reality is much more complex. Here's a fair analogy: A parent can forbid their teenager from having sex until they're able to handle the practical and emotional ramifications. But that doesn't ensure that the teen won't have sex. Instead, a parent could educate their teen about safe and responsible sex and hope this knowledge will have a positive influence.

And while Haidt's recommendations aim to protect adolescents' mental health, it is equally important to empower children, in age-appropriate ways, to make informed decisions about social media usage. Social media is not inherently harmful; it offers benefits such as peer connection, educational resources, and opportunities for self-expression. Teaching adolescents to balance these benefits against the risks helps them use social media in a way that enhances their lives without compromising their well-being. Educating them about the risks and benefits also develops the critical thinking skills they'll need to navigate the digital landscape. This will foster a sense of responsibility and autonomy, aligning with developmental psychology principles that emphasize granting young people the freedom to make choices and learn from their experiences. This approach leads to more mature behavior both online and offline.

As teens gradually access social media in more educated and supervised ways, emotion regulation skills will help them navigate the vicissitudes of their reactions. Such regulation could range from self-monitoring their length of exposure and how they feel, to knowing how to respond when hurt or upset, to seeking out sites that support their goals or well-being, and even to posting content in a way that aligns with their goals. By guiding adolescents on positive social media usage and teaching them emotion regulation, educators and parents can also help them develop other essential life skills in a digital context, including empathy, communication, and collaboration, fostering long-term resilience and balanced usage.

## 6. WE'D RATHER TREAT AILMENTS THAN PREVENT THEM

I'm talking here about emotional ailments, although this attitude applies to physical ones, too. Look at all the health problems that stem from poor diet and lack of activity: obesity, diabetes, heart disease, hypertension, even some forms of cancer. There are steps we could take to improve our odds against these serious diseases. But if our behavior is any indication, we'd rather live heedlessly, get sick, and then rely on doctors to save us. The prescription drug and medical industries are happy to comply, since effective prevention would decimate their profits.

We adopt a similar approach to emotional and psychological problems. We don't take the actions necessary to prevent situations we know will leave us feeling stressed and overwhelmed. Often, we don't even know there are things we can do to avert or manage difficult emotions. Instead, we allow ourselves to suffer.

The effects of this are everywhere, all around us. In the workplace, low engagement and depression cost employers a fortune in turnover and poor productivity. As a society, rather than provide universal mental health care, we wait until someone makes their illness clear—usually by acting out in a way that causes harm to themselves or others. That's when an ailment turns into a tragedy that could have been averted. Deaths from opioid overdose and suicide could have been avoided—but were not. Too often, rage and despair boil over into violence.

We waste money and resources keeping people locked up in prisons rather than treating them before they act out. One study tracked over four hundred thousand prisoners in thirty states after their release. About three-quarters were rearrested within five years. However, there was a 43 percent reduction in recidivism for prisoners who participated in education programs. The higher the degree they earned, the lower the recidivism rate: 14 percent for those who obtained an associate's degree, 5.6 percent for those who earned a bachelor's, and 0 percent for those who got a master's.

I've worked with a big-city school district that only serves students with serious emotional and psychological issues. In a meeting, one principal said, "We put infinite resources into helping kids who are in crisis. We intervene only *after* they're completely dysregulated. You're telling me they could actually learn skills to make some of these interventions unnecessary?" I could only shake my head in disbelief. Even the dedicated professionals seem unaware that it's possible to teach kids to deal with their feelings and thereby prevent the problems that upend their lives.

I'm also thinking here of a man I know, a total success when it comes to career, income, and prestige but who struggles as a parent role model, especially where the emotional life of his family is concerned. His teenage daughter is going through a difficult time with issues that starkly contrast with her father's accomplishments. It's possible that if the guy had been more emotionally present throughout her childhood, she might not require the extensive therapeutic support she now needs to overcome her battles with low self-worth, opioid abuse, and other forms of self-harm. While he is now investing heavily in her recovery, one can't help but wonder if earlier intervention might have made a difference.

Of course, we can't really put all the blame on the father. It's likely he was raised without a quality emotion education, and so he worked with what he had. He likely felt overwhelmed by his own feelings and, without knowing what to do with them, he shut down to protect himself from the pain of observing his daughter in crisis. It's unfortunate that his interest in the role of emotions in his daughter's despair was piqued only when she hit rock bottom.

The biggest problem with intervention-only treatment is that it doesn't reduce the number of new "cases" that enter the "system"—meaning that we need to do more than try to help people who can't manage their emotions. We need to find ways to prevent them from hitting that low point.

Simply put, building protective factors to promote good mental health reduces unnecessary suffering and is more cost-effective and improves outcomes.

## 7. THERE IS NO INSTITUTIONAL SUPPORT FOR REGULATION

Was there ever a time when we adults were expected to respond rationally to our emotions, even the challenging ones? It surely seems as though the general emotional climate wasn't always as tense and stressed as it feels today. Perhaps it was the COVID pandemic that made everything seem uncontrollable and uncertain. A 2021 study published in *The Lancet* estimated that the pandemic caused 53.2 million cases of major depressive disorder and 76.2 million cases of anxiety disorder globally.

Today, in the public realm, we're fed a steady diet of conflict and controversy, with the institutions we depend on roiled by dissension and chaos, and social media that feeds on outrage and offense. Suddenly we realize there's no powerful force restraining our worst impulses.

The youth mental health crisis began around 2010, and the pandemic just "poured fuel on the fire," according to US Surgeon General Vivek Murthy. In 2023, a panel of medical experts recommended routine screening of children for anxiety, and teens for depression. A diagnosis often leads to medication, which fails to address root causes. Kids' fears are rational. For at least a decade, most US teens have been stressed about school shootings, mass shootings, and gun violence in general, which is now a leading cause of death for this age group.

Workplace stress hit unprecedented levels in 2022, as Gallup reported. While 85 percent of executives surveyed by Harvard Business Review Analytic Services acknowledge the critical importance of prioritizing workforce mental health, a mere 27 percent acknowledge that their own organizations are effectively addressing it.

Based on all these indications, the experts agree that we're in the midst of a mental health crisis, but do we see government at any level treating this moment accordingly? Not that I can tell. In some areas of the country there is a one- to two-year wait for psychotherapy. Doesn't sound like a crisis we're taking very seriously.

Parents, caregivers, and teachers cannot be the sole bulwark against forces undermining our kids' development. The United States is ranked the least supportive of young people and families among forty nations by UNICEF.

The official war on social and emotional learning in some states reflects something larger and more worrisome—government's abdication of its role as a positive influence in our lives. I spoke recently with an educator in Alaska who reported, in tears, that her school board required her to sign a contract that forbids her from talking to kids about their feelings. If she does, she will be fired.

Another teacher in Florida sent me an email:

*I need to know if any of your new work provides educators with suggestions on how to address feelings students have when they experience deliberate exclusion, put-downs, name-calling, or unwanted and unwelcome physical contact. In Florida, the curricula for these programs have been revised to exclude important discussions regarding issues around race, gender, multicultural education, and migrant education. Would you have any guidance, leadership, or literature for us while we try to build capacity around empathy and compassion without addressing true issues?*

This message left me deeply concerned. As someone committed to emotional health and education, I find it disheartening to see vital discussions on empathy and inclusion being restricted. It highlights the urgent need to educate policymakers and support educators in fostering safe, compassionate spaces.

There's a trendy managerial-class acronym, VUCA, describing a world that's volatile, uncertain, complex, and ambiguous. That's where we all live now—in Vucaville. It doesn't sound like a place that values calm, purposeful emotion regulation, does it?

Okay, so take all seven of those reasons together, put them in a blender, and give them a whirl. Easy to see why we have so much difficulty dealing with our feelings.

But, of course, that's about to change.

# PART TWO
# DEFINITIONS

# 3.
# What Is Emotion Regulation?

*Not everything that is faced can be changed; but nothing can be changed until it is faced.*

—James Baldwin

I may have mentioned this once or twice already: Emotion regulation is *the* most important skill a human being can possess.

If we do it well, we vastly improve our chances for successful, satisfying lives, with healthy, loving relationships, meaningful achievements, and lasting inner peace (or as close as we're ever likely to get).

On the other hand, our inability or unwillingness to learn it will be the cause of virtually every problem we'll ever have, from the personal to the political to the global.

Unfortunately, it got stuck with a lousy name.

When I speak to groups and ask what they think *emotion regulation* means, here's what they say:

"It means to smother our feelings."

"It means controlling them."

"Fixing them."

("So," I reply, "does that mean you want to be smothered, controlled, and fixed?" Nobody likes any of those either.)

There's something about the word *regulation* that feels as though the emotion police are telling us what we may and may not feel.

We psychologists try to come up with more nuanced labels, such as *self-control, inhibition, managing emotions, modulating emotions, coping, impulse control,* and *delayed gratification.*

All perfectly fine, totally descriptive terms. But still, jargony and limited. They don't really get at what we're talking about: being conscious and intentional about your emotional life.

So then I usually say, "Well, what if I told you that the goal of emotion regulation is to learn how to use your emotions wisely, to get the outcomes you desire, and to have a more fulfilling existence?"

People sort of look at me as though I'm speaking a foreign language, which maybe I am, and then someone will ask, "What exactly do you mean?"

And with that, a new path forward begins.

Before diving into the intricacies of emotion regulation, let's first untangle the web of what we actually mean by *emotion*. How does it stand apart from its close relatives—affect, feeling, mood, and disposition? Understanding these distinctions is crucial before we can master the art of regulating them.

*Affect* forms the backdrop of our emotional life and fluctuates throughout the day; it's our general state of pleasantness and energy. An *emotion* (like anger, fear, or joy) is a mostly short-lived, automatic response to a stimulus (internal or external) that produces shifts in our thinking, physiology, and behavior. Emotions are intertwined with our upbringing and culture. Grief, for example, is experienced and expressed differently across cultures. A *feeling* is more reflective, analytical, and influenced by our personal experiences and the meaning we assign to things. You smile at me during a speech, and I feel like I'm making a difference. A *mood* is the result of an emotion or feeling that's longer lasting, less intense, and usually more diffuse. We can wake up in a good or bad mood and not quite know why. Finally, there's emotional *dispo-*

*sition*, or how a person is inclined to feel on a more stable basis. When we say someone is always cheerful or tends to be a downer, that's their emotional disposition.

Why do these distinctions matter? Because we need to be aware of all our affective experiences—from the fleeting to the enduring—and use helpful strategies to manage them. That said, because *emotions* and *feelings* are frequently used interchangeably in everyday conversation, we'll take the same approach throughout this book.

Okay, so what exactly *is* emotion regulation?

Emotion regulation means the total opposite of smothering, or controlling, or suppressing, or fixing. It starts with permitting yourself (and others) to feel and acknowledge every emotion, without judging it as good or bad or positive or negative. It's a feeling, and that's the only thing that counts. There's always a reason for feeling it. Your reason might sound totally irrational to me, or even to you. It might be impossible to fully explain it to yourself or anyone else.

Doesn't matter. It's a feeling. Feelings don't need permission to exist.

What *does* matter is what you do next.

James Gross, a leading researcher at Stanford University, defines emotion regulation as a process by which individuals modify their emotional experiences, expressions, and physiology and the situations eliciting such emotions in order to produce appropriate responses to the ever-changing demands posed by the environment.

Emotional intelligence theory emphasizes the goal orientation of emotion regulation. The first goal involves modifying the immediate emotional experience (e.g., reducing an unpleasant emotion). The second goal involves selecting one or more strategies to achieve a desired outcome—making a sound decision, maintaining a positive relationship, or completing an important task. Maya Tamir, a psychology professor at Hebrew University and leading emotion regulation researcher, emphasizes the cost-benefit analysis and motivation behind emotion regulation. Is it worth it? Will it pay off? Are there any consequences of not regulating?

All true, and we have some things to unpack, starting with "modifying" your emotional "experiences," to accomplishing "goals," to producing "appropriate" responses to the demands posed by "the environment."

Honestly, the concept of emotion regulation is simple:

Certain feelings—usually the strong, difficult ones that we'd rather not feel—will lead us to think and speak and act in ways that mess up our own lives and sometimes the lives of the people around us. "Regulation" simply means transitioning from unhelpful to helpful methods for dealing with those emotions. It involves moving from automatic or outside-of-awareness unhelpful reactions to more deliberate, mindful, and helpful responses that improve our lives. Or at least that don't do us (or others) any harm. We spend less time and effort regulating pleasant emotions, precisely because they bring us pleasure and so often go unnoticed, while unpleasant feelings demand our attention. Those are the emotions that have a stronger impact on our lives.

I can pretty much guarantee that if you've ever achieved any kind of goal—especially one that required patience or sacrifice or self-control—it was because you managed your responses to what you felt. You didn't call it "emotion regulation." You might not have given the mental process a second's thought.

But you regulated. Maybe somebody hurt your pride, but you refused to crumble. Or something made you anxious, but you found a way to push through. Or a setback filled you with self-doubt, but you maintained your momentum. Perhaps you decided to extend an arduous physical endeavor just so you could savor the sensations. Or you psyched yourself up for a challenging new enterprise.

You regulated.

The only thing left for us to learn is how to do it consciously, intentionally, and strategically, with a positive purpose in mind—not just once in a while, but whenever life requires it of us.

How often will that be?

We humans experience a nonstop flow of feelings, most of which come and go without us even noticing. Lucky for us, the majority of our emotions don't need to be regulated. It's a small minority of them—the ones that challenge our ability to act like reasonable, responsible human beings—that need help.

We're fortunate that many emotions are regulated automatically or implicitly. It's like a background app in your brain running without you consciously pressing Start. If someone says something hurtful and you don't react as strongly as you might have expected, it could be because your brain has already begun calming you without your conscious awareness. This is highly valuable because this form of regulation is less effortful and draining. You don't have to stop and think, *Okay, now I need to take a breath or reappraise.*

So, something happens. Could be anything.

You're walking outdoors and a delicious warm spring breeze caresses your cheek. You ask your teenager a question and get an eye roll and a snarky reply. You're driving and a car comes speeding by and cuts you off, nearly causing a crash. A rude individual at the supermarket with a full shopping cart cuts in front of you at the register. You try on the designer sweater you bought online and it makes you feel like a movie star. After fifteen minutes at the gym, you're exhausted and want to go home. As you're strolling down the street, a beautiful stranger smiles at you.

Like I said, could be anything.

Whatever it is, it provokes an emotion. Maybe a wonderful one. Maybe a troubling one. Maybe one so mild you don't even notice. Or one so strong it takes your breath away. Or a mixed one—maybe two emotions.

We don't always consciously perceive it this way, but every emotion is a two-part event—first we feel it, and then we respond to it. We have a response to every emotion, even when we don't realize it. Most of those responses are subtle and fleeting. Paying attention to every single feeling would be a huge mental burden. We wouldn't have time to think about anything else.

That beautiful spring breeze? You felt it, it made you happy, you kept walking, you forgot all about it.

But that highway bully? That inconsiderate person at the supermarket? Your precious little adolescent monster?

The feelings they evoke will mess with you.

In the course of a day, how many emotions will require regulation? Obviously, that depends on the kind of life you're living. Ideally, I think we'd all agree, the fewer emotions we need to regulate, the better. Because, as we've shared, regulation is mental work, and who wants more of that? If we perform too much emotional labor, a kind of weariness sets in, at which point we become overwhelmed and unable to regulate *anything*.

That's a big part of our problem in society today, I believe—we're all so worked up by everything going on around us that we're emotionally exhausted. That's when trouble follows. We give up trying to manage how we respond to all the things we feel. Maybe we let minor setbacks send us spiraling into discouragement and despair. Maybe disappointments we normally manage with ease now make us lose faith in the future. Maybe we rage at people whether they deserve it or not. Maybe we berate ourselves for being human and imperfect. We don't allow ourselves to enjoy an afternoon break or a summer vacation.

We've all been to that place. The job of emotion regulation is to keep us out of there.

It's also important to know what emotion regulation *isn't*.

It's not about denying or ignoring emotions. On the contrary, it's about embracing the idea that all emotions matter.

It's not a personality trait like introversion or extroversion or a tendency to be emotionally volatile or not. Someone who has a calm demeanor may be not so great at dealing with turbulent feelings. In fact, that person might struggle with regulation precisely because they do it so infrequently. And someone who seems always anxious might be good at it because they need to do it so often. You might recognize that you have trouble with anger, and so you'll keep that in mind, perhaps creating some space between you and the person who activated you. I am prone to feeling overwhelmed, so I'll be extra vigilant when the feeling starts to build and take a short break or go outside for a minute and get some fresh air.

The skills of emotion regulation are not capacities we're born with, though babies and toddlers try to regulate, even if they're not using adult-style strategies. Newborns let you know how they're feeling without a thought about how they might better express their need for a fresh diaper or nap or your attention. But they soon catch on to how to get what they want from their parents. Emotion regulation is 100 percent learned.

Regulation doesn't minimize the reality of difficult circumstances. Sickness, poverty, racism, and other damaging forces beyond our control create immense challenges. When we consider how people—especially children—navigate their emotions, we must acknowledge these realities rather than place the burden solely on them.

At the same time, external factors don't absolve adults of their responsibility to support children in developing emotion regulation skills. Too often, it's not children who lack the ability to regulate emotions but the adults in their lives—whether parents, teachers, or leaders—who struggle due to their own biases or lack of emotion education. I spoke about this with Dawn Brooks-DeCosta, deputy superintendent of Harlem Community School District 5 in New York City. She noted that while she is committed to addressing systemic issues such as homelessness and racism, she also recognizes that every child arrives at school each day with a full range of emotions. How adults respond to those emotions can either help or hinder a child's ability to learn. That's why teaching emotion regulation isn't about "fixing" kids—it's about giving them skills that empower them in an unjust world.

Emotion regulation is also about reclaiming power—not just for children, but for adults, too. When we understand and model regulation, we help create environments where children feel seen, supported, and capable. In the face of systemic barriers, emotion regulation provides tools to mitigate the effects of adversity, improving how people of all ages navigate their lives. While it doesn't erase injustice, it strengthens well-being, resilience, and agency in a world that often fails to do the same.

Emotion regulation is not about finding happiness. There will be times when life doesn't go the way we wish it would. Emotion regulation doesn't change reality. Nothing does. There will always be events that devastate us, that crush us with sadness or despair or loneliness. To be human is to experience the bitter along with the sweet. Emotion regulation helps with how we experience that reality.

Finally, emotion regulation isn't one-size-fits-all. The "correct" technique or tactic for dealing with a feeling depends on many things, including the emotion you're feeling, your unique biology and personality, your values, your culture, your history with the emotion, and the specifics of the moment, including who (if anyone) you're interacting with. Even time of day matters—our mental energy is different at 10 p.m. than it was at 10 a.m. I'll respond one way when dealing with a coworker and another with my six-year-old nephew. Likewise, what works for my six-year-old nephew will be different from what works on me.

I like the formula $ER(G+S) = f(E \times P \times C)$ as a way to capture the different forces at play when we regulate our emotions. It reminds us that emotion regulation includes goals (G) and strategies (S) and isn't just about picking a tool from a menu—it's a function ($f$) of the emotion (E), the person's (P) unique background, and the context (C) we're in. The same frustration might call for deep breathing in one context, humor in another, and direct problem-solving in yet another. If you've ever wondered why the same strategy doesn't always work for you and another person, this is why.

Regulation's task is to help us cope even during those toughest periods—not to transform them into "happiness," but to make it possible for us to get us through them as gracefully as humanly possible.

In psychology we talk about "hot" and "cool" cognitive processes that are choreographed by activity in the prefrontal cortex. As you can guess, hot means we're reacting impulsively to some emotional stimulus, and cool means we're thinking before we speak or act. The assumption is that cool executive function is almost always preferable for regulating. But importantly, there are times when "hot" processing is both appropriate and beneficial. It fuels creativity, deepens relationships through authentic emotional expression, and enables quick, instinctive reactions in high-stress or dangerous situations. It can also drive action against injustice, as moral outrage often sparks change. The key is balance—while "hot" processing is valuable in the right contexts, unchecked reliance on it can lead to impulsivity and poor decisions.

Janet Metcalfe and Walter Mischel of Columbia University describe the hot and cool processes like this:

> *The cool system is cognitive, emotionally neutral, contemplative, flexible, integrated, coherent, spatiotemporal, slow, episodic, and strategic. It is the seat of self-regulation and self-control. The hot system is the basis of emotionality, fears as well as passions—impulsive and reflexive—initially controlled by innate releasing stimuli (and, thus, literally under "stimulus control"); it is fundamental for emotional (classical) conditioning and undermines efforts at self-control. The balance between the hot and cool systems is determined by stress, developmental level, and the individual's self-regulatory dynamics.*

What they're describing is the difference between regulating our emotions and allowing our emotions to regulate us. So, the question during moments of intense emotional activation is, how do we get from hot to cool before we do something damaging?

Good question.

Your spouse just said something that irritates you. A lot.

You immediately reply with something just as irritating. Maybe more so. It's payback. You're justified.

And what's the result? Your spouse fires back something even worse. Something truly nasty.

So you react by . . . you see where this is going? Sniper warfare. Who's at fault? Does it matter? The fact is that you both had the opportunity to avert this moment of awfulness between two people who love each other. If only one of you had responded rather than reacted.

. . .

Okay, so how might you have regulated your irritation?

Well, that depends on several factors, as we've discussed, including your personality, your relationship, your mood, the setting, what happened earlier, how much sleep you got last night—a complex list that goes on and on. Later in the book we'll discuss precisely *how* we might respond to our feelings. For now, let's focus on *why*.

Most of the time, we respond well even to our unwanted emotions without overthinking it. I'm feeling groggy after slogging through a work project for six hours straight. I put my computer to sleep, grab my car keys, and go to the coffee shop. Or I flop onto the sofa and rewatch a few episodes of *Friends*. If I'm feeling claustrophobic, I put on my sneakers and go for a run. Doesn't take a genius to make those choices.

Now you're trying to read a magazine in the same room where your kids are playing a video game—a really loud, raucous one. They're screaming their heads off.

Your instant reaction is to yell at them to quiet down and behave. This is your house, too! You were in this room first!

Then you realize that you're about to sound like a seven-year-old yourself. And this is the only room in the house with a big-screen TV, whereas you can easily find a better place to read in peace.

So that's what you do—instead of scolding, you retreat. As an emotion regulation technique, it's brilliant. Simple. Effective. Fast. Your anger evaporates.

Now you're walking down a crowded street and a guy headed in the opposite direction bumps you and keeps going without a word. You're outraged! What makes this stranger think you can be treated with such disrespect? He has absolutely crossed the line.

So, what do you do? You punch him in the face! What did he expect? You can't let behavior like that go unpunished, can you? You immediately feel better. You regulated your strong feelings. Of course, now that other guy feels outraged and disrespected, and suddenly the two of you are in a brawl in the middle of the street, shredding your best suit *and* your self-respect, until finally the police arrive, at which point your troubles really begin.

I'm joking! Of course you're not the kind of person who goes around punching people in the face, even when the temptation arises.

Instead, you allow the ugly moment to pass. But you're left boiling with righteous rage.

Now what?

Whether you know it or not, you've already begun the process of regulating that emotional response in a way that serves your goals. It happened the second you restrained your impulse to slug the guy. Same as when you paused, then left the room to read elsewhere rather than harass your kids. And when you spoke gently to your spouse instead of trading potshots.

You've been taking that first step toward positive emotion regulation throughout your entire life. You just didn't know it had a name. But every time somebody or something triggered you, and instead of immediately reacting you paused and took a deep breath, or counted to ten, or bit your tongue, or turned the other cheek, you did it: You deactivated the difficult moment. You brought the unpleasant interaction to a halt. You de-escalated the drama.

It took effort. You didn't do it every time.

But you did it. You began making the switch from hot to cool and started the process of regulation.

The question is, what do you do next?

The problem is you don't automatically know.

Once you began cooling your emotional state, it was time to take the all-important next step.

Which is . . .

But first let me tell you about Aunt Hillary, who drives me crazy. Talking to her is so annoying that I can barely restrain myself from telling her to shut up. She has been a pain in the neck my entire life, at every family get-together.

Thanksgiving is in two weeks, and I know I'll have to deal.

(Before I go any further, I should point out that I don't have an annoying aunt Hillary, although we all have someone like her in our lives.)

What shall I do? Here's a better way to phrase that question: What emotion goals should I pursue? We can't really regulate our responses unless we know how, if we had a choice, we *would* feel. Because the fact is that we do have a choice.

When we've figured out what we wish to feel, we have the beginnings of a plan. Actually, five plans—and depending on the situation, we will use one, two, or more of them to achieve the desired result. Obviously, the fewer we need, the better. But it's best to know them all.

Here's my first course of action: If possible, I want to *prevent* the emotions Aunt Hillary brings out in me. That would solve the problem before it even exists. Perhaps I can just skip the traditional Thanksgiving this year and hang out with some friends for a four-day weekend. As in all matters of health, mental and physical, it's far better to prevent problems than it is to treat them. I know she's my aunt, but that doesn't mean I have to let her actions affect my happiness. So, that's my number-one goal—do what's necessary to prevent an unwanted emotion.

And if prevention is not an option? Then I'll try to *reduce* how unwanted emotions will affect me. If I get activated by something Aunt Hillary says or does at the dinner, I can decide to keep my distance from her the entire day—one quick kiss on the cheek and then I retreat to the opposite end of the table. Or I can create psychological distance by pretending I'm watching a movie where Aunt Hillary is a character. That would definitely help—I'll see her but not be as affected by her bad behavior. We can't always avoid being triggered by life, but there are usually ways to reduce the potential for further provocation.

I can also *initiate* pleasant emotions by actively seeking out experiences and situations I truly enjoy. By doing this I won't leave room for unwanted feelings. Today I'll reconnect with the cool cousins and their families. I'll pay more attention to the food and wine. Maybe I can join the noisy crowd in the den watching football on TV.

Okay, with those three steps I've done what I can to prevent and reduce unpleasant emotions and initiate some good vibes. Now I'll try my best to *maintain* those pleasant feelings, meaning I'll stay focused on having fun and not allow myself to get sucked into conversation with Aunt Hillary no matter how hard she tries.

Finally, I might find a way to *enhance* and add to the pleasant emotions I've managed to create. Maybe I'll duck out right after dessert and go to the movies or plan some late-night Netflix and chill. It's not enough to defend ourselves from unpleasant emotional situations—the best defense is a good offense. When we create enjoyable feelings, we crowd out the ones that make us miserable.

Again, the goal is to use these strategies one at a time, as needed. For your sake, I hope you won't have to use all five on a regular basis. But taken all together, they provide us with the big-picture goals of emotion regulation. Naturally, there's an acronym—PRIME—to make them easier to remember:

Prevent unwanted emotions, if we can.
Reduce them otherwise.
Initiate desirable emotions.
Maintain the feelings we want.
Enhance those whenever possible.

You may have noticed that the *P* and the *R* of PRIME are all about anticipating, avoiding, or shrinking emotions we'd rather not feel. That could be taken to imply that it's best to never experience challenging feelings. Which is absolutely not the case.

First, there are occasions when the emotions we think of as unpleasant are necessary. Even if it were possible to sidestep grief, for example, it would be a mistake. Grief is necessary to help us process the sad events we all must endure. In that case, regulation's job is only to keep the sadness from causing problems of its own.

There are also times when the most effective regulation techniques and tactics may themselves do us harm.

Say I have a coworker who annoys me practically every time he opens his mouth. Just the sight of him sets me on edge. When searching for a way to manage that emotion, I might ask myself, *Do I ever need to interact with this guy at all?* If the answer is no, there's my obvious solution—just stay away from him. Works fine, easy to do, a total win.

But perhaps I should stop first to wonder *why* this colleague affects me so intensely. Then I might realize it's because I am touchy when people openly disagree with me, which this guy does all the time. By steering clear of him, am I also avoiding having to deal with my inability to tolerate dissent? And if I *do* have a hard time with anyone who disagrees with me, could this also be affecting my relationships with family and friends? That's a good question to ask, one that might not have occurred to me if I hadn't been intentionally trying to regulate my response to emotion.

Or what if, when the noise and chaos at home drive me crazy, I escape to the gym and exercise? Sounds like a smart idea—I spare my family some drama and improve my physical fitness at the same time.

But what if working out works a little *too* well? If it prevents me from dealing with problems in my homelife, then getting in great shape does me no favors. Maybe I can learn to deal with my family *and* stay in shape.

There will be instances when simply muttering "Go #@&% yourself!" is a perfectly acceptable response to an emotion. If you're saying it to someone who just beat you out for a parking spot, and it dissipates your vexation, why not? They'll never know! But if you find yourself hurling invectives at other people numerous times a day, maybe you should examine what's going on with your mood.

At times it's possible that an outright, unapologetic display of some strong feeling—disappointment, disgust—will be the best emotion regulation technique. Perhaps once the other person understands exactly what you're feeling, your goals will be met. It may be the best first step in changing their behavior toward you.

In that case, reacting boldly and immediately would be the proper response. But only if you're doing it in an intentional, purposeful way, with a favorable outcome in mind. And only if you're tailoring your response to the situation, rather than just letting it rip because you couldn't stop yourself.

Every emotion response will be unique to the specific situation. The same tactic can be the absolute best or absolute worst choice depending on what's going on. You're holding a glass when it drops to the floor and shatters. You respond to the moment with a bit of self-talk, a very effective technique for dealing with feelings.

*Marc,* you calmly tell yourself, after you take a deep breath, *remember, nobody's perfect, not even you, and breaking a glass is no big deal.*

Or, without a second's pause you say, *Marc, you #@%& idiot!*

Same response technique of speaking to yourself as though you're another person. In the first case I'm my own best friend. In the second, I'm a masochistic self-saboteur.

I'm as susceptible to poor emotion regulation as anyone. Not long ago I was visiting a friend who is also a major donor to the center I lead at Yale (I shared this story with her before going to press!). I needed to talk with her about a new initiative that needed significant funding. These conversations are uncomfortable for me, especially with people I feel close to. As you can imagine, it's awkward.

As we sat in her living room chatting one evening, I held a big bowl of popcorn in my lap. Now, normally, because I'm a careful eater, I would limit myself to a small amount, if any. But on this particular night, as I fretted over when and how to bring up my fundraising mission, I ate a lot. I was anxious, and my anxiety was demanding to be fed.

Finally I found the nerve to bring up the project that needed funding, and once I finished my spiel, my anxiety began to vanish. I could have handled my mission that night without the help of popcorn, and I knew it even as I sat there gulping down great big handfuls of it.

I was lucky because I knew why I was anxious and what I needed to do to manage it. If compulsive binge-snacking becomes my go-to response to anxiety, though, I might be in trouble.

For most people whose anxieties drive them to overeat unhealthy food, the cause isn't so obvious. Stress eating is definitely a form of regulation. But it's not a helpful one. In fact, I believe it's a major but unnoticed force that's partly driving the obesity epidemic.

Even the ailments that are the top killers of Americans—heart disease, cancer, stroke, diabetes—can sometimes be attributed to our lack of healthy regulation skills. Recent research indicates that frequent feelings of anger can restrict blood vessel dilation, potentially causing damage over time and increasing the risk of cardiovascular disease or stroke. One study found that healthy individuals who frequently experience anger or hostility are 19 percent more likely to develop heart disease than those who remain calmer.

As you've no doubt noticed, when we talk about emotion regulation, we're usually managing unpleasant feelings like fear, sadness, disappointment, depression. But those aren't the only ones we need to modulate.

Why would you want to regulate a pleasant emotion?

Here's one reason. A happy, optimistic mood, research has shown, increases our confidence but leads us to disregard the details when making decisions. It causes what one study termed "a shallow and broad processing of information." You can imagine how that might lead to some poor outcomes—in our exuberance we assume that everything will continue to go right for us. Whereas in an unpleasant mood, we tend to focus more narrowly on the information at hand and look for reasons to be pessimistic, which might save us some headaches down the road. In the grip of high spirits, we could make snap decisions that we would have avoided had we felt sour and disillusioned.

Here's another scenario. You just landed an amazing job. It's a big step up careerwise and also a healthy bump in your financial status. You're bursting with the news. Who can you tell? Well, maybe this is a time to tread carefully where your friends and colleagues are concerned. Surely some of them will be happy for you. But others, only happy-ish. You may remember what Gore Vidal said: "Every time a friend succeeds, I die a little." Or maybe you relate to Bette Midler, who said, "The worst part of success is trying to find someone who is happy for you."

So, for the sake of your pals' egos, you might pause, then dial the celebration back. No boasting on LinkedIn. No videos on Instagram.

If this is difficult for adults, it's even tougher for kids.

I'm ten years old, and this weekend we're going to stay with my grandparents who live by the beach. I'm so psyched I can barely think about anything else. A wonderful state of mind. But on Friday morning I have a big arithmetic test. I'm not prepared, so I need to do some serious studying during the next couple days. How am I going to lower my ecstasy level to the point where I can focus? I'll have to downregulate my giddy emotional state so that I can master long division before dwelling on all the fun I'm about to have.

Of course, it would be a drag if we felt the need to downregulate—to *cool*—every strong feeling. Think of the times you've felt intense love, friendship, passion, joy, ecstasy. Now imagine what it would have been like if you'd had to stop, take a deep breath, and chill even those emotions before you acted on them.

Not much fun. But sometimes necessary.

There are also moments when we need to boost positive emotions in ourselves and others. I don't mean times when we're feeling bad—but when we need to feel better. The world of sports runs on that kind of emotional energy—we're always pumping one another up and building our self-confidence and envisioning positive outcomes. When something good happens and we're filled with pleasant feelings, we owe it to ourselves to do what we can to strengthen and maintain and amplify those emotions, so they last as long as possible.

## 4.

# Emotion Regulation in Action

*I'm not afraid of storms, for I'm learning how to sail my ship.*
—Louisa May Alcott

If emotion regulation really is such an important life skill, you might wonder, why haven't we all mastered it by now? If our success and happiness depend on it, how can it be that no one has ever bothered to teach it? True, we were instructed in good manners and proper behavior. But for the benefit of others, not ourselves.

This question has inspired me throughout my entire career as a psychology researcher. We make virtually no serious, organized attempt to learn this most critical ability or teach it to our children. It's as though we don't think it can be taught or learned—even though, clearly, it *can*, and must be, like any other skill. Either that or we don't truly believe there's any practical reason for mastering it. That's possible, considering how we usually think about emotion: as an uncontrollable, unruly force that gets in the way of our rational side.

It's no surprise that we feel that way. It's certainly true that our feelings often do cause us to behave in ways that run counter to our own best interests. But we seem resigned to that unhappy reality, rather than recognizing that our emotions can become useful and beneficial—which is, in essence, what regulation is all about.

This is what explains our inability to regulate. We don't make the connection between our feelings and our futures. We know that our actions determine the quality of our lives. And we understand that our feelings drive our actions. But then there's a disconnect. We don't appreciate how regulating emotional responses has a direct influence on our lives and those of the people we love.

Instead, we muddle through, wishing in vain that we could stand steady when the world seems determined to send us off the deep end. We admire the people who maintain their cool and their bearings no matter how they are provoked, but it never occurs to us that they weren't born that way—they had to acquire the talent somehow. And that maybe we can, too.

In a perfect world, we'd learn how to handle our wayward emotions at home—because then our education would begin while we are still in our most formative years. We would be absorbing helpful lessons in a (presumably) loving and nurturing environment, surrounded by people who want what's best for us. We would witness healthy emotion regulation on an ongoing basis, and before long its practice would become second nature.

Unfortunately, as many of us—me included—have learned, home is not always the cradle of beneficial regulation strategies and techniques. In some cases, it might actually be the exact opposite. Most of us learn our emotion skills by osmosis, absorbing them from our parents, who absorbed them from their parents, and on and on. And if the habits we picked up are useless (or worse), then . . . well, you can see how it might go for our children, and their children.

But it doesn't have to be that way.

Can't we teach regulation in schools? By now we depend on the education system, public and private, to transmit a long list of virtues and values to our children, way beyond simple academic instruction. But teachers already feel overburdened and overstressed. Realistically, can we assign them another task, especially one as complex and important as this? Is there a better choice? If emotion management isn't taught there, do we risk leaving the job to TikTok, Instagram, and AI?

Many of our schools already include what has come to be known as SEL. Our center at Yale developed an approach called RULER (for recognize, understand, label, express, and regulate), and thousands of schools all over the world use it to help educators, students, and families to identify and regulate their emotions. Research shows that RULER enhances educator and student well-being, engagement, and performance. Truthfully, it should be everyone's job to embody and embrace the principles of emotion regulation.

Want your children and grandchildren to live successful, happy lives? Make sure they learn to regulate their emotional responses, either in school or by watching how you regulate yours, or better yet, in both places. As a parent, express your feelings when someone makes you feel angry, or when a turn of events disappoints you, or during a situation that's making you worry, and then describe the strategy you'll use to regulate your emotion. What could be a better inheritance to hand down?

Amid all this discussion of what regulation is, and why we should do it, and what happens when we don't, we still haven't talked about the practical aspect—*how* to do it. The next sections of this book are a practical guide to the strategies and techniques and tactics for how and when to regulate our responses.

But it deserves at least a basic description here—a preview, if you like.

We've already discussed the critical first step of downregulation—stopping the action and deactivating the emotional moment. Bringing the proceedings to a halt gives us time to figure out what to do next.

To understand how that will go in real life, wait until the next time you feel a strong and unpleasant emotion coming on. One that's not so easy to manage. Could be anxiety, worry, fear, frustration, disappointment. One of the tough ones.

The instant you feel it, do this:

Pause.

The point of pausing, as we've already described, is to deactivate the moment. To keep it from making you instantly react in an unhelpful way.

Now during that pause, take a deep breath.

Take a few. Again, maybe count to ten or even higher. Perhaps, if you feel an intemperate response about to emerge from your lips, bite your tongue (gently). Or take a few steps back.

But otherwise, lengthen the pause.

Now ask yourself: *How do I want to feel right now?*

Okay, if you're performing this exercise in the middle of a conversation with your significant other, or during a meeting at work, or in line at Starbucks, coming to a complete and extended freeze might seem a little strange. Like you've gone comatose. Do your best to live with it.

Each of the following steps involves questions to ask yourself:

*Okay, I'm hurt. I have a right to feel hurt. But I'm choosing not to act from that hurt.*

What will you do instead? You're still doing nothing.

For how long? Long enough to feel your heart stop racing, and your breathing return to normal, and that fizzing in your brain settle down. This might take a little while, but don't rush it.

Okay, now you're ready to go to work. Each of the following steps involves questions to ask yourself.

**Step 1: Identify the emotion(s).** *What exactly am I feeling? Or what emotion do I anticipate feeling?* Emotion regulation strategy selection works best when we know what we're feeling (or might feel) before we decide how to deal with it.

**Step 2: Determine the goal.** *How do I want to feel? What do I want to do with this emotion? Is there a way to transform it into something I'd rather be feeling?*

**Step 3: Select and implement the strategy.** *Which plan will be most effective for me in this moment?* The strategy we choose is dependent on context (e.g., home or work) and is often rooted in our current needs and personality. For example, I am an introvert, and after a day of presenting, my preferred strategy is a visit to the gym or a yoga class and a quiet dinner. Helpful strategies are limitless, even for the same emotion, and we regularly employ multiple strategies, a technique known as polyregulation, to manage an emotion.

As the word suggests, the strategy is an overall plan of action—a purposeful way to meet the challenge of regulating each unique emotional response. Later in the book we'll go into seven research-based strategies:

1. Shifting our beliefs about emotions, including accepting our emotions as they arise and believing it's possible to regulate them.
2. Labeling emotions precisely to guide us in the right direction.
3. Quieting our mind and body by breathing in ways that help us deactivate strong emotions and practicing mindfulness.
4. Redirecting our thoughts to help us shift our attention or "reframe" our thinking about the situation.
5. Engaging with other people to gain perspective and comfort.
6. Managing our regulation budget, which includes sleep, physical activity, and nutrition.
7. Becoming the best version of ourselves, the ultimate step that includes making emotion regulation a core aspect of our identity.

Under each of those headings are countless techniques and tactics we can apply as we attempt to deal with our feelings. We've already discussed some of them, but there are many more. In truth, the list is infinite, because once you understand the basics, you'll be able to devise your own, suited to your particular needs.

There's one final step.

**Step 4: Evaluate the strategy.** *Did it work? Did it help me achieve my emotion goal?* This requires reflecting on the implementation of the strategy: *Did my action help to achieve a personal or professional aim? If not, why was it unsuccessful? Do I need more practice with the strategy, or do I need to replace it with a more helpful one?*

Choosing the best way forward requires intuition and creativity. A strategy that works one day might not work the next. One person might manage sadness easily but can't manage anger. Another is able to keep her cool under pressure but is racked by anxiety. You might struggle with depression but maintain your good humor while others are freaking out.

There's a natural tendency, during moments of extreme unpleasant emotion, to forget everything else you know about your life. Activation narrows our focus. There's likely an evolutionary reason for this. When you're being chased by a bear or an unfriendly fellow human wielding a club, you need to pay close attention to your pursuer and not notice what a beautiful sunny day it is.

The same dynamic is at work when a loved one has said or done something that brings up a difficult emotion. It's easy in those moments to forget how easygoing and accepting your spouse has always been, or how well-behaved your children were at dinner last night. All you can think of is how frustrated you are at this exact moment and that somebody else is completely to blame, and before you can stop yourself, you're yelling at the top of your lungs.

In a more perfect world, regulating our emotional responses would be as straightforward as we psychologists make it sound. You pause, label what you're feeling, choose the proper strategy and technique for regulating it, and voilà—instant equilibrium.

Unfortunately, our world today is anything but perfect. The more chronic stress we must withstand, the closer to the edge we all exist. Kids experience this more intensely than the rest of us, for the simple reason that they have so little control over the circumstances of their lives. You can understand how that might make learning more difficult than it ought to be.

Today, a lot of us exist in situations that fill us with fear, uncertainty, anxiety, hopelessness. I can't even imagine what it's like to be a child in an era when school shootings have become commonplace events. Now multiply that by all the dangers—real, imagined, exaggerated—that we live among today, the vague ambient threat that hovers over us all.

It takes its toll. It uses up emotional energy and leaves us unequipped to handle the feelings we experience in daily living. This gives us even more reason to focus on learning effective strategies.

We have one more factor to consider in regulating our emotional responses—perhaps the most important one.

Other people.

That's because more often than not, we experience our most intense and meaningful emotions during interactions with fellow human beings. It could be a parent or a child or a significant other; a sibling, a friend, a coworker, a neighbor, somebody on your softball team, your dry cleaner, the new barista at the coffee shop, or even that guy back at the beginning of the chapter who bumped you on the street.

Thanks to the power of TV and social media, it could even be someone you'll never meet, a public figure anywhere in the world. A celebrity! An elected official. Any of these might have the power to influence how you feel—for better or for worse.

We experience our emotional lives while interacting with other people who are experiencing *their* emotional lives. Their feelings cause their behaviors, which in turn trigger our feelings, which cause our behaviors, and around and around we go.

The term for how we influence one another is *co-regulation*. As a practical matter, it means that if you can surround yourself with people who are successful at regulating their emotional responses, they will make it easier for you to regulate yours. But if not, and if you're constantly among people who are incapable of regulating in healthy ways, you're in for a bumpy ride.

It's an infinitely complex web of relationships and emotions, as you can imagine.

## 5.

# What Is Co-Regulation?

*Life doesn't make any sense without interdependence. We need each other, and the sooner we learn that, the better for us all.*

—Erik Erikson

We're permeable. We pay close attention to one another. We listen and we watch, we take one another in whether we want to or not, and what we see and hear and feel affects us. We can't help it.

Sometimes we're improved by it; other times just the opposite. Either way, we react and respond to one another pretty much constantly, starting at birth and continuing until . . . well, for a very long time.

Our emotions are affected and influenced even by people we don't know and will never meet. Sometimes that's a good thing—like when we're inspired or uplifted by people we read about or experience from afar. Chance encounters with strangers occasionally leave us feeling fantastic. Other times, it's not so great—like when we are enraged or discouraged by public figures we see in our news feeds.

Demagogues are great at influencing the emotions of masses of people. That's pretty much the job description. If a demagogue can't rouse your most intense feelings and hype you up, they haven't earned the title. They can make us feel important, but they're not interested in us as individuals, or in improving our state of mind. Our connection to them is impersonal and usually the opposite of helpful.

Still, they get to us.

The same is true about the people we encounter in person but at a distance from our lives and concerns. That friendly bartender, the cop who pulled you over, the tech support person who tried to walk you through your latest digital disaster, the dentist who fills your cavities. They might momentarily make a difference in how we feel, but the ties are still impersonal. There's no commitment, no meaningful back-and-forth. If the relationship sours, you can always find another dentist.

And then there's everybody else—the people who truly matter to us. They have the power to affect us deeply, which means we can do the same to them. In a perfect world, we'd all use that power responsibly, judiciously, with love and kindness and care.

But our world is far from perfect. That's not our fault, although there are plenty of moments when we deserve some responsibility. We can all learn to do better. As with regulation, nobody is born knowing how.

For the purposes of our discussion, healthy co-regulation means regulating other people's emotional responses intentionally, while regulating your own, with a positive effect in mind. It means recognizing what other people are feeling and then acting in ways that will be helpful and possibly even improve the relationship.

Karen Niven, a professor of organizational psychology at Sheffield University Management School, is a top researcher of co-regulation, or what scientists who study adults call interpersonal regulation. She describes it like this: "You bump into a close friend while out for a walk and notice that they seem distracted and upset. What do you do? You might pretend all is okay and exit the conversation, but the chances are you don't—you most likely stay and try to make them feel better." This act of attempting to change the way someone else feels is *interpersonal emotion regulation*.

"The research that has developed in this area provides compelling evidence that the seemingly small behaviors we use to shape others' feelings can make a big difference to their lives—and to ours," she continues. "Interpersonal emotion regulation encompasses all and every attempt that a person might make to influence the feelings of someone else," including "attempts to elicit new feelings and to intensify, reduce, or maintain current feelings."

I was recently part of an academic working group focused on defining co-regulation among youth. Here's what we came up with:

A person who co-regulates in a healthy way:

- has curiosity in order to accurately imagine or understand the other person's needs;
- allows the other person to experience their feelings;
- is warm, supportive, accepting, and nurturing;
- coaches, models, and reinforces;
- offers comfort and empathy during tough times;
- supports achieving long-term goals by encouraging planning, awareness of consequences, and task completion;
- shares perspectives for problem-solving and decision-making; and
- ultimately, allows space for the other person, including when that is a child, to make their own decisions and experience the consequences.

Co-regulating starts with a series of questions: *What might this person be feeling and why? What might this person need right now? How might this person want to feel? Where do I want to help take them? If they're charged up but in a negative way, what can I say or do to validate, calm, and improve their emotional state? Or, if they're gloomy and despairing, how can I give them a positive, optimistic lift?* Once we have a goal in mind, we can use the tactics of emotion regulation to achieve it. We're all completely aware of the power of co-regulation, even if we don't call it that.

Sometimes, when I deliver a talk before a group, I'll start by saying, "Look, I know you're all focused on what I'm about to say, and you're alert and present and all that, correct?"

Nods all around.

"But then," I continue, "in a few minutes, your attention will start to wander. Maybe you'll notice that your chair isn't very comfortable. Maybe your stomach will start to growl. Or you'll feel your phone vibrate and you'll want to check your messages. All the usual things that take place when we're doing something else.

"And when that happens," I ask, "what will you do to remain focused? What strategies and techniques will you use?"

Here's how people answer:

"I'm going to take notes."

"I'm going to breathe."

"I'm sitting in the front row to make sure I keep up with you."

"I know I'm interested in this subject, so I won't have trouble paying attention."

And other polite replies along those lines.

"Okay," I say, "that all sounds good, but you know yourselves well enough to know that staying focused is going to be a challenge at some point while I'm speaking."

"Well," somebody will say, "isn't it your job to keep us focused? Aren't you supposed to be so interesting that we'll all listen to you?"

That's a pretty good answer. It's correct—during my talk, it's my role to engage my listeners. But I also like that reply because it says something about emotion co-regulation. As my audiences see it, my task is to recognize the things they might feel during the course of my presentation, and then do something about it. Meaning that I'll have ways of managing their emotions so they won't be bored or antsy or distracted.

We're constantly influencing other people's emotions. We're not always doing it well. We're not always aware that we're doing it.

But we're doing it.

Co-regulation is how we expect people who care about each

other to interact. Whether it's a parent to a child, one friend to another, spouses to each other, a teacher to a student, a supervisor to an employee—the list goes on. The truth is that you can't have a personal relationship that doesn't include co-regulation. Sounds simple enough, though nothing about how humans engage with one another can be described as simple.

Co-regulating flows back and forth between people, like a subliminal conversation—one that takes place beneath the literal meaning of whatever words we're exchanging. We use the most subtle cues imaginable to wordlessly say the things we choose not to speak out loud. Your overall vibe—your words and gestures and body language and facial expressions and tone of voice, the whole package of communication—amounts to an effort to move me from one emotional state into another, a better one (I would hope).

Even those of us who refuse to do anything at all are co-regulating, because ignoring someone's emotions is a way of influencing them. That may seem unfair: Why should I have to manage your emotions just because they exist? I surely didn't ask for that job.

But we're stuck with one another. If someone is in your life, their emotions are, too. There's no escaping it.

Not every response to another person's feelings can be called co-regulation. If my brother makes me so angry that I curse and slam down the phone, that's not an intentional action meant to regulate his emotions. That's me losing it and reacting in pure, heedless fury. Hardly co-regulation.

In truth, there are plenty of ways we can respond to other people's emotions by making them feel not better but worse. No surprise there. We'll call it *unhealthy* co-regulation and we'll discuss it just enough to make sure we learn to avoid it. Otherwise, there's no point in describing how to make people feel bad, is there?

It's not as though you'll say to yourself, *Okay, I want Marc to feel guilty about what he just did.* But if deep down you believe that Marc *should* feel guilty, or if you think that you might benefit if Marc *does* feel guilty, then you just might co-regulate him in that direction.

Of course, you probably won't do it blatantly, in so many words. You won't say, "Marc, you ought to feel guilty about what you just did." But by the time we're adults, we all know how to say things without saying them. You can call that passive-aggressive if you like, but a great deal of co-regulation happens passive-aggressively, which might actually be preferable to plain old unmitigated aggression.

That's co-regulation, too, but of a toxic kind.

It reminds me of the 1944 film *Gaslight*, in which the wicked husband, played by Charles Boyer, manipulates his vulnerable wife, played by Ingrid Bergman, into thinking she's losing her sanity so that he can rob her. The title refers to the gaslights in their home, which dim for no apparent reason. When Bergman's character notices this, her husband convinces her that only she can see the dimming, proof of her shaky mental condition.

That's a pretty good example of vicious co-regulation. I experienced it firsthand when I was a teenager.

My parents had come to visit me during my sophomore year of college. I was having a difficult time adjusting to life there and was in therapy with a counselor. I decided this was the time to finally tell my parents that I was gay.

My dad had a typical tough-guy attitude about most things in life. My mom was the opposite—every little bump in the road pushed her toward the nervous breakdown she was always on the verge of experiencing.

When I came out to them, their immediate response was to tell me I was wrong—I only *thought* I was gay due to the childhood sexual abuse I had suffered.

I remember wondering, *Could they be right?* They were my parents, after all. Maybe I *was* just confused?

Now I know better.

(Ultimately, everything worked out with my parents, though the journey was more drawn out than necessary.)

Today, the term *gaslighting*—popularized lately by my colleague and senior adviser Robin Stern, author of *The Gaslight Effect*—gets lots of use in personal relationships but also in the public realm. There must be a great deal of self-serving emotional manipulation going on in the world.

Anyway, if you live among other human beings and wish to have positive, loving, beneficial relationships with them, then you had better be aware of how well (or poorly) you co-regulate. It matters a lot.

This is the reason it's so important to model the skills of healthy co-regulation for our children. I often have this somewhat lofty—yet, to me, realistic—thought: If one entire generation of human beings everywhere in the world learned how to co-regulate smoothly, nearly all our troubles would quickly disappear.

I seriously mean that.

Because the generation that absorbed these skills would grow up using them, like second nature, and would in turn impart emotion regulation and co-regulation skills to their children, and so on and so on and so on.

Later in this book we'll talk about the role of schools and educators in teaching kids how to deal with their feelings. The first and best opportunity to teach it, however, is in the home. Of course, we can't teach what we haven't learned.

An infant sits in a high chair, face-to-face with her mother. Mom is smiling, talking, cooing, laughing, touching, and baby is responding in kind. At one point the child points to something behind her mother, and the woman turns to see. A typical moment of parent-baby bonding.

Suddenly, mom goes stone-faced. Absolutely impassive. Completely emotionless. Immobile. Baby keeps grinning and chattering away—for a moment. Then she also undergoes an abrupt change: Now she's frowning, whining, twisting and turning in her seat, obviously uncomfortable, extravagantly unhappy. This time, when she points, her mother's gaze doesn't budge.

It goes on this way for a few minutes. It's torture to watch.

Then, in a flash, the mother goes back to behaving normally. She's babbling baby talk, smiling broadly, laughing, touching. The child notices the change immediately and goes back to being the same happy baby she was at the start.

I'm watching the video of the famous "still face" experiment conducted in the 1970s by psychology professor Edward Tronick of University of Massachusetts Boston. You can find it on YouTube—it's a landmark in the study of early childhood development.

Here's what this experiment tells us about co-regulation.

First, it demonstrates the enormous importance of what we call *attunement*, even in the mind of an infant. When the mother withholds emotional cues, the baby freaks out, showing that infants fully understand the give-and-take of affection and connection. A newborn can recognize what psychologists call "the mother's violation of reciprocity"—meaning when the parent withdraws—as early as two to three weeks of age. That's a sure sign of how meaningful a secure reciprocal relationship is to a child's development.

That leads us to the second revelation: At a very young age, babies wish to be active participants in the flow of feelings that we adults take for granted. They understand the importance of interaction. The child in the experiment has already learned that she has the power to influence her mother's emotions and actions. When that power disappears, the baby suffers. She feels despair.

An older child, when faced with a withholding parent, might respond in kind, turning cold and shutting down. The infant doesn't yet have the ability to mask their feelings, so they can only react in honest, unregulated anguish. This suggests that adult involvement is absolutely necessary if a child is ever going to learn how to deal with challenging feelings. And finally, once the mother resumes her normal behavior, the baby instantly begins smiling and babbling as before—showing how easily emotional equilibrium can be regained, as long as the adult reengages and becomes involved again. What happens when it's not a psychology experiment? When the lack of emotional connection lasts not for a few moments but for years? For that, too, we have evidence, in a study that's also widely known and even more heartbreaking.

After the Romanian dictator Nicolae Ceaușescu was overthrown in 1989, 170,000 children were discovered living in the country's ghastly orphanages. Starting in 2000, a trio of scientists—Charles Nelson, Nathan Fox, and Charles Zeanah—began an assessment of 136 of those children, average age twenty-two months. They split them into two groups. One group remained in institutional settings. Those in the other were moved into foster homes. Then, over the years that followed, the researchers measured and compared the children, and wrote a book on their findings, *Romania's Abandoned Children: Deprivation, Brain Development, and the Struggle for Recovery*.

The institutionalized children, naturally, suffered most from their deprivation and lack of emotional engagement with the people who were supposed to be caring for them. Even their brains were damaged—they exhibited impairment in cognitive function, motor development, and language ability, in addition to abnormal electrical activity. They had more emotional and psychiatric disorders, too.

The children who had been sent to foster homes at the earliest ages fared somewhat better. They improved in IQ, social-emotional function, and language. They formed attachments with their foster parents and learned how to express their feelings.

It's through the exchange of emotional expression starting in earliest infancy that we attach to one another. That's when patterns are formed and expectations are created. The scientific concept of attachment originates from the work of John Bowlby, an English psychiatrist who started studying children with emotional issues in the 1930s. A colleague of his, a psychologist named Mary Ainsworth, made the case that we are born needing to attach to others as a means to survival. She defined four main "styles" of attachment:

The *secure* attachment style is a warm, loving, and consistent bond between parent and child. It prepares us to develop healthy, confident emotional relationships for the rest of our lives.

The *anxious-ambivalent* style of attachment makes children distrust caregivers, and this insecurity translates into a fear of abandonment and a strong need for approval. The same patterns that follow from childhood into adult life make us overly dependent on other people.

Children who acquire the *avoidant* attachment style learn to accept that their emotional needs are likely to remain unmet, and so they grow up feeling unloved and insignificant. They have difficulty understanding their own emotions and those of other people, and so they tend to avoid intimate relationships.

Finally, *disorganized* attachment combines the avoidant and anxious-ambivalent styles. Children in this group have a hard time controlling intense feelings, especially anger—these are the kids who throw violent tantrums and break toys and have strained relations with guardians. As adults they continue to be unable to manage strong emotions.

We each have our own version, our personal style of attachment, that began to form in infancy and sticks with us forever after.

In fact, I find that I'm pretty quick to accurately determine someone's attachment style moments after I meet them. One person seems anxious and forever seeking approval and agreement. Someone else gives off the vibe of avoiding personal connection altogether. The lucky ones seem relaxed and assured in how they relate to other people—neither overly attached nor distanced.

It's almost impossible to exaggerate the importance of attachment style to our future emotional and psychological health.

And how do our attachment styles develop?

Through our earliest experiences of emotion co-regulation. Through the interplay, the back-and-forth, the interactions that take place between baby and adult. According to Alan Sroufe, a developmental psychologist at the Institute of Child Development at the University of

Minnesota, co-regulation in support of cultivating a secure attachment is rooted in the deep, abiding confidence a baby has in the availability and responsiveness of their caregiver.

In infancy, co-regulation occurs even before self-regulation. In fact, it's only through the experience of being effectively co-regulated that babies learn to manage their own emotional responses.

From the beginning of life, newborns have a lot of stimuli to contend with and virtually no tools for coping. They're hungry. They're tired. They're cold. They're colicky. They're physically uncomfortable. They need to be fed or held or changed or soothed in one way or another.

They express it all in the only way they know how—by crying and whining and wailing. They're powerless to address their own needs or to express them in any other way. They can only signal to adults—*help me*.

Babies are not blank slates but are *experience expectant*, quickly absorbing information through every adult vocal utterance, facial expression, and act of response. They observe and learn how humans operate emotionally and watch for specific signals. Their brains are wired to expect interactions like being held, comforted, and responded to. These interactions develop neural pathways for emotion regulation and social bonding. If such experience-expectant interactions are missing or inconsistent, it can lead to difficulties in attachment and self-regulation.

A mother begins co-regulating her child's emotional state before birth (signals cross the placenta) and co-regulation becomes more formal at the moment of birth. And shortly after that, the child begins co-regulating her. That's how ingrained the exchange is in what it means to be human. And without learning self-regulation, children will struggle to develop meaningful relationships, communicate reciprocally, and succeed in school and, later, at work and in adult life.

Clearly, in our dealings with children, our own powers of co-regulation get a good workout. One adult to another, we're free to interact as we please, taking equal responsibility for our actions and reactions. But when we're with a child, we must strive to be the wiser one, more caring, more generous, more loving. As the parent, or guardian, or educator, it's our responsibility to teach the child positive lessons in emotion self-regulation—which we can do only by setting a good, beneficial example.

We need to think about temperament match. You're mellow and in control, but your child is excitable and volatile and voluble. This means you have to accommodate that difference and match your child's temperament with your own. To co-regulate that child you'll need to work on yourself first.

By the same token, if you're hyper and your child is not, you'll have to resist the urge to overstimulate your kid. You can't exhort a child to smile more or demonstrate their feelings with greater enthusiasm—you need to recalibrate your expectations and align yourself with your child's emotional reality.

When it comes to the tender feelings of a child, the ways we co-regulate in moments of emotional intensity can leave impressions that last for years, even decades. The attempts of our parents, guardians, and teachers—whether supportive or less so—shape how we view ourselves and others.

In a classroom, a child asks a question with a painfully obvious answer. Rather than replying, the teacher feels the need to belittle the student with a snarky comeback. That child will never trust that teacher again, for sure. But that's not the extent of the damage—every student in that room is now afraid of saying the wrong thing and receiving the same humiliation in response. Lessons like this ripple throughout the classroom.

Or at home, the kid announces, "I'm mad," and the parent replies, "So what's new?"

Where does the child go with that? How is that guaranteed to make them feel? It says, *I will use your emotional expressions as occasions for me to be witty and amusing at the expense of your feelings.* Or worse, *I don't care how you feel. Your feelings are annoying.*

The child's experience will linger for a very long time.

At home, a child announces her desire to be a professional singer someday. Mom smiles and nods encouragingly. The positive effect will linger no matter how realistic that dream might be.

But if her mother raises a skeptical eyebrow in response? I can guarantee that kid will be crushed, and when she's an adult—whether she's made it as a singer or not—she'll remember that awful moment.

Conversely, a friend told me about a lasting moment from his childhood.

He was at a birthday party, having a great time, until his father arrived to take him home—the first kid to leave. So of course he was furious.

On the walk home, that little boy made his anger known in the cutting way kids have when they're furious.

His father looked down at him and said, in a kindly voice, "I understand, but that remark was uncalled for."

My friend remembers being shocked—he fully expected his father to respond to his petulance with anger of his own, like any parent might. Instead, his dad showed sympathy and restraint that made my friend regret his sarcasm. To this day, he carries the vivid memory of that moment when, instead of the response he expected, he got something finer.

While it may feel like you get one shot at co-regulation, the truth is more nuanced. A single misstep doesn't define the whole relationship. Opportunities for repair—acknowledging a mistake, apologizing, and trying again—are themselves powerful forms of co-regulation. They teach children resilience, empathy, and the idea that relationships can withstand and grow from challenges. So, with our children, how do we proceed?

In the previous chapter on regulation, we discussed PRIME: prevent, reduce, initiate, maintain, and enhance. Just as these goals can help us to manage our own emotional responses, they can be used to guide us in co-regulating those of our kids.

First, we can try to *prevent* the child from experiencing unnecessary difficult feelings. We do this by anticipating and seeking to avoid a situation like bullying. (At the same time, it's important to remember that we can't shield children from awkward social moments, conflict, and navigating difficult friendships—experiences that help them grow and build resilience.)

Next, we can *reduce* the impact of the negative emotion.

Then, we seek to *initiate* an emotion.

We find ways to *maintain* or savor the good feelings we've engendered.

And finally, we do what we can to *enhance* pleasant emotions, to make them even stronger.

How might this work with a child we're trying to co-regulate?

We have to visit our complicated Aunt Hillary and know that Junior is going to be miserable once we get there.

We can *prevent* unpleasant emotions by making sure to bring his favorite toys and games so the fun can begin before the misery has a chance.

We can *reduce* unpleasant feelings by keeping an eye on Junior and removing him from Aunt Hillary's intrusive eyes if she happens to get activated.

We can *initiate* pleasant emotions by playing Junior's favorite music on the way to Aunt Hillary's home.

We can *maintain* the good feelings by recognizing when our visit is winding down and maybe ending it a little sooner than planned.

And we can *enhance* the positive vibe by reminding Junior how proud we are of his behavior during the visit.

Taken all together, so much attention to a child's feelings might seem like we're coddling or overindulging to a harmful degree. Are all these precautions and accommodations spoiling the precious little one?

Possibly. But interactions such as these are ways of teaching kids effective strategies for regulating their own emotional difficulties, now and in the future. And as we'll learn in future chapters, strategies for co-regulation are not about fixing or solving emotion-related problems; they're about co-constructing and building our regulation muscles.

But maybe the most damaging form of co-regulation is its lack—

ignoring the other person, especially a child, at a time when our presence is needed.

Or, nearly as bad, minimizing the other person's need.

"Come on, Junior, you're exaggerating!"

"Don't let Aunt Hillary get to you."

"She's your aunt, get over it."

"Be a big boy!"

"I've had enough of this."

Or, this bitter old-school shutdown:

"Stop crying or I'll really give you something to cry about."

It's tempting, for some reason, to take the emotional needs of children less seriously than those of adults. Maybe when people are small, the stakes seem smaller. Perhaps cuteness works against kids when they express their frustration and sense of unfairness with what the world dishes out.

At any rate, when we minimize the strong feelings of childhood, we do our children a disservice.

In childhood, our emotional response patterns are created. The lessons we learn in our first few years are carried forward into adulthood. They become entrenched and difficult, though not impossible, to change—it takes longer and more energy to unlearn them later on. And they are carried forward beyond our lifetimes, too, because as adults we pass along what we absorbed to our own children.

The ways we regulate and co-regulate are like inheritances. We receive and observe them in our parents, and that's how we learn them. They remain with us, and we use them in dealing with our own children, and the cycle continues.

# 6.

# Co-Regulation in Action

*As you grow older, you will discover that you have two hands, one for helping yourself, the other for helping others.*

—Maya Angelou

So, now that we know what co-regulation is and why it's so important, all that's left to learn is how to do it well.

As we've already said, healthy co-regulation with the people we care about begins with understanding what they're feeling, learning what they might need, and deciding on a goal—figuring out the best place for them to be, emotionally speaking. That alone requires a certain sensitivity on our part: How do we know what another person wants to feel? How can we tell if we're making the right call?

To a large extent, that relies on our relationship. Ideally, you know the other person well enough to understand something about their emotional makeup. If she's not likely to spill her guts, no point in pushing it. If he wears his heart on his sleeve, maybe asking him if he needs empathy or just another perspective will make a positive difference. If in the past a hug helped, give a hug.

When a friend's husband was dying, I knew she wasn't ready to talk about it. So, I sent her a text every couple of days—short, sweet, and easy, just to let her know she was in my thoughts, and that if she felt like unloading, I was there for her. Pushing any harder would have been exactly what she *didn't* need. In the grip of an intense emotion like grief, a little space and time to deactivate may be the only sensible first step.

But when my father died, a friend sent a text saying, "Listen, I know you're going through a lot, but I'm here if you need to talk—just give me a ring." What I really needed was someone who knew me well enough to know that I was unlikely ever to make that call. I wished she had called me.

Here's a good way to determine what to do when someone needs an emotional assist: Just ask. And then really listen. Not so we can fix everything, but to identify the strategy or strategies that will help them achieve their desired emotion—even if we're only helping them to "be with" their feelings.

The questions can sound something like this:

What's happening?
What would be most helpful to you right now?
What can I do to support you?
What do you think you need?
What would you like me to do?

We're most vulnerable to difficult feelings when we're weary, hungry, or thirsty. So maybe the first question should be, "Would you like to grab a bite? Do you need to sit down? How about a cup of coffee?"

Sometimes we'll just have to infer what would help, maybe by making suggestions:

Let's take a walk.
Let's breathe together.
Let's see a movie.
Let's go for a run.
Look out for the package I sent.

At other times, the feeling that requires co-regulation will be obvious: In those cases—in *many* cases—the best co-regulation will consist of practical problem-solving. That should always be option number one, for the simple reason that it sweeps away challenging emotions so efficiently.

I'm scared of my teacher, and I don't want to go to school.
Tomorrow is my annual job evaluation, and I'm a nervous wreck.
The doctor's office called to schedule a biopsy.
The responsibility for supporting my family is crushing me.
The way my colleague speaks to me makes me furious.

The person who's perpetually insecure at work? Maybe it's time to find another job. But that tactic won't help the child who dreads school, though perhaps a talk with his teacher and a fresh start will. Temporary uncertainty about your health will be resolved soon enough (even if it's replaced by unfortunate certainty). A rocky relationship between siblings requires more than soothing—it should start with an honest, possibly uncomfortable conversation.

Perhaps a friend is anxious about an important email he needs to send. Trying to talk him out of that anxiety would be useless; better to help him craft his message and give him confidence in what he's trying to say. Someone else fears for her safety in an abusive relationship. She needs support in removing herself from physical danger, not your heartfelt empathy.

People ask me frequently about if and how empathy works as a method of co-regulation. Does it mean we're trying to feel what the other person is feeling? That's impossible—we alone own our emotions. But can we attempt to understand someone else's experiences and motivations as a path to knowing how best to help them? That's achievable—empathy is a first step in the process. If a practical solution to a challenging situation isn't happening, then we turn to the same helpful strategies and techniques for co-regulation that we'd use in regulating our own emotional responses. Now, however, they're directed outwardly.

That makes a big difference.

Dealing with our own emotions is challenging enough. Engaging with someone else's can be downright scary, depending on the circumstances. It's hard being with someone who's furious. It's taxing to support someone in mourning. It can turn into empathic distress—a kind of dysregulation that happens when we have so much empathy we are not able to regulate the feelings that emerge.

But at its highest level, co-regulation pushes us to connect strongly with the people in our lives, especially when it makes us uncomfortable. And doing so is associated with better relationships and even benefits for the one doing the co-regulating—including better physical health, higher life satisfaction, and lower anxiety.

That's not the only difference. When we self-regulate, we may talk to ourselves, but when we communicate with others, we use the full vocabulary of human expression. Words and tone of voice are important tools but hardly the only ones. In fact, the nonverbal means of co-regulation can be quite powerful.

Our faces are fabulously expressive. They can hold entire conversations wordlessly. Just think of all you can say by narrowing your eyebrows, closing or popping open your eyes, winking, scrunching your nose, running through the full repertoire of your mouth and lips, or lowering, tilting, thrusting, or withdrawing your head.

It's a symphony of co-regulation. We study one another's faces obsessively. Compared to other forms of communication, our words are almost secondary. Our eyes see far more than our ears hear.

And our bodies? Pretty much our faces' equals. We can be all-embracing or in arm-crossed disapproval mode, in an obvious fury or a menace or a sulk. Again, we're co-regulating in ways that the other person will absorb far beyond the reach of mere words.

Psychologist Karen Niven asked adult research subjects about the techniques they use to co-regulate—how they make others feel better or worse or experience various emotions such as anger, sadness, or happiness. She and her team found that we have almost four hundred distinct ways of managing other people's feelings—roughly half of which are intended to make them feel better and the rest to make them feel worse.

The strategies we use, Niven reported, are of three main types.

The first is what she termed "relationship-oriented." This kind relies on the existing connection between the co-regulator and the person being regulated (whom she called "the target"). If you can help a friend navigate an unpleasant feeling simply by making them laugh, or taking them out to dinner, or giving them a hug, or changing the subject, then congratulations. Even if you haven't helped them solve anything, you've used your existing connection to change how they feel. Whatever works, works.

By the same token, of course, I can withhold affection or a cheerful word when you need it most, or turn humorless and unresponsive, and make your emotional state even worse. We can also co-regulate negatively by the words we *don't* say—like when someone needs full-throated support, and we offer a tepid expression. Or, in response to a romance that's ended badly, we say, "Come on, man, you two broke up six months ago, get over it!"

Is that meant to make me feel better? Understood? Are you truly trying to keep me from overreacting? Or are you saying that there must be something wrong with me to still be so hung up?

The other types of strategies are termed "problem-focused" and "emotion-focused." Problem-focused strategies attempt to change the situation or how the target thinks about it (for example, helping someone get out of a difficult moment like an argument or helping them find a different way to perceive the situation in order to modify their feelings). Emotion-focused strategies include trying to regulate the target's expression of emotion (by, for example, validating their anger or attempting to soothe or lower the intensity of the emotion). We'll dive more deeply into these tactics and techniques in part 3 of this book.

How we co-regulate depends a great deal on context. Am I in the conference room of a Fortune 500 company, or in the kitchen with my twelve-year-old, or in bed with my spouse, or speaking to an audience of two hundred fellow researchers? Big difference.

At one seminar I was leading, a man listened patiently but then said, "Look, just give me one strategy that my whole family can use."

"I wish it were that simple," I replied. I think he was missing the point—that there's an infinite number of good co-regulation techniques and strategies, and the right one depends on a long list of factors.

A simple way to make sure we'll receive helpful co-regulation is to surround ourselves, as much as possible, with people who know how to regulate themselves. That's partly because the same strategies, techniques, and tactics are used in both kinds of emotion regulation. It works the same in either direction.

But there's also another reason: Simply being in the presence of well-regulated people *is* a form of co-regulation. If you and your spouse are having financial difficulties, and you react in a panicky way, your spouse will take that as a cue to panic along with you. But if you appear to approach the problem calmly and with a clear idea about how to fix it, that becomes your form of co-regulation—a message that this is something we'll successfully tackle together.

The way we regulate our own emotions creates a vibe, an ambience, an energy. If you're around someone who reacts instantly and heedlessly to every emotion, the atmosphere will feel super-hyped. It might induce you, too, into responding without thinking. Or it might regulate you in the opposite direction—driving you into a defensive crouch where you refuse to acknowledge any emotion at all. Which could be just as worthless.

When we're near people who need co-regulation, we detect it easily—even at a chemical level. Strong, negative emotions alter our hormones and release pheromones into our sweat. When that happens, people who come into close contact with us will show increased brain activation corresponding to our own activated emotional state.

After a while, life partners' emotions automatically coordinate. In one study, just holding a spouse's hand reduced the physical pain people were experiencing.

In this sense, co-regulating is simply being a role model—setting an example for someone dealing with a strong emotion. When you offer a stabilizing influence during a challenging moment, your calm becomes contagious.

This is especially important when we're raising children. They watch how we handle our own emotions and learn to manage theirs.

Mom comes home from work exhausted and anxious, and once she's in the house there's a kid asking to play catch. The parent can say, "Not now," and head straight to the fridge to find refuge in a cold beer. Understandable. We've all had those days.

But put yourself in the child's position. What's the lesson in how to co-regulate when dealing with someone who loves you and needs your attention?

*Shut them down. And don't even try to explain what you're feeling.*

That's a form of unhealthy co-regulation the child will absorb and use someday, maybe on a child of their own.

Or, the mother could have said, "Sweetheart, Mom had a long, tiring day. Give me fifteen minutes to relax and I'll meet you in the backyard. I'd love to play catch with you. Go find the gloves and the ball."

Essentially the same outcome. But a completely different lesson has been learned.

Co-regulation really becomes a challenge when we have to do it on a large scale. Educators know this well—you've got a classroom full of children, each with their own personality and needs, and you've got to get them all pointed in the same direction toward the same goals and moving at the same speed. It's work, as any teacher will swear. Some of those kids will need to be downregulated and have their energy level lowered so they can focus and learn. Others will need just the opposite—they're sleepy, or bored, or have tuned out of classwork in favor of something else.

Try getting that room into the same emotional space. To do so, you might have to set aside your lesson plan and get creative. That probably won't happen if you're unable to regulate your own emotional responses and handle moving into the unknown.

Whatever co-regulation strategy we choose, we need to remember that emotions exist for a reason—they are the product of evolution just as much as anything else about us. Even the most difficult ones—fear, rage, anxiety, grief—serve a practical purpose. They are information about how we experience our lives.

So, co-regulation's role is not simply to make somebody feel "better." Happiness is not always a realistic goal, or even a desirable one. It's entirely possible that someone who's grieving will benefit from maintaining that grief and working through it rather than trying to smother it. A person fired up with righteous anger will get past it only by first exploring the reasons, then taking action to resolve it.

There's a danger in under-identifying or over-identifying with the people in our lives. We might fail to understand what the other person is feeling and why, which will limit our ability to influence their emotional state. Maybe we don't care enough to try. Maybe we can't read the cues. Maybe we're so intent on our own feelings that we have trouble perceiving anyone else's.

There's a sweet spot in co-regulating. We seek to understand the other person's feelings and engage with them in a helpful way. That can't be done from too great a remove. But it's also difficult when we're so close that we occupy the same psychic real estate.

Back when the world shut down due to the pandemic, I got a necessary lesson in this.

I was feeling the panic and anxiety we all shared. Would I get sick? Would the global economy tank and take my 401(k) with it? Would the Yale Center for Emotional Intelligence, to which I had devoted so much of my life, go under due to our supporters' and benefactors' financial suffering? Inside, I was freaking out and shutting down, so fearful of the worst possible outcomes that I felt unable to articulate my fears even to myself.

Then I remembered that I had a staff of people who were depending on the Center—and on me. And they were feeling all the same things I felt. Maybe worse because they had even less control than I did. It was my responsibility to help them address their emotions right then.

So I did, but not by sugarcoating anything. If I hadn't been honest, they would have picked up on it in a second and begun to worry even more. We convened (online of course), and I and my leadership team talked openly about the scary possibilities we all faced. Calmly, we enumerated our fears in as much detail and specificity as possible. And I also shared all that I was doing to regulate. That opened the floodgates—in a good way.

Suddenly I began hearing about all my colleagues' efforts at regulation.

"I've learned every park in New Haven," one of my coworkers told everyone.

Another colleague shared, "My husband and I made a pact to try new recipes together. It's the first time we've cooked meals together in years."

"I've had Zoom drinks with friends I haven't seen in years," said another.

It went on that way for a while. We learned a lot about one another.

Another benefit: The fact that we could talk calmly about what we all feared made the worst case seem less likely. If you can openly discuss what frightens you, the unspoken message is that you believe everything will be okay in the end. Once you honestly own your insecurities and anxieties, they automatically become less threatening and easier to manage—to yourself and to the people around you. The mere presence of someone we view as caring reduces our stress and makes things feel more manageable, even if no obvious solution emerges.

That underlies the truism of co-regulation—it begins with managing your own emotional state. If you can't self-regulate, you'll never be able to co-regulate. But keep in mind, even if you can self-regulate, it doesn't guarantee you'll be good at co-regulation. Both take practice.

. . .

Before we move on, let me offer an exercise my colleague Robin Stern and I have developed to help you think about how you co-regulate:

On a piece of paper, create what's known as a sociogram—a visual representation of the people in your life, with you in the middle.

Represent yourself however you like, as a stick figure or a circle or just your name.

Next, represent the five to seven people with whom you spend the most amount of time currently. Consider your emotional closeness to them in how you depict them in the sociogram. In other words, position their name or circle at a distance that reflects how emotionally connected you feel to them. Then, connect yourself and your people with lines.

Once you're done, spend a few minutes looking at your drawing and thinking about how exactly you interact and engage with each person on the page.

Ask yourself: How helpful do you tend to be at co-regulating with this person? Are you an emotion enhancer or a squasher? Do you tend to offer helpful advice or behave critically toward this person? Engage with kindness or make unnecessary comments?

How does that affect your relationship?

Given all that we've learned about co-regulation, what might you now do differently?

# PART THREE

# BUILDING BLOCKS

## 7.

# The Hidden Driver of Regulation

RETHINKING YOUR BELIEFS ABOUT EMOTIONS

*You are what you believe yourself to be.*
—Paulo Coelho

When I was a kid, I was horrifically bullied. If I walked around school smiling, my tormentors would be like, "Hey Brackett, what are you so happy about?" If I ever seemed at ease, it would only bring down more abuse upon my head. There was not a lot of joy in my life.

So you can see why even today I have conflicted feelings about being happy or carefree or accepted. I honestly believe my childhood traumas are why I have a complex relationship with feeling good today.

Naturally, I would much rather be happy than not. And thanks to lots of support and work on myself, I am happier than I've ever been. But I'm still slightly uncomfortable with that feeling—I subconsciously expect that someone or something is going to ruin it for me.

Today, I give talks and conduct seminars regularly, usually before large groups. Recently I noticed that I start out full of confidence, but by the end of a session I begin feeling insecure. I realized it's because when I finish, I usually get enthusiastic applause and thanks from people who come up and speak to me. But like a lot of people, I'm not totally comfortable accepting praise and positive feedback.

I've taught myself over time to manage these feelings and graciously accept the nice things people say, mostly because they deserve to have their compliments acknowledged. Meanwhile, though, as I deliver my talks, I'm scanning the room for the one person who seems unimpressed or bored, or who looks like they think I'm not saying anything useful. It's as though I want to wreck any good vibes before someone else does.

Want more? I grew up in a home with a father who made no attempt to control his rage. I loved him but feared him, and so today I'm still somewhat uncomfortable with anger—other people's but even my own. I hope anger is not as scary to you, because from time to time we all must face that difficult emotion. And anger can even be a force for good, when properly deployed. Just not when all it does is frighten us.

My point here is that we all have feelings, and we also have feelings about our feelings, like my fear of happiness and anxiety about anger. There's even a term for that: *meta-emotions*. I like to think of it as having relationships with our emotions: Some we greet happily, like old friends; with others, the encounters are more complicated. Some we welcome, and some we shun, and the choices don't always make sense.

Run through the list below and for each emotion, take a moment to reflect honestly: How does experiencing it truly make you feel? Does it energize you, drain you, motivate you, or leave you conflicted? You might surprise yourself with what you discover. Pause and think carefully before answering.

Anger
Sadness
Fear
Joy
Pride
Envy
Contentment
Surprise
Disgust

Anxiety
Guilt
Shame
Hope

I'm going to wager that you're more comfortable with some than with others, and it's not necessarily the "negative" ones that make you squirm, or the "positive" ones that make you smile. For example, I've met people who swear that hope is what keeps them going, and others who argue that it only makes them impatient and frustrated.

Some of us go out of our way to experience unpleasant emotions like horror, sorrow, or angst. We ride on terrifying roller coasters, watch gruesome movies, play dangerous sports; we read tearjerkers and listen to morose love songs; we scroll through social media looking for posts that rile us up and make us hate people we'll never meet, seeking conflict and outrage. These are all feelings that emotionally healthy people would presumably wish to avoid. Yet we all indulge.

When researchers in one study asked subjects how they felt about certain emotions, here's how they replied:

"I like the feeling I get when expressing my anger."

"I enjoy movies that stir up feelings of sadness."

"When I see something disgusting, I look at it again on purpose."

"I love doing things that scare me."

It's human nature, and it speaks to the complexity of how we feel about how we feel.

After all, joy is wonderful, but can you imagine life if you were constantly joyful? Even when you have to make important financial decisions? Or when you find out about a loved one who is sick or in trouble? Too much joy sounds exhausting. And it's proper to mourn when circumstances call for it, but you don't want to be mournful on a daily basis.

Anxiety has its benefits when it prompts us to fix whatever's making us worry. As we think about it, we tend to worry about things we care about. Anger is useful when you've been treated unfairly and need the will to fight back. But being constantly anxious or angry is no way to live.

Part of the problem is the belief that some emotions are "good" and others are "bad." That idea is totally counterproductive: Naturally, most of us would prefer to experience mostly pleasant feelings and never be troubled by the unpleasant ones that challenge us, but life is an emotional roller coaster. So we need to take them all as they come and deal with them as equals—because good and bad are tricky concepts when it comes to emotions, and as I've said, each emotion has something to offer. For example, it's fair to say that we Americans value happiness above all else. Its pursuit is even enshrined in our founding document, the Declaration of Independence. In other cultures, where people have more modest goals for their emotions, that principle would be startling.

And of course, because happiness *is* such a wonderful emotion, we wish to experience it as often as possible. To settle for less would be like giving up on the good life—at least in our eyes, where mere contentment just doesn't cut it. Go to the self-help section of any bookseller, and you'll find a bottomless supply of advice on how to attain happiness—which also suggests how elusive it must be.

And in fact, research tells us that placing too much value on happiness and trying too hard to get there might actually increase unhappy emotions like discontent, loneliness, and depression.

Now, let's look at a feeling most of us experience more often than we wish—stress. Nobody loves stress, correct?

But what would our lives be like without it? Think of athletes, for instance, at a critical moment when they must perform at the absolute peak of their powers. It sounds stressful. But without that stress, would any athlete achieve greatness?

Even when we ordinary human beings are under stress, it pushes us to perform. We might not always get to where we want to go. But thanks to stress, we may come close—closer than if stress never existed. We anguish over money, so we spend less or earn more (or both). We feel deadlines looming, so we buckle down and work. There's an endless supply of outside stressors in our lives. We can use them to improve our lot, or we can succumb to them, be immobilized by them, give up all hope of positive outcomes. The difference depends solely on our feelings about the feeling.

When we view our stress as bad, "We either check out or freak out," says Alia Crum, a former member of our Center who is a psychology professor at Stanford. But if we see it as an opportunity, stress will keep us focused on our goals and how to reach them.

And there are more reasons we might find it difficult to face up to our emotional realities.

To many people, there's a distinctly feminine aspect to certain feelings, which could place them firmly out of bounds depending on how you feel about femininity. Rather than acknowledging our most sensitive emotions, we'll intellectualize them. Instead of "I feel," we'll say, "I think" or "I believe." Someone made a remark that hurt your feelings? Safer to say, "I'm mad!" than to admit, "I'm wounded." You're distraught over the death of a loved one? Less vulnerable to shrug and say, "It sucks!" than to shed a tear. Pressure on the job makes you fear getting fired? Rather than admit it, better to say, "I have a lot of stuff going on at work."

Here's one more factor that influences how we manage our emotions. On my own, I feel completely able to deal with my feelings. I realize I've been slacking off at the gym? I rededicate myself to my workouts and before long I'm back on track. I possess a near-bottomless belief in my power to respond to my emotions in positive, productive ways.

But what about when my feelings involve other people? When I'm fighting with my husband and we haven't spoken for an entire day? Or if a formerly close colleague at work is now gossiping about me? And when it involves my best friend, he and I can't be in the same room for ten minutes before we start arguing over things that happened thirty years ago.

Suddenly, my faith in my powers of regulation vanishes. The fact that there's another human being involved means I can no longer call all the shots and handle everything in ways that feel comfortable to me alone.

Instead of being confident and in control, now I'm in an emotional crouch, on the defensive. This is what happens when we feel threatened.

So we need to accept each of our emotions as they arise, but it's equally important to believe it's possible to regulate them.

We can't be victims of our feelings as though they're a force of nature, like hurricanes. Yet I talk to people all the time who tell me that's how they feel—that their emotions are beyond their control and have the power to screw up their lives. Here's what they say:

"I'm insecure and I fear rejection, so I don't ask people out on dates."

"Because I secretly believe I'm no good at my job, I try too hard to please my boss."

"I keep good news about work to myself because most people I know dislike their jobs, and I don't want them to feel bad or envy me."

"I can't restrain my anger, so I don't complain about how badly my partner treats me."

"I'm so anxious about my finances that I dread opening the mail."

As a result, these people believe—with some accuracy—that their emotions prevent them from achieving goals in their personal lives, their careers, everywhere. And if we have difficulty handling our own feelings, we probably have a tough time dealing with those of the people we care about—children, spouses, family, and friends.

When we talk about emotion regulation, here's the big question: Are emotions fixed—meaning, are we unable to manage how we experience them and how they affect us? Or are they malleable—so that we have a big say in how they will influence us and our behavior?

If we believe it's pointless to work on our emotions, it's no surprise that we'd view them warily. There's a certain logic to it: If your emotions can force you to take unhelpful actions, it's wise to deny them whenever possible.

But even with so many challenges, there are plenty of occasions when we all manage to control how we respond to our feelings.

Do I feel like waking up early?
Do I feel like walking the dog when it's raining?
Do I feel like doing a third set of burpees?
Do I feel like writing that disappointing sales report?
No, no, no, and no.

Yet we do them all. At some level we're all capable.

But we don't all believe we can do it every time, or for every emotion, especially the difficult ones. As a result, some of us don't even try. You can see how this might be a problem when it's necessary—for our own good, if for no other reason—to regulate how we deal with what we feel.

*Mindset* is a fairly recent concept in emotion studies. It was pioneered by Carol Dweck, a professor of psychology at Stanford who has been studying it for decades and wrote a bestselling 2006 book with that one-word title and the subtitle *The New Psychology of Success*. She coined the terms *fixed* and *growth* to describe people's beliefs about the nature of intelligence. In her research, Dweck would ask participants if they agreed or disagreed with statements such as "Your intelligence is something very basic about you that you can't really change." Or "Everyone, no matter who they are, can become a lot more intelligent."

Her questions were designed to reveal her participants' attitudes about how much control they have over their intelligence and to what degree it's either fixed or malleable.

People with what Dweck called *growth mindsets* see their own and other people's mental capabilities as malleable and changeable. They believe that with effort they can learn, improve, and grow. They are like students with learning goals: They employ *mastery-oriented strategies* such as asking for help from other people. They believe in effort and practice. These are our friends who tend to be strategic and persistent in the face of challenges. They study more deeply and recover from failure with an optimistic "I can do it" attitude. Their mindsets shape their motivation to learn and change.

Those with what Dweck called *fixed mindsets* tend to see their skills or abilities as nonmalleable and resistant to change. In her research, these people cared more about performance than improvement. They were highly competitive and more interested in getting top grades than in learning. They needed to look and feel capable at all times. Failure was their number-one enemy, and even the thought of it was terrifying.

It might seem obvious that in any endeavor, we do better by making a great effort than by not trying at all. Yet to Dweck's participants with a fixed mindset, putting in effort was not a compelling incentive. They wanted to do well but were not willing to struggle and try.

This was not due to laziness, Dweck said, but rather because students with a fixed mindset believe that if you're really smart you shouldn't need to try hard, and if you have to make an effort to excel, you must not be so smart. They believe that things come easily to people who are truly gifted, and when they look at successful individuals, they see people whose achievements were thanks mostly to talent.

In one of Dweck's studies, her team analyzed students' brain activity while reviewing errors they made on an exam. Those with a fixed mindset showed no activity when going over their errors, whereas those with a growth mindset experienced what's called *processing activity* as they looked at their mistakes. This means their brains were working to analyze the errors, understand why they occurred, and figure out how to deal with them or avoid them in the future. This active mental engagement is critical for learning and growth.

How does this relate to emotional life?

In essence, the person with a growth mindset about emotion says, "My feelings are an important part of who I am. They help define me as a person. They tell me and other people how I experience life, and the information they contain can be useful. And emotions can be changed depending on how I think about them."

The person who leans toward a fixed mindset about emotion says, "My feelings are often the source of my flaws and problems and difficulties. I can't help how I react to my emotions, so they usually dictate how I act. If something causes me anxiety or fear or insecurity, I can't do anything about it—except to try to ignore what I feel. I am unable to resist their influence over my thoughts and my actions."

Ironically, people with a fixed mindset are often *more* emotional than those with a growth mindset, not less. You could even describe them as hyperemotional, for the way their feelings control them rather than the other way around.

In general, studies show that people who believe that "emotions are more hindrance than help" tend to have worse psychological health, including greater anxiety and depressive symptoms, and lower overall well-being. According to the research, that fixed mindset also predicts heightened negative responses to stress. It's easy to see why individuals who hold that belief lack faith in their ability to handle stressful situations well. If our feelings aren't navigable, why even try to manage them? Those with a growth mindset are more likely to persist in the face of setbacks and achieve more positive outcomes.

In a study of incoming university students, Maya Tamir and her colleagues found that participants with a fixed mindset about emotions were less able to manage their feelings during the transition. Their mindsets were measured with a scale adapted from Dweck's research by having them rate their agreement with statements such as "No matter how hard they try, people can't really change the emotions they have." Participants kept weekly diaries throughout their first academic term, and those with a fixed mindset reported more negative emotional experiences than other students. They also said they had received less support from their new friends. By the end of freshman year, these students showed more symptoms of depression and lower levels of social adjustment.

By contrast, those with a growth mindset believe they can overcome difficult emotions, and so they are more likely than people with fixed views to work harder to cope with challenges. In Tamir's study, the students with a growth mindset about emotion were more likely to use helpful strategies to regulate emotions, such as cognitive reappraisal, or what's commonly called reframing.

Additional research shows that when individuals with a fixed emotion mindset experience intense feelings, they often try to disengage altogether. This pattern is inherently unhelpful: Ignoring difficult emotions and pretending not to be upset is associated with a variety of mental health problems, including depression.

In another study, researchers gave adolescents a smartphone app on which they completed a survey on their emotion mindsets and then reported on their emotional experiences multiple times a day for two weeks. The researchers then examined what the participants did when negative emotions arose. Here's what they found:

When adolescents with a growth mindset experienced an unpleasant emotion, they were more likely to think deeply about what was wrong, try to see the situation in a different light, and understand other perspectives.

But when adolescents with a fixed mindset experienced negative emotions, they tried to hide their feelings and pretend all was well. Six months later, they were more likely to report symptoms of depression.

It's interesting to note that according to at least one study, belief that emotions are manageable *decreases* from childhood to adolescence. There are a few reasons why that might be so.

Teenage years are a complex period for the development of emotion regulation skills. Numerous areas of the brain, such as the reward and social-affective circuitry, are remodeled by changes in hormones and neurotransmitters like dopamine, serotonin, and testosterone. Neurological changes that occur in the "social brain network" increase the need to belong, activate concerns about social status, and stimulate identity formation—all of which make regulation harder.

But probably the single greatest factor is that younger children rely more on parental support during trying emotional moments. Because adolescence stimulates the need for independence and exploration of new social networks, it makes teens more emotional and volatile. It's no surprise that adolescence is a sensitive period for the emergence of psychiatric disorders. It makes you wonder what might be different if we placed a greater emphasis on early and ongoing cultivation of emotion skills.

Ultimately, treating adolescents as though their occasional inability to regulate their emotions indicates a problem will backfire. The same is true if we try offering them advice when it's not wanted. But leveraging their growing sense of independence and agency, and their desire for prestige and social competence, can work wonders. For instance, instead of immediately stepping in when a teenager is upset about an argument with a friend, a parent might say, "I know this is tough, but I trust that you'll figure out the best way to handle it. I'm here if you want to think through this together." This approach acknowledges the teen's capability and supports their independence, making them more likely to come to you for advice when they really need it. By doing this, the parent is respecting the teenager's autonomy while also reinforcing their confidence in their ability to handle relationship challenges.

While we wish to encourage a growth mindset in all age groups, researchers have uncovered an intriguing, not entirely positive aspect. A study found that people who believe emotions are controllable are slightly *less* empathic and compassionate when responding to other people's difficulties. Perhaps this is because they believe everyone can—and should—be able to regulate their emotions and handle all challenges. That attitude could lead to a brand of tough love that does more harm than good, especially when dealing with children or people in desperate moments.

So, we need to cut one another—and ourselves—a little slack when necessary. The growth-versus-fixed mindset picture isn't as black-and-white as we might wish it to be.

Since our mindsets are so important, we need to ask: Where do they come from?

There's evidence that they begin to form in early childhood and depend at least in part on parental feedback when a child either accepts or avoids challenges. At those pivot points, there are two basic approaches a parent can take: performance praise or process praise.

Performance praise is when we compliment children for attributes and abilities that come easily. "You're such a great ballplayer" to a child with natural athletic ability. "You're so beautiful" to one with good looks. "You're so good at math" to the kid with an aptitude for numbers. It encourages the child to take on tasks where they excel. It's clear why this is so attractive—it allows us to win easy praise from the people who matter most, our parents.

Giving process praise means changing a child's value system, away from flawless performance and toward hard work, multiple strategies, and improvement, not just achievement. Process praise takes the focus off outcomes and puts it on learning and striving.

Process praise sounds like this: "Nice choice. What are you going to try next?" "Great persistence, you're getting closer!" "I love the way you focus. It led you to some great ideas." "It was a smart idea to ask your sister for help."

In studies of children aged four to twelve, Dweck found that when they were praised for their abilities after a success, they were more likely to avoid challenges and falter or become defensive when trying difficult tasks. Again, it's only natural—who doesn't prefer success to struggle?

But when these same children received praise not for performance but for process, they were eager to take on new challenges and were persistent in the face of difficulties. Their sense of their own abilities was not diminished by having to try hard to succeed.

When mothers give process praise like, "You're trying so hard to put those blocks together. Good job!" to babies aged one, two, and three, it predicts the child's growth mindset and desire for challenge five years later, in grade school. In a follow-up study, researchers found that it also predicted the children's math attainment and reading comprehension in fourth grade.

When we value process, direct praise becomes unnecessary. Simply asking children questions about the methods they tried and the strategies they chose is reward enough. It implicitly shows what we value most—learning and growing.

Praising process instead of accomplishment actually increases motivation and perseverance. It reminds kids that they are not perfect and can always improve. It teaches them to manage failure without becoming discouraged or giving up. When a child's self-talk fails them, a parent might say, "Let's think of other things you might say to yourself or do to help you feel less angry or fearful or worried. Try one of those next time. They seem like they'd be really helpful. We all mess up, and that's okay. What matters most is that we keep trying."

Dweck also has done research on the power of the word *yet* in the lives of young people, like in the phrase, "You haven't figured out the way to solve the puzzle *yet*."

Using the word as a rallying cry increases students' persistence and confidence that they will succeed eventually, she has found. The word *yet* puts a growth mindset spin on the defeatist things kids sometimes say:

"I'm not a math person . . ."

"*Yet*."

Or "I'm no good at soccer . . ."

"*Yet*."

Or "I tried to answer these chemistry questions, but I couldn't . . ."

"*Yet*."

We can teach students that when they try hard things, the neurons in their brains form new, stronger connections. Children with a fixed mindset come to believe that if major effort is required, it means they're not very smart. Instead, they need to understand that effort and struggle will make them even smarter.

At Yale, I see firsthand evidence of dysfunctional relationships with praise and performance—but of a different kind.

Students there are mostly the offspring of high-achieving parents. Starting in childhood, these kids are taught that any time they're goofing off and having fun, other students will be studying and learning. So, doing anything enjoyable will hold them back. They come to feel that happiness means they're falling behind the competition. No wonder feeling contented makes them uneasy, while feeling stressed, overworked, and overwhelmed tells them they're on the right track.

But which track *is* it? Ten or fifteen years after graduation, they'll have the jobs they wished for at Goldman Sachs or Google, they'll work eighty hours a week and neglect their families and themselves, and all because they're more at ease with unpleasant emotions than pleasant ones. The lucky ones will retire at forty and become yoga teachers. The rest will keep going that way until retirement, disability, or death.

We performed a study at the Center, led by James Floman, an associate research scientist, to see if mindfulness training might help students relax a little, shift their mindsets, and enjoy their nonacademic lives. We received a grant and offered students a stipend to take part in an eight-week program that included a weekly one-hour session and daily self-guided practices.

Here's what happened.

Somewhere around 70 percent of the participants dropped out of the study before it ended. Most of the remaining participants took part when working with an instructor, but almost none of them practiced on their own, even though they knew it was important and would benefit them.

Their reasons? Not enough time to do that and everything else they had to do. Students would stay up late working on their term papers but couldn't find fifteen minutes to still their minds. In theory, the students said they saw the benefits of being relaxed and peaceful, but the time cost was too high, they said, so they gave up. They've been told all their lives that achievement is what matters most and they need to do whatever it takes to get the top grade.

Feeling tension and dissatisfaction, on the other hand, means they're headed toward success. The sense that they're not naturally excellent will push them to try ever harder. These students are smart enough to manage both success and contentment. But no one has ever shown them how. It's no wonder there's been a consistent rise in anxiety and depression among college students over the last decade.

That fear of contentment isn't a facet only of overachiever Ivy

League undergraduate life. At the Center we had a postdoctoral researcher from China, Shengjie Lin, who taught me a lot about how culture influences belief about emotion. "I like feeling relaxed at home, but not at work," he told me. "In Chinese culture, particularly in Confucian philosophy, we're taught that self-perfection is highly desirable. That translates to mean that if I feel comfortable, I'm not cultivating myself, I'm not pushing myself. For that reason, I feel my best and most productive when I'm feeling stressed at work. That means I'm on the verge of accomplishment."

Another colleague, Mariam Korangy, grew up in a Persian home. In the mindset she grew up with, relaxing means you're lazy. "My parents didn't want us sitting around doing nothing," she said. "They'd say, 'You'd better find something to do or here's your math workbook!' Now, as a parent of two children, when I see my kids relaxing on the couch, I have to work hard at regulating my response. I now have a different set of values from my parents, but that mindset of 'relaxed is bad' is ingrained in me."

Time will tell if she manages to regulate her response, as she puts it—to allow her kids to excel but also to enjoy the fruits of their excellence.

Growth mindset is the necessary precursor to emotion regulation. You can't have one without the other. With a fixed mindset, regulation seems elusive, if not impossible. It's as though we're being held hostage by our own feelings. With a growth mindset, managing how we respond to our feelings becomes attainable—a practical, practicable skill.

It's not as though people with a fixed mindset are completely incapable of managing how they respond to their emotions. My father always felt entitled to his anger. That attitude became his excuse for not even trying. But let's say a police officer pulled him over for speeding; I can assure you that he'd be as ingratiating and humble as any other driver seeking to talk his way out of a hefty fine and points.

We're all capable of restraining our emotional responses from time to time to manipulate other people and get what we want. But that's emotion regulation on a strictly transactional basis—not as a practice meant to benefit our own lives and the lives of others. Big difference.

We at the Center have come up with a list of statements that people with growth mindsets around emotion regulation and co-regulation tend to believe. Take this abbreviated self-assessment to measure your own. Score yourself from 1 (strongly disagree) to 5 (strongly agree). The higher the score, the more you lean toward having a growth mindset.

I can get better at dealing with my feelings.
I can learn strategies to manage my emotions more productively.
I can get better at assisting people in dealing with their feelings.
I can learn strategies to help people manage their emotions more productively.

Okay, what was your score? I hope reading this chapter made you think differently about these questions and your responses. How motivated are you to shift your beliefs about emotions and your ability to regulate them? And if you are raising children, which of these beliefs are you trying to pass along?

8.

# From Chaos to Clarity

## LABELING YOUR EMOTIONS PRECISELY

*The limits of my language mean the limits of my world.*
—Ludwig Wittgenstein

How hard can it be, you might wonder, to know our own emotions well enough to put them into words?

It's not so easy, I've discovered. Maybe you've noticed it, too.

Socrates famously said, "The unexamined life is not worth living."

Of course, he said it just after he had been sentenced to death, which probably gave the idea of self-knowledge a bit more urgency than we feel about it today. Still, his words remain a touchstone of civilization and an ideal we can all aspire to.

In theory, at least.

In practice, not so much.

I was reminded of this during a seminar I gave at a business school to a bunch of executives from an engineering company.

As I usually do in these sessions, I instructed the group, "Describe the difference between the following emotions: anxiety, fear, stress, pressure, worry, and overwhelmed."

"No difference," one man said almost immediately, and the others around him nodded.

"Hang on," I said. "Clearly, they're not all identical. Let's split up into groups and discuss this, and then we'll come back together to see what everybody thinks."

A little while later we reconvened.

"They're on a continuum," one group reported.

"Some are high energy, some are low," said another.

"They differ in how much control we have," said a third.

"Those aren't definitions," I said. "They're descriptions. I want you to define each one of them the way a dictionary might."

"Well, maybe one is internal and the others external..."

"Or one is weaker, and the others are stronger..."

I gave up.

"Anxiety is uncertainty about something that lies ahead," I said. "We feel fear when we're in actual, immediate danger. Stress is too many demands and not enough resources to meet them. Pressure is when something important depends on what we do next. Worry is concern about a temporary situation. And we're overwhelmed when we feel overcome by our emotions about whatever's going on in the moment."

They looked back at me blankly.

"Do you see how those differences might matter?" I asked.

"No," most replied.

"Okay," I said. "But don't you think that *how* we handle those feelings might differ depending on what's causing them?"

They still seemed unconvinced.

"Okay, let's go back into groups and talk about that," I said. And away they went. And then came back.

This time, at least a few had begun to see how defining emotions and identifying what causes them could be useful. But it was like pulling teeth.

Now, you could say that these were all type-A alpha dog businesspeople who had learned over the course of their lives to ignore any inconvenient emotions that got in their way.

And I would agree with you, except they weren't so different from the rest of us—maybe just a slightly exaggerated version of what I hear when I talk to various kinds of people around the world about their emotional lives.

So, let's start here: Why *does* it matter whether we can describe with precision and specificity the emotions we feel? Let's be honest, Socrates—it didn't do you much good. It sounds like a lot of work for an intangible benefit.

At the Center, our motto is "You have to label it to regulate it." Catchy slogans aside, it's the undeniable truth.

In fact, this task—labeling—is supremely critical to the process of learning to respond positively to our most intense emotions. Because if you don't know exactly what you're feeling and why, how can you choose an effective way of dealing with it? It would be like prescribing a medicine before you know why you're sick.

Labeling is the link that connects our internal lives—our feelings—to our outward actions—how we react to those feelings. I'm not exaggerating when I say that mastering this skill is what ultimately gives us the power to control our own fates. A pretty important thing.

Given all that, why are we so bad at it?

A number of reasons.

Here's a big one: We lack motivation. We see no reward for understanding the exact emotions we feel and then hanging a name on them. And labeling, as we witnessed with those businesspeople, can be work. It requires self-examination and careful analysis.

Even if you wanted to, who has the time?

And if we do it, it's not as though anyone else cares. Think about how many times a day you ask someone, "How are you?" Imagine what would happen if they each gave you a highly detailed, exhaustively considered answer. You'd never ask again.

So, how are *you*? I'm fine! I'm great! Doing okay! All good!

We tend to use just a few basic words—angry, sad, stressed, anxious, depressed, meh—to signal the entire spectrum of negative emotions.

And even fewer terms to express neutral or happy feelings—fine, good, okay, great, happy.

When you consider the vast and fascinating complexity of the human psyche, it makes sense that we'd need more than a handful of words to accurately describe how we feel. And we often feel more than one emotion at a time!

As a result of not utilizing our full emotion vocabulary, it's become impoverished. It's like any other language—if you don't use it, you lose it. English in particular is lacking when it comes to defining emotions. The terms we adults use to describe our feelings don't vary much from the ones we employed as children—*I'm happy, I'm sad, I'm mad* . . . There's no verbal evidence that as we've matured our emotional lives have gotten any deeper or more nuanced.

Compare ours with the lexicon found in other languages. German is a fine tongue for expressing psychological complexity—we English speakers regularly find reason to use their word *Schadenfreude*, the pleasure one takes in the suffering of others. In Norwegian, *koselig* is a feeling of deep contentment and well-being, something more profound than mere happiness. The Dutch describe the refreshing emotion that comes from walking in the wind as *uitwaaien*. In many Bantu languages, kindness to others based on our shared humanity is called *ubuntu*. And let's not forget the German portmanteau word for the joy of driving, *Fahrvergnügen*, that Volkswagen coined for an ad campaign.

Think back—when's the last time you told someone you felt peeved, or alienated, or blissful, or vexed, or buoyant, or wistful, or any of the other subtle emotions that we all feel but for some reason never put into words?

Author David Brooks published an amusing essay expressing doubts about the advice from psychology experts (me included) to closely label feelings. He wrote,

> *As I got deeper into the emotions of different cultures around the globe, I was kind of relieved to be a happy and shallow American. We don't*

*have words for some of the dark varieties of despair that seem more prevalent in other places. The Greeks have* stenahoria *to describe a feeling of hopelessness, constriction, suffocation, and doom. The Russians have* tocka, *which is a kind of spiritual anguish. The Pintupi people in Western Australia have* ngulu, *the dread you feel when you suspect that someone is seeking revenge against you. The Japanese have* age-otori, *the feeling of looking worse after a haircut.*

(But haven't we all wished we had a word for that emotion?)

Here's another reason we're reluctant labelers: We still tend to admire the strong, more-or-less silent type, the stoic who can cope with life's ups and downs calmly and capably, without making a fuss—as opposed to our inner whiny, self-obsessed child pleading for understanding and accommodation. We start beating that person out of ourselves early on:

"Be a man!"

"Grow up!"

"Get over yourself!"

"Stop acting like a child!" (Even to children!)

And my current least favorite response when kids express disappointment or a sense of unfairness:

"You get what you get and you don't get upset."

Which of course is total nonsense—as children *and* adults, we are often dissatisfied, dejected, and upset by what life dishes out. But we're taught that it's a sign of maturity to swallow those feelings without saying a word or expressing an untidy emotion. Nobody really believes those unhappy sentiments will instantly vanish. Instead, they fester inside—to come out another day, perhaps in another form even more disruptive than what we would have expressed had we just immediately complained and then moved on.

Even as an exercise in arithmetic, labeling feelings can be a chore. On the free How We Feel app (howwefeel.org), which I developed with Pinterest cofounder Ben Silbermann and our respective teams, we've included 144 possible feeling words and their definitions. That's a lot to shuffle through before you settle on the absolutely perfect label for what you're feeling. You can see how this could be challenging in the heat of the moment—in the middle of an argument or a breakup or some other highly emotional exchange.

One final reason we might dread examining our feelings closely is an insidious one: Often, our most sensitive emotions arrive with a quiet accompaniment of shame.

Think about it. When we come face-to-face with our fears, insecurities, or uncertainties, we tend to view them as frailties and flaws. It's difficult to admit when we're less strong or able than we wish to be. From an evolutionary perspective, weakness leaves all creatures—humans included—vulnerable to enemies and predators.

No wonder we'll go to great lengths to avoid seeming weak, even to ourselves. In those moments, we might prefer to indulge in a little self-deception. Someone said or did something that hurt your feelings? Better to couch your emotion as anger than admit to being so easily wounded. Far safer to sound furious than to say, "I am really hurt by what you just did—and I'm also ashamed that I feel hurt."

So we avoid owning our most tender feelings, and therefore we never learn to respond to them in healthy, positive ways. The shame becomes even more powerful than the original emotion.

This dual-emotion dynamic can be particularly challenging for parents. Your child is having a problem? He's a bed wetter? She's being bullied at school? Like it or not, you (and perhaps others) may view this as a reflection of your qualities as a parent and a human being. You can see how such shaming might make you hesitate to examine the emotions your child is feeling and then label them.

But that poor kid is going to sense your shame, I guarantee, so now neither of you can be honest about what you're feeling.

There's an even more concerning reason some parents are reluctant to understand their children's emotional lives. This may sound hard to believe, but in candid moments mothers and fathers have admitted it to me: They're actually afraid to know what their children are feeling.

They're so scared of what they might learn that they'd rather not hear anything at all. And these are people honestly trying to be good parents and role models.

What exactly do they fear? Aside from not wanting to find out anything that reflects poorly on themselves, the bigger issue is that once they learn how their kids feel, parents are obliged to do something about it—to take action. Too much truth might provoke some uncomfortable conversations. It could even lead to involving other people, like a school counselor or psychotherapist, at which point the exploration of that child's emotional life could become *seriously* honest.

This is something lots of us, I'm sorry to say, would rather avoid. Parents don't know how to begin the conversation, and they don't know how to deal with what might come up. Just the thought of talking about it brings up unprocessed feelings of their own.

Taken all together, we find many excuses *not* to label our feelings or help other people to label theirs. Luckily, there are more—and more powerful—reasons for doing it.

Okay, so what are they?

Let's begin with a really basic one: We all ought to have as much clarity as possible about who we are and what goes on inside our own heads.

Makes sense, no? Putting thoughts into words that can be shared with other people is in our human DNA. It's who we are. So of course we need to understand our feelings and those of the people around us. Our emotions contain important information about how we experience life. They provide the motivation for every action we take. So why *wouldn't* we want to know exactly what we're feeling? What could possibly matter more?

Naming an emotion externalizes it—turns it into something that exists outside ourselves, so that we might consider it at a slight remove, see it from different perspectives, ponder it a bit. This also takes away some of the feeling's power to control our reactions. Once an emotion is an object we can examine, we can calmly take its measure and ask—is it beneficial or harmful? Urgent? Relevant? Do I feel like I am able to handle it? How much will it matter tomorrow? All important considerations when searching for a helpful way to respond to an emotion without underreacting or blowing it out of proportion. We can determine whether this feeling is transitory, likely to pass soon and be forgotten, or an insight into something deeper and more serious.

This is a key role of accurate, highly specific labels—they help us to distinguish fury from mild irritation, panic from minor worry. They help us to see what's going on beneath the surface, because appearances can be deceiving, and it's easy to mistake one similar emotion for another.

As psychologist Susan David, author of *Emotional Agility*, explains, "We need a more nuanced vocabulary for emotions, not just for the sake of being more precise, but because incorrectly diagnosing our emotions makes us respond incorrectly. If we think we need to attend to anger, we'll take a different approach than if we're handling disappointment or anxiety—or we might not address them at all."

Here's a good example. You're driving the family to a day at the zoo. For weeks, your kids have been crazed with anticipation. On the way, the car breaks down. Now you're parked on the side of the road, waiting for a tow truck. That's bad enough, but your children are having a meltdown. They're furious—understandably—and they're looking for someone to blame: you!

If you automatically define their tantrum as anger—which it surely looks, sounds, and feels like—you'd be justified by responding in kind.

"It's not like I *wanted* the car to break down on the way to the zoo!" you might yell right back.

But what if you calmly consider their outburst for a moment and correctly identify the emotion behind it? It's disappointment. The car trouble came as a total shock to them, because children haven't yet learned all the ways reality can let us down. Hence, a tantrum, superficially anger, is something else entirely.

They're disappointed. They expected something wonderful and got something terrible instead.

How might that accurate label change anything? Well, suddenly you see that their emotion is not aimed at you personally. With that in mind you could show a little sympathy, and then attempt something to quiet their crying and dispel their disappointment. Something like "Kids, I know you really want to go to the zoo, and we'll go soon, I promise. I didn't want the car to break down either. But how about if tonight we go to the movies and see the new (fill in whatever flick they've been dying to see)?"

At the very least, you're addressing their true emotion and trying to help them respond to it, rather than mistakenly reacting to their raging with raging of your own.

Will this approach do the trick? Possibly not. Disappointment isn't easy for children to manage. (It's not so easy for adults either.) So perhaps the movie offer doesn't make a dent—today. But maybe next time a similar situation arises, carefully labeling emotions will pay off. It's possible that your kids will always remember the time they expected you to yell at them for yelling at you, and instead you responded in a different—kinder, more loving—way.

Even someone like Brené Brown, who has a tremendous understanding of the human psyche, can mislabel emotion.

Not long ago I was on her podcast.

"Hey," she said to me, "let me ask you a quick personal question for my own therapy. Resentment is in the anger family, right? Because when we're resentful we seem kind of bitter and angry."

"No," I told her. "Resentment is a function of envy."

She was startled. Here's how she talked about it later:

"That completely changed my life," she recalled. "Because now, instead of looking at someone and saying 'Hey, look, I'm working sixty hours a week, why aren't you?' I'm thinking, 'Oh, they're taking the weekend off.' I'm not mad because you're not working. I'm mad because

*I'm* not taking the weekend off. And so, there's a knife up against my throat—but I'm the one holding it."

She found an important distinction that's easy to miss. Next time you feel the need to blame other people for your emotion, pause and examine your reasoning—like, in Brené's case, by asking what exactly it is you resent. That led her to identifying her true feeling, which was resentment, and how to resolve it (by taking some time off).

The stakes can be serious. A physician who was familiar with our work told me about a patient who reported feeling anxiety over some serious family issues. Usually, the doctor would have prescribed an anti-anxiety medication, but she had a sense that something more was going on. Asking the patient why she was anxious, she discovered that the woman was feeling incompetent and incapable of managing one of her children, a really difficult kid. The patient used the word *anxiety* because it's an easy term that we all toss around—incorrectly in this case, since it refers to uncertainty.

In reality, the woman was feeling stress—which we define as having too many demands and not enough resources—and overwhelmed, meaning so stressed that she could barely function.

Recognizing this, the doctor didn't write a prescription—instead, she advised her patient to find a therapist who could suggest better ways of dealing with that child.

There's research showing that physicians sometimes diagnose anxiety in women who have complaints that turn out to be symptoms of heart disease. Occasionally, as you can imagine, these cases end tragically, when cardiological intervention is required but never received. Another reason it's important to be precise when we talk about how we feel.

If all those reasons for labeling emotions aren't persuasive enough, I can direct you to the large body of scientific evidence that makes the case. As you might expect, we psychologists do a huge amount of research into how people perceive their emotions and how labeling affects outcomes.

One word we in the field use a lot is *granular*.

Psychologist Lisa Feldman Barrett defined *emotional granularity* as "the adaptive value of putting feelings into words with a high degree of complexity," thereby mirroring our inner lives. In her experiments, the participants she dubbed "granulars" were less likely to lose their cool or rely on alcohol when under stress, and more likely to find positive meaning in negative experiences. They were also better at regulating their emotional responses in order to achieve desirable outcomes. The subjects who were low in granularity—"clumpers," she called them—did worse on all those counts and tended to be psychologically and even physically ill at a higher rate than the granular group.

Studies show that naming your emotions immediately releases their grip over you and reduces physiological distress. In an experiment conducted at UCLA, people with arachnophobia—the extreme fear of spiders—were split into four groups. One group received no instruction at all. A second was told to try and change their thinking about spiders. The third group was asked to distract themselves from their fears. The fourth group was encouraged to label as specifically as possible what they were feeling.

The researchers then measured skin conductivity of all four groups—and found that group four had the lowest response to their phobia. Labeling had taken away some of the spiders' power to strike fear into their hearts.

Simply saying the words "I feel ____" helps you bring your reactions under control and move on, instead of spiraling into distress, studies have shown. Acknowledging feelings—rather than dismissing them—is crucial to lowering emotional reactivity and improving your overall mental well-being.

There's even a physiological benefit to it, one that has been measured in the lab. Research shows that what psychologists call *affective labeling*—applying specific words to feelings—is linked to lower activation of the amygdala, the region of the brain that indicates strong, mostly unpleasant feelings. And it increases activation of the ventrolateral prefrontal cortex, which supports emotion regulation.

Along with supportive social relationships, positive job performance, and psychological well-being, emotion understanding has been associated with good physical health.

So even our biology appreciates the benefits of naming emotions. Our mentalities just need to catch up.

Once we can see the importance of understanding what we feel and why, and then labeling our emotions, just one final matter remains: How do we do it? What are the steps we must take to acquire this necessary skill?

Identifying our emotions well enough to label them starts with this realization: Often, our feelings are responses to underlying causes that are not completely apparent, even to us. We've already touched on this. Brené Brown didn't recognize that her resentment was an expression of envy. Those kids on their way to the zoo seemed angry, but their emotions' true source was disappointment.

We call these underlying causes *core relational themes*. This idea was researched most significantly by a psychologist named Richard Lazarus and is based on his "appraisal approach" to understanding emotion. Lazarus maintained that there are themes that explain why we feel what we feel. And it's important to understand these themes if we're going to label our emotions properly.

In a research project conducted in our Center, we summarized the research on some of these themes. Of course, not every emotion's theme lies beneath the surface. Many, especially the pleasant emotions, are obvious. Not all, however. For example:

Anger is often a response to injustice or unfairness, whether to ourselves or to someone else.

Frustration arises when we feel as though someone or something is blocking us from achieving our goals. Sadness emerges when we perceive a meaningful loss, whether it's the loss of a loved one, a missed opportunity, or something we deeply cherish. Shame usually occurs when we behave or appear in ways that we would condemn in other people, especially regarding ethical or moral behavior. Shame lowers our self-esteem the same as it would lower our opinion of other people.

Anxiety, as we discussed, is uncertainty about something in the future—a situation or event that might turn out badly if proper action isn't taken.

Embarrassment is feeling exposed to shaming by others, but it's based on the assumption that they view us as we would view them in similar circumstances.

Joy is when we feel free to engage in play or have fun, or when we receive favorable news.

Contentment is experienced when a person feels that their basic needs are met, that they are in a safe and stable environment, and that there is no pressing need to change or improve their current mood or situation. Gratitude is the appreciation for an altruistic gift or someone's generosity.

Compassion arises when we notice someone else's suffering and feel a genuine desire to help, accompanied by a sense of empathy and connection.

Pride comes from perceptions of earned achievement from effortful action.

We need these themes to have a common language to talk about emotion. If we don't have a common understanding that anger is about injustice, and disappointment is about unmet expectations, it'll be impossible to communicate and understand one another.

But emotions are also subjective—no two people experience reality in the exact same way. A great deal of that subjectivity is due to factors such as culture, family history, power dynamics, and more. We see this today in public life—we all perceive events differently depending on things like our gender, race, economics, political affiliation, social prestige, and so on.

So, what angers me might not anger you. What excites you might leave me feeling bored, and that's perfectly okay. What matters most is that we remain curious and make the effort to understand (and don't judge) what makes each of us feel the way we do.

Okay, now we are prepared to label.

First, we must determine whether our overall state feels pleasant or unpleasant, comfortable or uncomfortable. Recall that we want to avoid labeling emotions as positive or negative.

Next, we ask ourselves: Am I feeling energized or depleted? Here's what that means. Are we feeling charged up or mellowed out? We often use the word *activated* to describe feeling alert, aware, and ready to take some action. Interestingly, there's no commonly used term for its opposite—we don't usually say *deactivated*. But it's what we mean.

To imagine the landscape of our emotional state, we can visualize the Mood Meter (a square divided into four quadrants).

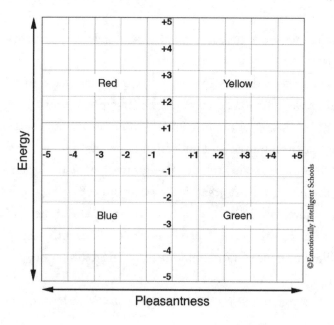

Let's devote the two quadrants on the left side of the square to unpleasant emotions and the two on the right to the pleasant ones.

Now, let's call the top two quadrants *high energy*, and the two on the bottom *low energy*.

Okay, we're ready to make the first decision of labeling: In which quadrant do we belong at this moment, emotionally speaking?

You're feeling energized but unpleasant? That indicates you're in the red and feeling something like irritated or furious or annoyed or resentful or jittery. An active emotion, but not one you'd describe as pleasant. You're in the top-left quadrant.

Feeling unpleasant and low energy? That's blue and includes feelings like sadness or dejectedness or loneliness or apathy or discouragement or pessimism. Again, not something you want to feel often. You're in the bottom-left quadrant.

If you're energized and pleasant, it could be anything from thrilled to confident to hopeful to cheery. Go straight to the top-right yellow quadrant.

Low energy and pleasant? Now we're talking about serene or contented or blissful or balanced or thankful. You're in the green bottom-right quadrant.

Okay, now that we've narrowed it down and found our quadrant, we're ready to get granular.

As we said before, there are literally thousands of words we can use to label our emotions. A lot to remember, but each one of us will have a smaller palette of terms we're comfortable with—our own personal repertoire, you could say.

That's labeling. Like any skill, it improves with practice.

As I mentioned earlier, I worked on a free app called How We Feel that provides lots of options. You can begin there, just to juice up your emotion vocabulary. Ideally, you won't always have to consult your phone every time you need to label an emotion. At some point you'll develop your own lexicon suited to your emotional makeup.

Not everybody goes through life feeling exuberant, or desperate, or enraged.

There's one last step we can take to make sure we've settled on the proper label. It has to do with something psychologists call *ideal affect*. It means the emotion that we would prefer to feel at any given moment.

In conducting research, we often ask participants, "What do you wish you were feeling right now?"

People usually find it easy to answer this question—quite a bit easier than telling us what they're actually feeling.

In the workplace, we often hear this: "I want to feel valued and appreciated."

What's the message in there? That this company has a problem making its employees feel that they are respected for their contributions. As we've learned through our extensive work consulting with corporations, this is a serious issue. It's why some firms suffer from high turnover.

So when we ask this question and get this answer, we learn something valuable. Even in nonbusiness settings, asking what we wish to feel provides insight into our emotional state.

Ask yourself, right now, what you wish you were feeling. Make a list of the emotions you'd like to feel at home and at work. Some might be the same, but it's likely that many are different.

Using that list, you should be able to infer what it is you're actually feeling. If at this moment you say you want to feel secure, ask yourself if there's a reason you feel insecure. If you say you wish to feel cherished, or respected, or serene, or joyful, do the same thing—figure out if you're feeling the opposite of those emotions.

This method works even when we're feeling good. For instance, almost everyone wishes to feel "happy." But that emotion means different things to different people. At some point the word becomes almost meaningless, so a one-size-fits-all version is impossible. Some people find happiness when they feel calm and tranquil. Others need a more stimulating and energetic vibe. It's important to know that before you try making everyone happy.

I'll end our discussion of labeling with a final reason for naming our emotions as precisely as possible: It feels good.

Labeling frees us. It makes us honest. It gives us integrity because we suddenly have nothing to hide or hide from. Depending on the emotions we're feeling, it can be like coming out from under a great, burdensome weight.

At the height of the pandemic, I was invited to be on a national TV show to share how people might deal with their anxiety and fear. I knew that millions of people would be watching, and so I felt the need to perform at the highest possible level. I had only one day to prepare and one shot at getting it right—no do-overs. Kind of like being asked at the last minute to sing the national anthem at a televised ball game.

How exactly did I feel? I was dealing with a whirlwind of emotions—anxiety, stress, pressure, and embarrassment (my head looked like a Chia Pet since I hadn't had a haircut in months). But once I named my feelings, I was able to start to tame them, even though they all rushed in at once, as feelings often do.

In the end, I realized I was mostly overwhelmed; I was saturated and needed some time to decompress. Just before the interview, I cleared my schedule, took a walk, did some slow breathing, and reminded myself that I've been doing this work for a long time and have been interviewed many times. The fact that I had successfully completed dozens of interviews in the past reassured me—and this one turned out to be successful, too.

This is the seeming contradiction at the heart of labeling emotions. It takes confidence to admit that you're feeling insecure or overwhelmed. You need bravery to confess that you're terrified. But by labeling unwelcome emotions, we take away some of their power to control us.

In the end, to label or not to label is a binary proposition—an either/or. Either we choose the easy way out and never determine exactly what we're feeling and why. Or we examine our feelings as they arise and learn to name them. The first choice makes it unlikely that we'll consistently behave in ways that benefit ourselves and the people around us. The second option prepares us to act with wisdom and intention every time a challenging emotional moment comes along.

# PART FOUR

# STRATEGIES

# 9.

# Quieting Your Mind and Body

*Feelings come and go like clouds in a windy sky.
Conscious breathing is my anchor.*

—Thích Nhất Hạnh

We start out full of resolve and good intentions for dealing with our feelings in positive, beneficial ways.

And then, in the heat of the moment, all our wonderful plans go flying out the window.

"Everybody has a plan until they get punched in the face," heavyweight boxing champion Mike Tyson famously observed. It may seem strange to be taking emotion regulation advice from someone who fights people for a living. But, as someone who practices martial arts, I can assure you that being physically attacked triggers your emotions like nothing else. It's a great lesson in how we react under pressure of any kind—physical or psychological.

With that in mind, it's time to learn the two things we must do *before* we're fully ready to deal with our feelings.

There's a reason that all over the planet, reaching back to ancient history, how we breathe has been considered an important part of spiritual fitness. Long before there was any scientific research to support this idea, we knew that regulating our breathing gave us the power to manage our bodies and minds.

I think it's meaningful that we're all familiar with the term *breathing room*. It shows how we associate breath and space—the psychological space we create when we breathe deeply and calmly. When we feel challenged, we can use our breath to still ourselves inside and create room to think about what action, if any, we should take.

That room is the space between stimulus and response.

Breath work is likely the oldest emotion regulation strategy in the book. When you feel like you're about to flip out or melt down or totally lose your grip, you stop yourself and you take a deep breath. We all do it, at least some of the time.

Years ago, I came up with a phrase: "You have to deactivate to regulate." Deactivation begins with inhalation.

It works almost instantly on two levels. First, if you're breathing slowly and deeply, it's impossible for you to speak or act in a way you might later regret. Second, that breath triggers several physiological changes in your body, all of which help you better navigate the challenging moment.

To explain this requires a brief review of the sympathetic and parasympathetic nervous systems.

These systems work together to regulate a long list of involuntary physiological processes, like heart rate, blood pressure, respiration, and digestion. The sympathetic nervous system takes over whenever we feel threatened. It releases neurotransmitter chemicals like cortisol and epinephrine that initiate the ancient fight, flight, or freeze response: Heart rate increases; blood vessels constrict; breathing becomes rapid and shallow; focus narrows onto the threat before us and blocks out everything else. We're in emergency mode, ready to battle for our lives, run like hell, or just freeze in terror (not the most helpful response under most circumstances, but nobody's perfect). The memory of the scary event is then locked into the brain's hippocampus region so that we'll react even faster the next time it happens.

The parasympathetic nervous system acts as a counterbalance, promoting relaxation and restoration once the fear subsides. It slows down the heart rate, calms the breathing, and restores the mind and body to homeostasis. In healthy individuals, there is a dynamic interplay between sympathetic and parasympathetic activity, allowing us to respond to emotional stimuli without excessive arousal or sluggishness.

Under normal circumstances, cortisol, the main hormone that regulates physiological arousal, peaks in the morning and slowly declines until bedtime. But being under constant pressure or stress disrupts this flow so that cortisol stays high throughout the day. This leads to dysregulation of the nervous system and contributes to various emotional and physical health problems. Cortisol also crosses the blood-brain barrier, directly impacting the brain and its various networks and functions, which burns out executive functioning ability and other higher-order cognitive functions supported by the prefrontal cortex. When this happens, we lose the ability to reason calmly, which of course makes healthy emotion regulation impossible.

Early in my life I received an education in the function of the sympathetic and parasympathetic nervous systems. I would come home from school and tell my mother, "Mom, I hate it there. The bullies are always picking on me and—"

"Marc," she'd interrupt, "who do you think you are, talking to me like that? Go to your room right now and do your homework!"

It's obvious to me today—she was totally triggered by what I was experiencing. It drove her into an immediate panic. But she couldn't get past her feelings about my feelings and behavior to try to help me. Classic flight reaction.

My father, on the other hand, went directly to fight. When I told him how I was being bullied, he was furious—at me—for not being the kind of tough guy he would have been in my shoes. He reacted as though I were the one in the wrong.

You may never have heard of your vagus nerves, despite their great importance to healthy human function. There are two of them—they start out in the brain stem, pass through your neck, and travel down your body to your large intestine (in Latin, *vagus* means wandering). They manage most of the work of the parasympathetic nervous system.

How we breathe affects the vagus nerves—if we can control our respiration, the vagus nerves will make it easier for us to act in helpful ways when triggered. If we ignore our breathing, our vagus nerves won't be doing us any favors. Stimulation of the vagus nerves has even been shown to alleviate symptoms of anxiety and depression. And when those symptoms diminish, our overarching need for regulation decreases.

In the method of dealing with feelings we developed at the Yale Center for Emotional Intelligence, deep breathing is a critical first step in gathering our inner resources before we say or do anything else.

Maybe it will help if we start by listing the breathing habits that get in the way of finding calm when we need it.

> *Shallow breathing*, mostly in the upper chest rather than lower from the diaphragm, increases feelings of stress and anxiety. It signals to the body that you're in danger.
> *Rapid breathing*, or hyperventilation, is associated with panic and fear, and can lead to dizziness. It disrupts the balance of oxygen and carbon dioxide in the blood, causing confusion and anxiety—even headaches.
> *Breath holding* usually follows that sudden gasp of inhalation in moments of surprise and distress or those intense moments when we're in deep concentration. It disrupts the normal flow of oxygen to the brain and body and induces sensations of fear and anxiety.

So it's clear that the effects of different ways of breathing are as much psychological and cognitive as they are physiological. Failure to manage how we breathe during emotional moments prevents us from responding as we'd like to.

Breathing is unique among our involuntary bodily functions because, unlike digestion or heartbeat, we can manage it.

How? Like anything else in life—by doing it. By practicing how to breathe, something we all do naturally but not always in healthy ways, we can reap its benefits.

Not everyone is comfortable performing breathing exercises. They can make some people feel *more* anxious, because focusing on the breath can draw attention to the physical sensations that come with emotional unease. Additionally, some individuals who have experienced trauma may feel panic when they concentrate on their breathing. (For them, movement-based practices and visualization exercises often help.) For others, it's frustrating to sit still and regulate how they inhale and exhale, to the exclusion of everything else.

Nevertheless, the benefits are clear for most people, and the scientific research bears this out: A range of breathing exercises improves vagal tone, which is associated with a greater ability to relax, reduced inflammation, and better emotion regulation. It enhances respiratory function, reduces blood pressure, and contributes to cardiovascular health. Researchers also have found that slow, intentional breathing aids brain function and brings about positive changes in our emotional and cognitive states.

Training people to work with their breathing so it is deeper and slower has been effective in reducing depression, anxiety, and stress; decreasing pain; improving physiological function; elevating mood; and enhancing learning ability. High school students who were taught breathing exercises reported lower stress and higher levels of effective emotion regulation. An eight-week study of healthy adults showed that controlled breathing improved attention and lowered cortisol levels.

There are quite a few kinds of breathing exercises. Some are more complicated than others. At least one is battle-tested. The most important thing is that we incorporate them into our daily routines and do them several times a day, especially when we're not activated. If we try to deploy them only when we need them—in moments of high emotional activation—they won't do us as much good. Breathing with intention is an ability that needs to be second nature. We must get to the point where habit and muscle memory run the show.

And the only way to get there is by rehearsing. We can do it in ways that fit in seamlessly with the rest of our lives—it doesn't have to be a big deal, or one more chore to add to your list.

Maybe you'll do it the moment you wake up, before you even get out of bed. Or on your morning commute to work. It's easy to do while listening to a podcast or walking down the street. Find the spaces in your daily life where practicing breathing exercises makes most sense and do it then. The important thing is to do it when it's not necessary, so that it will be there for you when it is.

Here are some breathing practices to try. Feel free to be creative and find the ones you like. In the beginning, I recommend following these basic guidelines for safety:

- Keep your body relaxed. Tension disrupts breathing.
- Stay hydrated and make sure you've eaten before doing breathing exercises, as low blood sugar can worsen hyperventilation symptoms.
- Begin with shorter sessions and gradually lengthen them as you become more comfortable.
- If you're unsure about your technique or if you have underlying health conditions, seek guidance from a qualified instructor.
- If you feel uncomfortable, dizzy, or lightheaded, return to normal breathing.

Okay, now we're ready.

One simple technique is to imagine a tranquil scene and then match your breathing to what you're seeing. For me, it's a calm lake on a gorgeous spring morning. I'm standing alone on the bank, completely at ease, taking in all the sights and sounds, breathing as deeply and slowly as I would in real life. A minute or two of that and I'm good.

Another simple technique is to take two inhales and then one long exhale—like a sigh—and then repeat that for one to two minutes. This reduces carbon dioxide levels, slows your heart rate, and leaves you calmer and more focused.

We can try what Navy SEALs do in extreme situations. Visualize a square with four equal sides—like a box. Focus on one side as you inhale for four seconds. Now picture the next side as you hold that breath for the same amount of time. Visualize the third side of the square as you exhale for four seconds. And then focus on the fourth side as you hold your breath for four seconds. Repeat that pattern over and over, picturing the square while maintaining a relaxed, tranquil state of body and mind.

The SEALs call it *box breathing* and they use it to control how they react during life-threatening events. We're unlikely ever to face the emotional challenges they endure. But we can use the same breathing technique to get through our own stressful moments. Box breathing has roots in pranayama, the yogic practice of breath control. It's been around for thousands of years. Its popularity in Western contexts, especially in military and tactical training, is often credited to its simplicity and effectiveness in promoting relaxation and focus.

Similar to box breathing, *coherent breathing* draws from ancient practices found in yoga, tai chi, and other mindfulness traditions. The term gained prominence through the work of Stephen Elliott, a researcher and practitioner in the field of biofeedback. He and his colleagues studied the effects of rhythmic breathing patterns on heart rate variability, which is the amount of time between each beat of the heart. Longer time between beats makes us calmer.

To do it, sit comfortably with eyes closed and take a few deep breaths to center yourself. The goal is to take no more than six breaths in a minute—five seconds to inhale and five to exhale.

Yogis will be familiar with *alternate nostril breathing*: First we use the thumb of the left hand to block the left nostril while we inhale through the right. Then we use the index and middle fingers of the same hand to block the right nostril while we exhale through the left. Next, not moving our hand, we inhale through the left nostril, then block it with the thumb and exhale through the right. It sounds more complicated than it is, trust me. People have been using this technique for thousands of years, so there must be something to it.

As someone who's been doing martial arts, yoga, and Zen meditation for nearly forty years, I've come across many kinds of breathing exercises. The ones above are some of my favorites. People make claims that one is better than the other, but I don't buy it. In fact, researchers have begun to test the relative impact of different breathing exercises. A 2023 study, for example, compared coherent breathing to normal, deep breathing in a carefully designed experiment. After four weeks, stress levels were no different between the two groups. But there were overall improvements in stress, anxiety, depression, and well-being for *all* participants.

The key is to stop what you're doing for a moment and just consciously breathe. Try different techniques, find the ones you like, and use them daily.

I think of breathing exercises like I do about cardio: It doesn't matter whether you're walking, running, swimming, cycling, jumping rope, rowing, or dancing—they *all* get your heart rate up. All these breathing exercises will do just the opposite: They will quiet your entire body down, especially your nervous system, and allow you to be fully present in emotional moments as you choose how to deal with your feelings.

But even breathing has its limitations. Whatever *caused* your emotion didn't go away while you were breathing. It's still there, waiting to be dealt with.

You inhaled.

You exhaled.

Now what?

In many instances, that pause for a breath *will* be enough—mostly when the emotion is so minor that it practically resolves itself. These are the moments when you take a deep breath and silently ask yourself, *Is it worth it? Is this worth me getting upset and doing something about it?* Somebody unimportant to your life says or does something that rubs you the wrong way. Before reacting, you take that deep breath and pause—and realize that this provocation is so beneath your dignity that you need not even acknowledge it.

But that's not always the case. So we need to take the next step.

Mindfulness was developed thousands of years ago within Buddhist contemplative practices to reduce suffering. Its tenets can be found in most religious traditions, including Christianity, Hinduism, Islam, Judaism, and Taoism. Yet, most mindfulness practices today are secular in nature, emphasizing the psychological and physiological benefits without imposing any religious or cultural beliefs.

Mindfulness refers to both a state of mind and a set of skills that help us cultivate these things:

- Attention and awareness of the present moment
- Nonjudgmental observation and acceptance of all emotions—our own and others'
- Curiosity and openness
- Compassion for oneself and other people

Breathing exercises, like the ones we discussed, are often used to help us relax. While mindfulness can lead to relaxation, it has a larger goal of teaching us not to react to each and every emotion. It allows us to sit with our emotions, even the uncomfortable ones, the kind we'd rather not experience. With mindfulness we can create that moment of calm inaction before we decide how or if we'll respond.

Mindfulness allows us to live in the moment. That expression confounds some people, who will say, "I'm *always* in the moment, where else *could* I be?" But think about it—how much of your life do you spend thinking about either the past or the future? About what you could have done before, or what you should do next, or what else you ought to be doing this minute? Those thoughts are the source of a great deal of the anxiety we all live with.

I'm no exception. Even as I'm writing this book, I'm getting distracted thinking about how the publisher will react when I submit it, or what I'll have to do next to make it better. It's as though I can't fully experience what I'm accomplishing this minute, and maybe even enjoy it.

While we can't (and don't want to) shut our minds off when practicing mindfulness, first we try to filter out distractions—the noise. I don't mean only the sounds that intrude on our awareness. I mean the visual noise, too, and the informational noise. Anything unnecessary that gets in the way of calm consideration of the moment at hand.

As in martial arts or the boxing ring, we must learn to observe our emotional provocations without feeling personally assaulted by them. It's almost as though you're watching a movie where you notice everything that's happening but don't feel overwhelmed by it. You're in the moment but not *of* the moment. There's a big difference. Practicing mindfulness offers us greater presence of mind to respond to our emotions constructively and with intention, rather than reacting to them out of habit. In this way, it gives us more agency over our lives. No matter what happens to us, we can create a space to thoughtfully respond to events in ways that are healthy and purposeful for us.

Sounds like work, right? It surely is. That's why it has to be learned. And, as we're about to discuss, practiced. But with small amounts of practice over time, it gains its own momentum and becomes an invaluable tool to navigate your emotional life.

"The nearer a man comes to a calm mind, the closer he is to strength," the Roman emperor and Stoic philosopher Marcus Aurelius wrote in his aptly titled *Meditations*. Of course, he died in the year 180, when there were, presumably, many fewer distractions to deal with.

Being mindful today is more challenging than ever thanks to technology. A study conducted twenty years ago found that participants kept their attention on a single screen for an average of two and a half minutes. Today, it's forty-seven seconds. Our digital lives, spent scrolling, surfing, swiping, and gaming, have conditioned us to move fast and expect instant results and constant dopamine hits. That's unrealistic in the flesh-and-blood world, so we're caught in limbo between the two, and our brains and social and emotional lives pay the price. It's even tougher if you're young—that's always been a skittish time of life but is even more so today thanks to social media and smartphones. Research conducted by Ian Anderson and Wendy Wood at the University of Southern California reveals that habitual or compulsive social media users often engage with platforms out of routine rather than for rewards. This behavior can result in a disconnection from the consequences of their actions (consequences that can include the spread of misinformation, for example) and can diminish people's sensitivity to the negative impacts of social media consumption on their mental health.

Additionally, frequent social media use has been strongly associated with poor sleep quality, including nightmares and increased anxiety. The compulsive nature of social media engagement exacerbates these effects, making it increasingly difficult for users to disconnect from these platforms.

In the midst of all that noise, practicing mindfulness can be a reprieve and relief, though challenging to establish. We have to set aside time to train ourselves to be as fully present as possible—for ourselves and those we care about—not distracted by nonsense, not multitasking, not thinking simultaneously of the past, present, and future. This kind of discipline can only be acquired in the same way we learned to breathe properly—by practicing until it becomes a habit. By cultivating mindfulness when we don't need it so it's there when we do.

It's obvious that becoming more mindful and still, more fully present in our lives, will be beneficial, and there's plenty of science to back that up. In 2021, Richard Davidson and his colleagues at the University of Wisconsin-Madison published a comprehensive randomized controlled trial (a systematic look) at studies of mindfulness-based interventions. They found that these interventions reduce and prevent the relapse of depression, anxiety, and other mental health conditions, and even offer benefits for chronic pain and heart disease. This research and hundreds of other studies conducted in laboratories around the world indicate that mindfulness training can enhance attention span and short-term memory, reduce stress and negative emotions even in people suffering with serious disease, increase empathy and compassion, foster neuroplasticity (allowing the brain to remain adaptable and resilient even into old age), and enhance the skills of emotional awareness and regulation.

Perhaps the first step in becoming more mindful in current times is to reconsider some of our screen-related choices. Maybe we'll go on a media diet—limit the time we spend watching cable news, turn off Wi-Fi except when it's necessary, close the laptop earlier than usual. This is especially important in the hours after dinner and before bedtime, because healthy sleep is key for mental health and well-being. When you're tempted to check your email (which research shows we do about seventy-seven times per day), go have a conversation instead, even on your phone. Stretch, breathe (you now know some good techniques), read a book—one that doesn't fill you with anxiety or dread. Still yourself and see how it feels to miss all the angst you currently experience right before you're supposed to drift off to dreamland.

You might notice how you're feeling right now—curious, engaged, bored, resistant, or maybe even questioning why you're reading this at all. That's okay. These moments are opportunities for you to pause and practice the very skills we're talking about. Take a breath. Let yourself settle for just a moment. Then, when you're ready, come back to these words with a fresh perspective. This isn't just reading; it's a chance to gently train your attention and nurture your focus in real time.

Now we're ready to begin actively cultivating mindfulness along with the mental and emotional benefits it offers. How does this happen? In a number of ways.

There are both formal and informal ways to practice mindfulness, and I recommend you try both. Formal mindfulness exercises include meditation, yoga, tai chi, mindful walking, "nature bathing," and many other methods. We'll cover a few practices below; there are innumerable books and guides you can consult.

Informal practice really just means taking a moment in your day to be aware of what is happening and how you feel—not necessarily trying to change anything. Every so often, it helps if we ask, *What's going on in my body? Am I tense, am I relaxed? What's going on in my mind? Am I feeling depleted or energized? Do I feel like attending this meeting or do I wish I could avoid it?*

At the Center, we use a tool called the Mood Meter, as we discussed in the last chapter. Are you in the green quadrant, signifying a pleasant, peaceful frame of mind? That's good to know, because it suggests that you might be able to handle even intense feelings when they come your way. Or are you in the red quadrant, meaning you're feeling activated in an unpleasant way, say anxious or overwhelmed? If you're there, it might be a good idea to figure out why and either allow it to pass or find a way to address it. Spending too much time in the red practically guarantees that you'll be easily triggered when difficult moments arrive: Your brain and body are preparing for the fight-flight-freeze response even when it may not be useful. You can also begin to anticipate moments when you're likely to have feelings that will need managing.

By focusing on your momentary experiences, you can start to discern your large emotional patterns, and then be proactive in regulating them.

In the morning, take stock of the day and identify encounters—a job interview, a doctor's appointment, a talk with your child about some misbehavior—where a little emotion regulation might come in handy.

Learn to recognize the signals that you're about to be triggered. Somebody says something and you feel yourself immediately tense. Your heart begins to race. Your focus zooms in. These are signals that you need to find stillness now, before you pass the point of no return.

Maybe you can just sit with the experience and notice it with a curious mind. Then let it go and move on with your day. Maybe you'll need an additional strategy.

By being more aware of our triggers and priming ourselves to be ready at the start of the day, we can be less reactive and more mindful in the moments when we are triggered. Our expectations play a big role in our emotions, and if we adjust them for the day ahead, we can adapt better.

The quest for stillness and being present, open, and curious underscores a truth about emotion regulation: It can't be something we practice just in the heat of the moment, when it's necessary. It must be integrated into our lives, throughout our waking hours, so it's not only something we do—it's who we *are*.

Now we're ready to delve into some exercises to help cultivate mindfulness and mental stillness. Here are four widely practiced ones to start.

Ch'an or Zen meditation revolves around posture, breath awareness, and mental focus. My first exposure to this came from a workshop I attended thirty-five years ago. I ended up becoming a disciple of a Taiwanese Zen Master named Sheng Yen for many years.

How do you begin? Bring your attention to your breath. Breathe naturally and without force. Focus on the sensation of the breath as it enters and leaves your nostrils. Pay attention to the rise and fall of your abdomen with each breath.

The basic exercise requires us to still our minds by counting our breaths, from one to ten. If we get briefly distracted, we refocus on breathing and continue counting. But if we get lost in our wandering thoughts, we start over. The goal is to be able to return to that clear, present mind any time we wish. Start with five minutes of practice and work your way up to ten or fifteen minutes or even longer.

Over the years, I've taught this meditation to thousands of people. Not everyone manages to still their minds with it. In the beginning it can be trying. But with practice, it's possible. And the benefits of a clear mind make it worth the effort.

Next is Vipassana, or insight meditation, which I learned from Joseph

Goldstein, a renowned American meditation teacher. Like Zen meditation, it begins by getting comfortable and bringing our attention to our breath. But instead of trying to block out the world around us, we open our awareness to every bit of our surroundings, including our thoughts (even the random ones), feelings, bodily sensations, and background sounds. Give yourself a few minutes to be present with whatever surfaces in your consciousness.

In this form of mindfulness, we allow all stimuli to arrive and then depart, without getting caught up in them. Notice each thought or sensation as it arises—observe it without interference or judgment. Allow it to linger as needed, maybe label it if you want, and then gently let it go. Resist the urge to push away thoughts or cling to them. By adopting this observer's stance, our minds naturally become quieter, and we are more fully present. We also can begin to identify the habitual patterns that dominate our reactions and see more clearly how our mind operates. The more we practice, the finer our awareness will become. This deeper understanding enables us to engage with life and people more deliberately and kindheartedly, choosing responses rather than falling back on automatic reactions.

I learned this next technique, often referred to as conscious breathing, on a retreat with Zen Master Thích Nhất Hạnh over thirty years ago. I use this mindful exercise often, especially when I feel overwhelmed, get irritated at someone, or have trouble sleeping. As with all the others, it starts in a relaxed position, usually seated or lying down, and breathing deeply and slowly. When we inhale, we silently say the word *in*. On the exhale, the word is *out*. In the next breath, the words are *calm* and *ease*. On the inhale after that we smile gently and then we say *release* to ourselves on the exhale. These phrases are then repeated for a few minutes. When I teach this technique, people report that it makes them feel calm, peaceful, and balanced.

Finally, there is the loving-kindness meditation made popular in the United States by Sharon Salzberg. This practice can be thought of as a cousin of the other, more direct mindfulness practices that specifically target present attention and open awareness. The goals of fostering a present, open, curious, and nonjudgmental stance toward all people and things are shared. However, loving-kindness explicitly focuses on cultivating an attitude of compassion and feelings of love toward oneself and others.

It starts with a comfortable physical position and calm, deep breathing. Then silently repeat these phrases (there are many versions of this):

*May I be safe, healthy, happy, and live with ease.*

Next, bring to mind someone you care deeply about, and extend the phrase to them:

*May you be safe, healthy, happy, and live with ease.*

Now, imagine that person offers loving-kindness back to you:

*May [your name] be safe, healthy, happy, and live with ease.*

Next, imagine a friend, family member, or colleague who's doing well right now:

*May you be safe, healthy, happy, and live with ease.*

Now, picture a friend or colleague who's struggling:

*May you be safe, healthy, happy, and live with ease.*

Next, think of people who are suffering:

*May you be safe, healthy, happy, and live with ease.*

Finally, imagine all living things everywhere:

*May all beings be safe, healthy, happy, and live with ease.*

Ultimately, this form of meditation seeks to dissolve barriers that separate us and to promote empathy, forgiveness, and harmony in all our relationships, including the one with ourselves. There are even versions that include thinking about someone you are having difficulty with and sending them good wishes. Some people also prefer to start by focusing on sending well wishes to the "beneficent other" rather than oneself. There's no single correct formula.

When I teach this, people share that they feel warm, blessed, peaceful, grateful, and connected. Some even get tears in their eyes as they reflect on various people in their lives. This is well supported by research that suggests that loving-kindness meditation practices increase feelings of compassion, decrease intergroup and implicit biases, and change the network in the brain that underlies our empathy and kindness.

You might be wondering which of those mindfulness exercises is best. The answer is that it depends, and I've shared only a few of the many hundreds of practices available. They all produce benefits, but recent research suggests some important nuances.

In one study, researchers found that employees practicing breath-based meditation improved their *cognitive* understanding of others' perspectives. By contrast, those engaging in loving-kindness meditation enhanced their ability to empathize and *connect emotionally* with others.

A related study asked over 1,400 online freelancers to recall a time they had wronged someone. They then engaged in either breath-based or loving-kindness meditation. Those who practiced breath-based meditation were less inclined to make amends than those who practiced the loving-kindness technique or did not meditate at all.

This suggests that loving-kindness meditation might foster empathy and a focus on others, while breath-based meditation might ease feelings of guilt but also reduce the drive to apologize or correct past mistakes. This also tracks with cognitive neuroscience research that suggests that some mindfulness practices activate and develop executive functioning networks crucial for attention, memory, and self-control, whereas loving-kindness practices differentially activate brain networks important for feeling what others are feeling and experiencing empathy.

To be sure, all forms of mindfulness can help with stress and compassion. But some mindfulness practices that calm our minds or alleviate anxiety may differ from those that make us more empathic and connected individuals. Using one method of mindfulness meditation as a universal stress reliever might lead to avoiding issues that need addressing, potentially leading to unintended consequences in our relationships. The idea is to begin thinking creatively and strategically about how to cultivate mindfulness.

Try the exercises I've shared and others and see what works for you, given your specific goals. Here are some additional tips:

**Integrate mindfulness into existing daily activities.** Try "stacking" or performing your mindfulness practice alongside daily activities such as brushing your teeth, exercising, making dinner, folding clothes, or walking the dog. This helps embed new mental exercises into your everyday life, enhancing their benefits across your daily routines. Research tells us it is easier to build on an existing habit than to start from scratch.

**Establish a mindfulness routine.** Choose a consistent time and place for your mindfulness practice. Even brief but regular sessions of five to ten minutes daily can be more effective than longer, less frequent sessions, according to new research. Basketball legend Kobe Bryant said that starting his day with a few minutes of mindfulness meditation was essential for grounding himself. Consistency makes it permanent (that's how new neural connections are formed!).

**Be mindful in interactions.** When engaging with others, work toward being present and attentive. Make eye contact, breathe naturally, and give your full attention to foster genuine connection. Put your phone away. Also, try being open-minded and curious even if you don't agree with others—this will help to bring nonjudgmental awareness in your relationships.

**Embrace mindfulness as a practice.** The goal is not to become "good" at mindfulness but to bring a present, open, and curious awareness to daily activities. Don't stress over whether you're doing it "right"—that defeats the purpose. As long as you're trying and being kind to yourself even if your mind continues to wander, you're succeeding. Pay attention to which practices feel most natural, under what circumstances, and why. Explore and rotate through various techniques to find the ones that suit you best.

**Practice with other people.** Many people who practice mindfulness benefit significantly from being part of a community of fellow practitioners (called a sangha in Sanskrit). Group practice provides a supportive environment in which people can share experiences, difficulties, and insights, fostering a sense of belonging and mutual understanding. This also helps reinforce regular practice, as members encourage one another to stay committed and consistent.

A final note.

This is something I run into all the time, with adults in seminars and children in classrooms. They've heard all about the importance of taking that deep breath. They understand the need for stillness and mindfulness, including the benefits. But they're hazy on what—if anything—comes next.

I say to people in seminars, "Tell me exactly what you think taking a deep breath is supposed to accomplish, especially when you are triggered. We all agree that it's an important first step to calm your body and mind. But then what will you say or do?"

More often than not, I get blank stares.

In a middle school classroom I visited while writing this book, I said to the students, "Okay, you got into a fight, and you feel really bad because you said something mean and cruel to the other person. What do you do?"

A boy said, "I would take a deep breath."

"But how does that help with the guilt you're feeling or the other student's hurt feelings? How does that help to resolve the conflict you have with the other student?" I asked him.

He couldn't say.

Breathing and mindfulness have an important role. But we can't rely solely on breathing and mindfulness to regulate our emotions, cultivate positive relationships, and solve problems. If we do, we can become so focused on calming ourselves and seeking inner peace with meditation and yoga and breathing that we stop thinking about taking action. And breathing and mindfulness exercises don't resonate with everyone.

No one method, no matter how effective, will help us to manage the complex array of emotions and social challenges we face. Some approaches help at some times and in some settings, and not in others.

Research suggests having a rich repertoire of emotion regulation strategies is key for well-being and resilience.

I've been studying these concepts and practicing them for almost four decades now, and it's still a challenge for me at times. I do my breathing and mindfulness exercises and think I've got my body and mind in a good place. And then someone says something that irritates me, and I have to lecture myself—*Marc, don't say it, don't react to this, it's insignificant, stop and take a few deep breaths.* It's not easy.

## 10.

# Redirecting Your Thoughts

*What holds attention determines action.*
—WILLIAM JAMES

Now we're going to use our imaginations to improve how we deal with our feelings. I don't mean we're going to reinvent reality or anything weird like that. Instead, we'll tweak how we respond to the things that make us angry or anxious or hurt and learn techniques to "downregulate" unwanted emotions and "upregulate" or initiate the emotions we want to feel. These strategies can be most helpful when we're in situations that are beyond our control, or when we don't have a trusted friend to help us think things through. Regardless of how tough the moment is or the situation seems, we can protect and buffer ourselves just by changing the way we interpret what's going on.

A lot of what we'll cover in this chapter has its roots in cognitive behavioral therapy (CBT), which has been used successfully all over the world since the 1950s. According to the American Psychological Association, CBT was founded on the idea that "psychological problems are based, in part, on faulty or unhelpful ways of thinking." It empowers therapy patients to reframe and reimagine emotionally negative experiences.

By doing so, they learn to better manage stress, fear, despair, and all the other unwanted feelings that make life more difficult than it needs to be.

One of CBT's pioneers, Albert Ellis, called it "disputation," meaning that we learn to dispute how we initially see events and find other, less damaging ways of interpreting them. The therapist guides the client through a series of questions that challenge their negative perceptions, like these:

- Do I have actual evidence that my thoughts and beliefs are true?
- Is the critical comment that person made to me a universal opinion?
- Is my way of thinking about this helping me or hurting me?
- What's another way of viewing it that will help me achieve my goals?

Along with that, we need to be reminded of another concept from the study of psychology. Two researchers, Paul Rozin and Edward Royzman, first coined the term *negativity bias* in 2001. They found that we all tend to pay more attention to negative experiences in our lives, allow them to dominate positive moments, and remember them better. Negative events, they said, are even more contagious than positive ones.

Negativity bias shows up in numerous ways, and as a result we're often more pessimistic than we need to be when we evaluate things that happen to us.

It's why, whenever the phone rings, some of us—I'm thinking here of Aunt Hillary—automatically ask, "What's wrong?"

It's why, whenever we kids were fooling around and having fun, my grandfather would warn us, "You're laughing now; you'll be crying later."

Or any time we would talk about a future plan, my grandmother would interject, "God willing!"

Negativity bias explains why, if your significant other hasn't texted you all day, you think it's because they're falling out of love—not because they've been swamped at work, or they lost their phone, or some other benign reason. If the vet wants to run a follow-up blood test, it's because your cat has a terminal illness, not because a lab technician lost the test tube, or Tiger has some minor deficiency that can safely be ignored. The bank is calling? Obviously, it's because somebody hacked your account and stole all your savings, not because you forgot your ATM card at the teller window.

Evolutionary psychologists suggest that negativity bias has roots in our prehistoric past and may have provided survival advantages. People who were more alert to the presence of predators or rivals were better equipped to respond quickly and adapt to changing circumstances. This heightened sensitivity to negativity helped our ancestors navigate a world where survival often depended on avoiding harm.

Negativity bias is why we might remember criticism and insults better than praise. The one person who was rude to us sticks in our memory long after we've forgotten the many who were kind and polite. A single rejection stings more than the pleasure of a dozen welcomes. After a while, those unhappy experiences begin to influence all our expectations and color our experiences.

It's also likely that our negativity bias is amplified by cultural and social factors, including our personal histories. Today, the constant flow of worrisome news and brutal social media content reinforces the negative spin on life. This may result in an exaggerated focus on threats that are not necessarily life-threatening but are distressing all the same.

Now, if you're crossing the street and you see a truck bearing down on you, negativity bias is not to blame for your fear of getting squashed. But most of the time, I'll wager, your negative feelings are caused by less tangible forces—by how you perceive normal, everyday occurrences.

The connections among CBT, negativity bias, and cognitive strategies for emotion regulation are evident: We're already tweaking how we view our experiences—but unfortunately, we're often imagining them in negative ways.

We want to keep using these cognitive strategies, but now we want to swap that negativity for more helpful and productive ways of thinking. Imagine the effect that might have on your emotional state and your ability to deal with your feelings. And let's not forget that cognitive strategies are also used to evoke and prolong pleasant emotions.

Here's the main thing to keep in mind: It's totally acceptable to use anything we can come up with—humor, distraction, even avoidance—to create a little psychological distance from difficult moments. We don't always have to deal with challenges head-on, and there's no rule that says we need to address them the instant they present themselves. Making a tiny bit of mental space, carving out a short delay before we react, can allow us just enough room to respond rationally and come up with sensible solutions. And sometimes we need a bit longer to decide on a strategy. We need time and space to process and think through how we want to approach the feeling and situation.

Cognitive strategies help us see that our lives are much bigger and richer than any one specific moment that's causing us pain. They work best when used in situations where we have little or no power to change what's happening to us. These techniques are most effective when someone or something unpleasant is coming straight at us. They create space—not the kind you can measure with a yardstick, but psychic space. They allow us to put whatever's triggering us into another dimension altogether. Some place where it can't touch us or drive us crazy.

Here are five research-based approaches to help us redirect our thinking that I've found especially helpful:

1. *Spatial distance*: Mentally placing ourselves at a physical distance from the emotional stimulus
2. *Temporal distance*: Viewing a negative experience from a future perspective
3. *Distanced self-talk*: Viewing our experiences through the eyes of an outside observer
4. *Reappraisal*: Shifting how we think about a situation to modify its emotional impact on us
5. *Visualization*: Creating or recreating an image or experience in our minds

## SPATIAL DISTANCE

This strategy involves imagining physical space where none exists. I'll give you a personal example.

My father was an air conditioner repairman whose three sons earned doctorates. He was proud of that. He even came to watch me defend my dissertation.

But he was also resentful. He was constantly on the lookout for anything that seemed like snooty behavior or that suggested that I or my brothers thought we had become in some way "better" than him. When he sensed that, he would be vicious with his angry put-downs, even at family gatherings. It made for some extremely uncomfortable spectacles for everyone and humiliations for me.

So here I was in my late thirties, standing there in the middle of a family birthday party, and my father was going off, and I was embarrassed, but what could I do?

I could have yelled right back and turned it into an all-out screaming match. Definitely not my style.

I could have stormed out of the house. Not my style either.

I could have stood there silently, on the verge of tears, with all our relatives confused by what they were witnessing.

None of those would have helped me handle the horrible way I was feeling.

Then, one blessed day, I tried another approach.

I pretended I was watching a performance—like a scene from a play or a movie (I call this the "TV screen" technique). There I was, calmly viewing a make-believe madman character going off on his undeserving son in a bad domestic drama. Instead of standing a few feet away from my father, absorbing all his fury, I was off in a corner of the room, watching a tiny old man go ballistic on a TV screen.

Suddenly, my father wasn't so scary. My heart stopped pounding. A feeling of calm came over me. I felt grounded and in control.

Now, did choosing that response actually fix anything? Did it show him the error of his ways and teach him to do better? Did it take away my pain at being treated so harshly by my own father?

No, none of the above. It was beyond my power to do any of that.

But here's what it did: It got me through an extremely painful moment without losing my grip or sobbing uncontrollably or storming out of the house.

I took charge of the only thing I *could* control in that encounter—how I experienced what was happening, and how I responded to my feelings.

Spatial distance also came in handy late one night when I arrived in Australia to give a talk. I had been on planes for an entire day and wanted only to collapse into bed. But the landlady of the bed-and-breakfast where I was staying had other ideas—in a slightly drunken rant, she felt the need to tell me everything she disliked about the organization that was sponsoring my trip.

I was trapped. So as I stood there seeming to listen, I imagined myself in the basket of a hot-air balloon rising up into a blue sky. I looked down at the earth and watched as a tiny woman whose voice I could barely hear grew smaller and smaller until finally she was just a gesticulating little dot on the landscape.

Eventually, she wore herself out and left me in peace.

Another spatial tactic is imagining that whatever is happening is not happening to you. Someone is speaking to you harshly or judging you in extremely negative terms. If you were the one being spoken to in that way, if you were the person who deserved that kind of treatment, you'd feel wounded.

But since you're *not* that person, it doesn't bother you as much.

A couple of decades of science supports using these techniques. In one study, researchers asked two hundred adolescents to think of a time they got mad at someone. Then they were told to imagine viewing that scene from a distance—as though they were watching a movie in a theater. They reported feeling less angry, sad, hurt, and rejected. And when they imagined the incident from a distance, they blamed the other person less, too.

Like all emotion regulation strategies, spatial distance is an effective way to keep from being overwhelmed by our feelings. But here's a note of caution: It can be *too* effective. By this I mean that in certain circumstances, it's not such a great idea to redirect our thinking in order to avoid dealing with emotions.

With my father, my rationale for using the spatial strategy was that he was old, not well, and unlikely ever to change no matter what I said or did. I refused to allow him to keep upsetting me. But I wasn't going to cut him out of my life. So, my little game of turning him into entertainment on a TV screen did neither of us any harm.

Same was true of that B&B tyrant. I would never see her again, but I didn't want to be rude and tell her to shut the hell up and let me sleep. Up and away in my beautiful balloon, I was patient and serene.

But what if I were dealing with someone who was a significant part of my life—like a spouse, or a dear friend, or an important colleague? Sending them into another dimension on a regular basis would do us both more harm than good. In that circumstance, this would be a very poor choice of emotion regulation strategy, as it leans toward avoidance. When considering various strategies and trying to figure out which might be most helpful, it's important to keep in mind that every technique and tactic in this book can be used to help or to hinder. The potential for downside comes when we find ourselves using these strategies too often—it means we're avoiding situations that we probably need to address. Otherwise, we'll have created so much space that we can no longer see one another. This underscores the importance of being a good emotion scientist. We need to understand what's going on before we can choose the proper strategy. And after we use a strategy, we have to honestly evaluate its effectiveness.

So, despite the occasional temptation, I allow the people closest to me to remain where they are, spatially speaking, and when necessary, I find other strategies for dealing with the feelings they provoke.

## TEMPORAL DISTANCE

As Einstein said, space and time exist on a continuum, and so it makes sense that we can make use of a temporal—time-based—strategy, also referred to as "mental time travel."

Here's what that means: When you're about to freak out over something that's happening, you stop and imagine your future self, and then you ask, *How much will this moment matter tomorrow? In a week? A month?* Sometimes, our immediate, knee-jerk reactions to sudden events cause us to ignore the fact that whatever's going on isn't a big deal.

For example, you're rushing through the airport and hear an announcement that your flight has been canceled. Disaster! It means you won't get home tonight, and you won't be able to keep the appointments you made for tomorrow. And you're about to wind up in some airport hotel instead of your own bed.

Then you stop, take a deep breath, and project yourself into the future. *Two days from now, will this inconvenience still affect me?* you ask. *Am I going to miss anything important at home tonight? Can I easily reschedule those appointments? Will there be any lasting damage? Will I even remember this next week?*

In many cases (though not all, granted) the answer will be, *No, I guess not.* And the fact is that even if this mishap does screw up something important, there's nothing we can do about it. Once we acknowledge that, we can begin to deal with our feelings in a more productive way.

Here's a situation from the contemporary workplace that I hear people complain about from time to time.

We're at an obligatory office meeting on Zoom with maybe a hundred people in attendance. In our opinion, it's totally unnecessary, a complete, annoying waste of time. If you work in a big organization, chances are you know what I'm talking about.

If we could skip it, we would, but we can't.

We might feel better if we were to interrupt the session and speak our mind. There's even a chance—slim, we realize—that if we were to express our opinion it could lead to change, assuming that other people feel the same way.

But we doubt it. And speaking up could actually make things worse for ourselves and everybody else. It would make the meeting even longer. And it would put a target on our back. We could go to our boss and complain about how much work we can't accomplish because we're stuck in that useless session. The only problem is that he might not know what to do about it either.

This is when we do a little mental time travel and project ourselves into the future by two hours—by which time this meeting will have ended. And so instead of paying attention, we begin drafting a plan for a new project or do some other useful things while we're sitting there.

Suddenly, our exasperation over the meeting begins to fade. As with the canceled flight, this strategy doesn't change anything except our emotional response—which is the point. That's the only thing we can control.

In a series of studies conducted at the University of California, Berkeley, researchers found that people with high scores on a measure of temporal distancing had greater life satisfaction and fewer depressive symptoms. The research also showed that good temporal distancers respond to annoying interruptions during difficult tasks with less anger than those lower in this skill.

Other experimental research has found that cueing people to think about how they might feel about a current stressor in the distant future (ten years from now) versus the near future (a week from now) led them to experience less distress. These results held true for both serious and minor experiences, and regardless of whether the negative events had already happened or were ongoing.

Why does temporal distancing work? Focusing on how we might feel about our current troubles in the future can hasten emotional recovery by increasing our awareness that our current thoughts and feelings might fade with the passage of time—a process known as impermanence focus. It also helps us to avoid enacting an unhelpful reaction that we might regret.

Here's a great example of this strategy from my friend Jewel, the Grammy-nominated singer-songwriter and mental health advocate. She reminds us that no feeling, positive or negative, lasts forever. Remembering just that could make it easier to respond to certain challenging moments. If this emotion will soon be gone, how much of my anguish does it really deserve?

On my *Dealing with Feeling* podcast, she recalled,

*In my late teens, I was in a lot of pain, everything was very confusing, and it seemed like there was no way out. I was sitting on a bluff, and in Alaska there are huge tides that go out for a mile and then come in. I probably sat there for eight hours, paralyzed. But while I was sitting there and watching this tide go out and come back in, it suddenly dawned on me that the one constant in the universe is that things change. The culmination of nature is change and the arrogance and hubris that it took for me to think that I was the only thing in all of nature that wouldn't change became laughable. Like I was sitting there going, "Wow, that is a really selfish, strange thought to believe that my bad feelings, the crazy knot that I'm in, won't ever change." As if I alone existed outside the laws of physics. I was part of nature and that comforted me. Even if I wasn't parented properly, I was part of nature, and that gave me a tremendous amount of anchoring, connection, of feeling like I belonged. And because I was part of nature, these feelings I had would change. I called it buckling myself in—I just had to wait and things would change. Physics would take care of it, somehow. But in the meantime, was there a way that I could influence how it changed? Could I maybe influence it into changing sooner, by going toward something instead of running away from it?*

While working on this book, I also interviewed another friend, Ethan Kross, a well-known researcher on emotion regulation and author of *Chatter: The Voice in Our Head, Why It Matters, and How to Harness It*. He explained that thinking about events as temporary reduces distress by making you realize your current feelings and thoughts are temporary, too, which lessens their emotional impact. It also helps us discern what is truly important and what doesn't really matter.

One caveat in using the temporal distance strategy: We need to be careful not to minimize our emotions to the point that we disregard the truth they contain. Sometimes, when we ask *Will this really matter?* the answer is *yes*.

### DISTANCED SELF-TALK

We all talk to ourselves from time to time. But usually we do it like this:

We drop a glass and think, *I'm such a #@&% klutz!*

We make a wrong turn while driving and mutter, *That was really #@%& stupid.*

Or we're attempting some challenging task, and we start by saying, *Okay, let's see if I can do this and not &*#@ it up.*

So, self-talk already comes naturally to us—just not always in helpful ways. We need to do it differently.

If you were in the kitchen with your grandmother who dropped a glass, you wouldn't yell, "You idiot!" And if you were in the car with someone and they made a wrong turn, you wouldn't say, "That was really stupid." (At least I hope you wouldn't.) And there's no normal circumstance under which you would tell someone, "Try not to screw this up."

The imaginative leap involved in this self-talk strategy requires us to pretend, as we speak to ourselves, that we're addressing someone else. By doing this, we create psychological distance that allows us to see situations without the stress we feel when we're the ones under pressure. It's as though we're witnessing someone else's struggle—which makes it easier for us to respond calmly and rationally.

That's the key to positive self-talk—doing it as though you're trying to help someone you love, which—theoretically, at least—you *are*.

I was talking with a woman who tried this strategy with her son after attending a workshop I led on emotion regulation. She described driving the boy to a dentist appointment. The poor kid was scared, and nothing his mom said could console him.

Finally, she asked him, "If your best friend felt this way about a dentist visit, what would you tell him to make him worry less?"

Her son began rattling off a dozen things he'd say to his buddy to make him feel better.

"Okay, honey," his mom said, "how about telling yourself all those things and seeing how you feel?"

The kid was quiet for a moment. Then he said, "Mommy, you're a genius."

The seeds of negative self-talk are planted early. We hear parents and other authority figures speak critically about themselves and us, and so naturally we internalize those views and those voices, and then we carry them forward. In a study of elementary school children, researchers found that kids whose parents and other adults spoke positively to them showed higher positive self-talk and lower negative self-talk than children whose parents and others spoke to them negatively.

It's easy, when provoked by something we've done or failed to do, to instantly exclaim, *I'm such a dope!* It's harder to pause, take a breath, and then say, *Marc, don't worry about it, it's only a glass.* Or *Marc, you've taken on bigger challenges in the past, you'll do fine.* Even that little grammatical tweak of using the second person instead of the first (*you* instead of *I*) can make a significant difference.

I've also noticed that people's negative self-talk, often manifested in a response to a compliment, is subtle. It manifests in ways that may not seem immediately harmful but can impact our confidence over time. Here are some examples:

"Anyone could have done it."

"It's pretty good."

"We all get lucky sometimes."

"Let's see if they like it."

Recognizing these patterns is the first step toward changing them into more constructive self-talk. This all reveals a sad truth: Most of us are much nicer to others—more forgiving, more understanding, more accepting, more supportive—than we are to ourselves. But with this strategy, we can change that.

*Psychology Today* reported on a study conducted at the University of Michigan where participants had to compose five-minute talks about why they were qualified for their dream jobs. They were all informed that people tend to use self-talk to ready themselves for stressful tasks such as the one they faced, but half were told to do it using first-person pronouns (*I* and *me*) while the rest were to use second- and third-person pronouns (*you* and their own first names).

Then they delivered their talks (before a panel of experts, while being videotaped, just to amp up the pressure). The researchers found that the second group—those using impersonal pronouns—performed significantly better. Not only that, but they were less emotionally stressed while they prepared their speeches as well as after they delivered them.

When I speak to groups of parents, I'll sometimes ask what they say to themselves after they've mishandled some interaction with their kids. Here's what they report:

"Damn, I'm an idiot."
"I'm a shitty parent."
"I'm a failure!"
"Ugh, I wish I hadn't said that!"
"I botched it."
"I'm really screwing up these kids!"
"I'm just like my mother!"
"I am such a jerk."
"I really screwed that one up."
"How can I undo what I just did?"
"I hope I didn't just mess her up for good!"

More than a reflection on their skills as parents, this shows the kind of self-flagellation we're all capable of performing. You can imagine what a confidence destroyer this brand of self-talk represents.

Ethan Kross, the psychologist whom I introduced earlier, shared with me, "Introspection is a superpower. It's the reason we are capable of doing amazing things as a species. But it's also one of the biggest challenges we are faced with. It makes it easy for our self-talk to go south. Too much introspection can actually backfire. It's easy to go down a rabbit hole."

Psychology has a term for our inclination to offer good advice to others while struggling to heed the same wisdom ourselves. Igor Grossmann, a psychologist from the University of Waterloo, calls it "Solomon's Paradox." King Solomon, the leader of the Jewish kingdom, was renowned for his wisdom and judgment, attracting people from afar for his counsel. But his personal life was plagued by poor decisions and unchecked passions. Sound like you?

It's rare, I've observed, to find people whose self-talk is filled with affirmation, admiration, and congratulation. At the same time, there's such a thing as self-talk that's *too* positive. Avoiding honestly assessing our behaviors and thoughts undermines our ability to grow. In fact, there's research showing that self-criticism—because it prevents us from being overconfident—increases our motivation to do better. It's all in *how* we talk to ourselves—thinking, *What could I have done differently?* isn't the same as saying to ourselves, *You'll never get this right!*

While we don't want to be too hard on ourselves, we also don't want to delude ourselves. We're all familiar with "toxic positivity"—the kind of talk that insists we're always happy and energized by positive thoughts. This occurs when people make statements such as "It's fine!" or "Don't let it get to you!" or "Stay positive!" That's dangerous because it doesn't reflect anyone's reality. We all experience unpleasant emotions, and we need to acknowledge and accept them before we can deal with them. Positive self-talk isn't helpful when we use it as a barrier to honest appraisal.

## REAPPRAISAL

The next two strategies both fall under the category of *reappraisal*, which means consciously choosing to reassess a difficult moment in a way that generates a less negative response.

We react with strong emotions to plenty of things that are beyond our control. We all know the big ones—climate change, war, school shootings, political strife. In our individual lives, we find the same—realities we have to deal with that we had no hand in creating.

While we can work our entire lives to create larger change, we can't change those things instantaneously. But if we try, we can come up with more than one way of dealing with our feelings about them. That's a big part of what's called for here—creativity. It involves changing our initial reaction to unpleasant moments by asking ourselves, *Is there another way of seeing this? Is it possible to interpret this in a way that's less damaging, less triggering?*

This is the wisdom of cognitive strategies: When we can't change the world, it's time to change the way we view it.

Research in the field of positive psychology has shown that how we perceive and interpret the events in our lives plays a key role in shaping our levels of happiness. People who adopt a positive outlook, practice gratitude, and focus on the bright side of things tend to experience higher levels of happiness and well-being.

One highly cited 2005 study conducted by Sonja Lyubomirsky, Laura King, and Ed Diener shows that using helpful regulation strategies to change one's perspective or outlook can account for up to 40 percent of individual differences in happiness levels.

Brain imaging studies conducted using functional magnetic resonance imaging (fMRI) technology found that reappraisal significantly dampens activity in the amygdala, an area of our brain that becomes activated when we experience strong emotions. Instead, reappraisal activates the lateral temporal cortical regions of the brain, which help us to modulate how we respond to our feelings.

In one of our Center's studies, led by Jessica Hoffmann, an assistant professor, we showed that reappraisal effectiveness (the extent to which reappraisal improves one's emotional state) is significantly associated with originality (the extent to which the reappraisal was novel). In the study, high school students were given the following scenario: "Right before a presentation you must give, the organization tells you that it expects you to speak for twice as long as you originally planned." They were then asked to write reappraisals following this prompt, "How could you reframe this situation in a positive way?" Experts then rated the appraisals for their originality. For example, "The more I speak, the more I might be remembered, winning greater public admiration" was rated as more original than "This is a test to determine how skilled I am." As expected, the most effective or helpful strategies were the more original ones.

Reappraisal use is strongly associated with many indicators of well-being, such as greater physiological health, optimism, life satisfaction, and active attempts to repair negative mood, as well as lower experience and expression of depressed mood and negative affect. Here, we'll cover two approaches.

The first reappraisal strategy we'll consider is called *reconstrual*.

According to the *Oxford English Dictionary*, the verb *construe* means "to interpret a word or action in a particular way." Implicit in that definition is the idea that there's more than one way to view the meaning of words and actions—that nothing is completely fixed. In which case, we have choices to make: How will we construe our lives?

You go to the coffee shop and order in your usual polite, friendly way, and the cashier gives you a withering look and a curt reply. Now you're left wondering—*Did I do something to deserve that?*

That's one interpretation, one construal: You're to blame.

But what if instead you allow for the possibility that the cashier just goes through life with a chip on her shoulder? Or maybe she fought with her boyfriend that morning? Or maybe she got bad news from her sister?

So, you reconstrue the moment: Her attitude has nothing to do with you. And so you move on, unscathed.

Or you applied for a job you really want. It would make a big difference, not just in your paycheck but in the rest of your career. You feel qualified. Your hopes are high.

And then you get the dreaded email: They picked someone else.

If you've ever been there—and by a certain age most of us have—you know the immediate sensation. You weren't good enough, smart enough, cool enough, something enough. The news lands like a kick to your self-esteem. It's going to leave a mark.

Okay, that's one way to construe it.

Here's another—the person doing the hiring was just unable to see what a high-quality employee you would have been. Perhaps there was another candidate who had the inside track for one reason or another—like being somebody's relative.

But reconstrual doesn't have to be solely defensive.

Try these interpretations instead: Sometimes, stuff just happens. Some things work out and others don't, and either way it's not the end of the world. Nobody gets everything they want. In the past you've been the one who gets chosen, and you'll be the chosen one again. Perhaps you were totally qualified but for some other reason it wouldn't have been a great fit. In which case, neither you nor the person doing the hiring was an idiot, and now you can move on, still feeling good about yourself.

On my podcast, I interviewed the actress and musician Emily Kinney, best known for her role as Beth on *The Walking Dead*. We spoke about how she has managed rejection in her career. It's clear she's mastered the reappraisal technique:

> *Part of being an actor is rejection. You don't want it to harden you. I've learned over time that no audition is your only chance to succeed. That gives you perspective. And as someone who has gotten many parts, I've seen it to believe it. When I don't get the part, I give myself time to grieve. I take a walk, analyze it, allow myself to feel sad, but then I let it go and move on. I don't let the rejection define my identity as an actor. And once I decided I would be doing this work into my old age,*

*the rejection didn't mean that much. It still hurts, but not getting a part doesn't decide my entire life or career, just that job. You don't know what will happen next. And many times I've gotten the job other actors wanted as much as I did.*

Those are just some of the possible ways of seeing what happened. Undoubtedly there are many more. We must learn to strategize effectively and find positive versions of reality to reconstrue negative experiences. Either that or we go down the emotional black hole of *I'm not good enough, smart enough, et cetera.*

The key thing here is to choose the construal that will benefit us going forward. This is *the* most important aim of every emotion regulation strategy we'll discuss in this book: We want to deal with our feelings in ways that will bring us closer to our life goals. We owe it to ourselves.

Here's another example. You arrive right on time for pickleball with a friend. You've claimed a court and now you're waiting . . . and waiting . . . and now you've been here for twenty minutes and no friend—and no text or call explaining their lateness.

It's happened before with this particular person. What do you make of it? Maybe they love you, but they don't really respect you. Or they believe their time is more important than yours. Or they're dragging their heels because they didn't want to play in the first place.

Now your blood is starting to boil, and what should have been a fun occasion is doomed.

But what if, instead, you stopped your pessimistic guessing game at the very start? Instead, you begin thinking of alternate explanations that would totally salvage your emotional state. Maybe something urgent came up—a worrisome phone call from their child's teacher, or an email from their boss. Maybe there was an accident that required a detour on the way to the gym. Imagine all the things that can go wrong, and then allow for the chance that today one of them actually did.

Now, at least for the moment, you've talked yourself out of feeling disrespected. You can relax a little and patiently wait—even though you know in all likelihood none of those things *did* happen. You can choose to feel resentful if that's what you prefer, but it won't do you any good and will only make things tense once your friend does show up.

Instead, you had a choice, and you chose wisely. Of course, when your friend arrives and you learn the reason they were late, you can forgive them or have the difficult conversation.

The other, related form of reappraisal is called *repurposing*. It means examining a negative experience or emotion and finding—and focusing on—the positive one hiding inside. It allows us to assign a different meaning to an experience that would otherwise just bum us out.

So, you missed your train? Just think: Now you have even more time to prepare your notes for that meeting before you arrive at work.

Or your kids are clamoring to go to the local amusement park. You've taken them there often enough to know the routine: They beg to go on one ride after another, and then they plead for all the junk food that everyone else is devouring, and there goes your Saturday.

It's really a major annoyance. It's tempting to tell them to clean their rooms and watch TV instead.

But then you think about it a bit, and alongside the negative you find a positive: how much joy you will be giving your kids if you go. And you remember when you were a kid, and you clamored for the amusement park, and your parents indulged you. You can still recall how happy it made you. And you realize that here, today, you have a chance to bring that same happiness to your own kids.

And so, you go to the park, at peace thanks to the positive repurposing you just performed. You're not going to love the amusement park experience. But you'll love what you've gotten in return.

Here's another example from my own life. (You can tell that I spend a lot of time using emotion regulation strategies.)

A huge part of my career as an academic studying how we deal with feelings has been devoted to talking about it—to groups of educators, business leaders, government officials, concerned parents, and other people, all over the world, in person and online.

I love presenting, but at certain points—especially when I'm traveling long distances, and jet-lagged, and feeling weary and totally talked out—it's a challenge to keep it up. I sometimes think to myself, *Is this the best way to spend your time?*

I've had this conversation with myself more than once.

But then I remind myself that while the message may be familiar to me, it's going to be new to everyone else in the room. And they've all come to hear me because they think the topic I'll discuss is an extremely important one. Urgent, even. Tonight I'll be addressing five hundred school superintendents from the state of California. Five hundred school districts equals how many hundreds of thousands or millions of students? How many futures will my talk be influencing for the good? And it's not just the educators and the schoolchildren—how many families will benefit because of something I'll say in the next two hours? How many years from now will my words still be making a difference?

*Okay!* I tell myself. *Let's go!* Now I feel psyched. I looked past my exhaustion about the task ahead of me and found something I could genuinely get excited about. And that feeling of excitement carried me into the auditorium and prompted me to give my all.

## VISUALIZATION

This emotion regulation strategy was widely recognized after the 1984 Olympics, when Russian researchers found that athletes who had employed visualization techniques experienced a positive impact on their performances.

The power of visualization in enhancing sports performance is strongly supported by empirical research, including a comprehensive meta-analysis conducted by James E. Driskell and colleagues published in the *Journal of Applied Psychology*. The researchers examined thirty-five studies and concluded that mental rehearsal, including visualization, significantly enhances performance, particularly in tasks with a cognitive component. They found that while the impact of mental practice is generally smaller than that of physical rehearsal, it still serves as a valuable tool, especially when combined with physical training. The authors highlight that mental imagery alone can lead to measurable improvements, underscoring its role in skill acquisition and performance enhancement. These findings support the concept of mental rehearsal as a form of conditioning that can prepare athletes for high-pressure situations and improve their execution during competition.

Golf legend Jack Nicklaus once said, "I never hit a shot, not even in practice, without having a very sharp, in-focus picture of it in my head."

Even beyond the world of sport, science backs up the life-changing power of creating images in our minds. According to a 2021 study that surveyed the uses of visualization in CBT, "imagery can have profound effects on emotions, cognitions, beliefs, and behavior," and in ways we're still discovering.

Studies of brain function show that thoughts of actions can produce the same neural effects as physical actions themselves. Mental imagery influences cognitive processes such as motor control, attention, perception, planning, and memory. It can even activate the release of dopamine and endorphins, which are associated with feelings of pleasure.

It's almost as if our brains can't tell the difference between visualization and reality—a phenomenon that works to our advantage.

There are several ways we can use visualization to deal with our feelings. The most effective of these helps us to regulate emotions we have yet to experience—future emotions.

For instance, you know you're about to face a challenging moment, a sensitive conversation with your spouse, a showdown with your kids, or a delicate salary negotiation at work. Perhaps you're going to deliver a speech before a large audience.

These all have the potential to provoke intense feelings and cause us to react emotionally rather than with calm and purpose.

We need to recognize those events *before* they take place and then visualize them happening in the best way possible. In our mind's eye, we watch as each event, each discussion, each meeting plays out smoothly, rationally, with no discomfort for anyone involved. In those instances, visualization is like a rehearsal, giving us confidence in our ability to deal with what we'll feel when the moment of truth arrives. Our anxiety fades because now we're in control.

When my previous book was published, I was, like any other first-time author, suddenly facing appearances on TV shows—a nervous wreck. I worried about how I would sound, and if I would be able to explain my ideas clearly, and how I would look.

So, here's what I did. I imagined a TV studio complete with the chair where I'd sit and the cameras aimed at me. I saw myself wearing my sharpest suit, with my hair in perfect form. I watched as the show's host asked me questions, which I answered flawlessly, speaking clearly and cleverly, totally at ease, as though I had been doing it all my life.

For two weeks before my first appearance, I ran that video in my head every day. My performance kept getting better.

But then, people would say to me, "Are you nervous about going on those morning shows? I'd be a mess. I'd freeze like a deer caught in the headlights."

"No, I'm not nervous," I'd lie. But their fears began to chip away at my imaginary calm.

So I'd have to go back and rewatch my mental videos, where I performed like a veteran TV star. And sure enough, when I did that, my confidence would return. By the time I began appearing on those programs, I felt like I had done these interviews many times before. For a beginner, I think I did pretty well.

Here's another example. I've studied martial arts—a Korean style called hapkido—for thirty years. A former martial arts student of mine told me that a friend was spreading nasty rumors about him. He would have been justified in confronting the person and even getting angry, but that's not what he did.

"I used my martial arts training," he said, but not in the way you might be thinking. "I took control of the situation by using his momentum against him—in my mind, I grabbed his arm and flipped him onto his back and then I walked away, leaving him sprawled on the ground. I didn't need to speak to him or take out my anger on him. I solved the problem by myself and that was the end of the friendship."

He says he's used that trick more than once—visualizing dispatching anyone who triggers him, and calming his negative feelings before he says (or does) anything extreme. Again, this strategy works best when it's someone you are not going to see again or can break ties with. It doesn't solve the problem of a person who spreads rumors, for example, and thus problem-solving might also be required once the initial intense emotions have been managed.

We can also use visualization to create scenery that evokes calm and serenity when that's what we need. Instead of reacting emotionally to some event, we pause and envision ourselves in a canoe on a pond, surrounded by trees and flowers, with birdsong filling the air. Or in a mountain meadow of the greenest grass on a beautiful spring morning. Find the paradise that works for you.

And don't just picture it, really place yourself in the middle of the image, filling your senses with the sights and sounds and smells and textures that surround you. During moments of extreme emotional activation, summoning up peaceful landscapes and pausing there can make a big difference once we do speak or act.

In one study, researchers found that participants who engaged in guided imagery experienced significant reductions in stress compared to those who did not engage in visualization. By mentally imagining calming scenes, we downregulate negative emotions like anxiety, anger, and sadness. Research shows that this leads to decreased cortisol levels and increased parasympathetic activity, contributing to a sense of calm and equilibrium.

This afternoon, you have your annual performance review at work. Your new boss is a stern taskmaster. You have no idea what to expect, so naturally you're anxious. In your most pessimistic fantasy, the meeting starts like this: "I have to be honest and tell you that, in my opinion, you're not cutting it."

No wonder you're anxious!

Now, what if, instead of that scenario, you imagine a totally different one. You see the two of you seated across from each other, separated by the boss's enormous desk.

"I have to be honest," he begins. "You're doing a tremendous job here—much better than I expected. I'm going to suggest that you get the maximum raise and be put in line for a promotion when the next step up becomes available."

Picture how you'll feel going into that meeting after this scenario plays out in your head. It has to increase your confidence, which will be obvious to everyone, the new boss included.

Here's a recap of the cognitive strategies and when to use them:

*Spatial distance*: When something unpleasant comes at us more intensely than we'd wish, we jump in our hot-air balloon or banish the scene to a TV screen, to view it from a distance. From afar, it turns into a blip in a life that's otherwise perfectly okay.

*Temporal distance*: As seen from a safe distance into the future, those sudden, challenging experiences seem infinitely less dire and more manageable.

*Distanced self-talk*: When you speak to yourself as your friends and admirers would speak to you, you immediately feel more capable and powerful and able to handle whatever life has just thrown your way.

*Reappraisal*: When my instant perception of an event is discouraging or negative, I set it aside and imagine several alternative—more helpful—ways of looking at it, such as finding a new purpose hiding inside it, and use that to lift my spirits.

*Visualization*: Imagine the most positive scenario possible of some emotional moment you're facing and replay that video until it becomes your reality.

Now, keep in mind that as useful as these cognitive strategies are, they are not foolproof. There's even research showing how challenging they can be to put into practice. And there is the risk of a slippery slope. If I construe my boss's verbal abuse as a bad pattern he learned from his boss or parents, I will end up tolerating it and explaining it away. If I continuously construe my failure as someone else's idiocy, how will I ever grow? As I've shared, we have to evaluate our use of cognitive strategies like emotion scientists to ensure they are working for us and not against us.

For instance, what if we go into our annual job performance review expecting praise and a big raise and instead get negative feedback and an admonition to do better? In that case we need to manage our disappointment without falling to pieces. It's time to look honestly at how we're performing and either do better or find a job more closely suited to our abilities.

So, consider the upside of negative encounters—they require us to fire up our imaginations and consider alternatives, often when we're feeling stuck. They provide us with some power in situations that sometimes seem (or are) beyond our control. And they also put us in the right psychological place to formulate a plan about what we might need to do next.

You can see how acquiring these skills might be worthwhile.

## 11.

# Cultivating Your Emotional Strength Through Relationships

*Our lives are connected by a thousand invisible threads, and along these sympathetic fibers, our actions run as causes and return to us as results.*
—Harriet Beecher Stowe

My life as a psychologist who studies and writes about feelings started at age twelve, thanks to Uncle Marvin.

I've written about him before, and I speak of him often. I had an extremely challenging childhood that was only made tougher by parents who couldn't manage their own emotional lives, let alone help me with mine. I felt alone and in crisis until Uncle Marvin came along and saved my life. That's not an exaggeration.

Here's what he did first: He gave me permission to feel.

That's a strange concept, I know. We can't help feeling what we feel, whether or not anyone gives us "permission." But the message I got from everyone around me was that my emotions were the problem, and we'd all be better off if I just ignored them, or swallowed them, and pretended they didn't exist. That I (and my family) would be happier if I could only deny the powerful, horrible things I was feeling.

That's a lonely, scary place for a kid to be.

Uncle Marvin told me it was okay for me to feel all those things, and then he taught me something else, equally life-changing—that our relationships with other people can be a powerful tool to help us deal with emotions that might otherwise alienate us and leave us alone and in despair.

Here's what he did.

First, he asked me how I was feeling, and he listened to me. Really listened. He didn't interrupt me or cut me off or try to anticipate where I was going with my story. He didn't rush me. Nothing about his body language made me think that he had better things to do. He looked me in the eye. His facial expression was kind. He sat still while I spoke. He wasn't pretending to listen while figuring out how he wanted to respond. Everything about his bearing made it clear that he believed me and was taking my words and my emotions seriously. For me, this was a new experience.

After I had talked myself out and said every painful thing that was in my heart, he spoke. But even then, it was not what I had come to expect from adults.

He talked without judging me for anything I had told him—and believe me, some of the things I had to say back then were tough to hear.

The questions Uncle Marvin asked were open-ended. There was no right or wrong answer, no good or bad emotion. I never got the sense that he blamed me or found fault with anything I said. He asked questions in a way that made it obvious that he truly wanted to know what was going on.

He didn't try to tell me how *he* would have felt if he were in my position, or what he would have done. He never flipped the conversation around to talk about his experiences. He kept the focus on me.

Finally, he showed what I'll call *active compassion*, meaning that once he understood my feelings, he made it his mission to say and do all he could to help me understand and regulate them as a path forward. With his help, I felt secure knowing I wasn't alone and I would get through my traumatic experience *with* him. The role Uncle Marvin played in my adolescence, and the lessons he taught me, have been hugely important factors in everything that's happened since, personally and professionally. I can't even imagine what my life would be like today were it not for him back then.

Let's see why.

Earlier in this book, in chapter 4, we talked about co-regulation—meaning how the people in our lives influence the way we feel and how we respond to our feelings, especially the intense ones.

Co-regulation makes sense. We humans, by nature, are social creatures. We evolved in groups—families, tribes, communities—and many of our emotions exist as a result of our interactions with one another. In some cultures, emotions are even viewed as shared experiences rather than individual internal states.

For better *and* for worse, we're constantly influencing one another.

This form of influence starts long before we understand anything about our feelings and how we respond to them. As soon as we're born (actually before) we begin relying on other people, our parents or guardians, in times of emotional activation. We're hungry, or tired, or uncomfortable, and in our distress we turn to the ones who can bring us comfort. When toddlers fall, they look to the nearest adult's reaction for a cue before deciding on their own. In that instant, a parent's smile works wonders toward calming a child's response. As I've shared, simply having a caring adult present lowers the stress response in children and is one of the strongest predictors of later resilience.

Throughout life, we turn to people we know and trust to provide ways of viewing our own experiences. In the heat of the moment, it may seem to me as though I'm facing a disaster. To you, it looks like a temporary setback, one I can easily overcome. Your reaction encourages me to reconsider my own.

"Never worry alone" is a catchphrase in discussions of emotion regulation, especially among children. In challenging moments, involving other people improves how we deal with our feelings. Often, when beset by worry, frustration, or despair, we isolate ourselves. This makes it more difficult for us to handle those emotions in healthy, beneficial ways. The research backs this up—even physical pain is felt less sharply in the presence of someone who cares. Getting another brain involved can elicit a solution that wouldn't have occurred to us. It can help us identify compromises or better ways to handle difficult moments.

Personal connections have many of the same effects as proper nutrition, sleep, and exercise. Membership in a community—any community—is an important factor in mental, emotional, and spiritual health. Carefully controlled public health studies reveal that the positive effects of close social relationships on health are comparable to or even greater than the negative effects of well-established risk factors like smoking, excessive alcohol use, and obesity.

Research has repeatedly shown that isolated individuals are at greater risk not only for depression and anxiety but also for disease and death at rates that are equivalent to smoking four packs of cigarettes a day. Individuals lacking strong connections often experience feelings of isolation, which can lead to emotional dysregulation, including internet addiction, anxiety, and depression, and in extreme circumstances suicidal ideation. Social neuroscientist John Cacioppo states that chronic loneliness increases the odds of an early death by about 20 percent. It is also associated with increased odds for anxiety, depression, and dementia. Even bruises have been found to heal more quickly when we have strong social bonds than when we are isolated.

The harmful consequences of a population that lacks social connection can be felt in our schools, workplaces, and public life in general. A 2022 study found that only 39 percent of US adults said they feel socially connected to others. Recent studies have found that about 50 percent of adults report feeling lonely, with even higher rates among youth.

According to the 2021 American Perspectives Survey, men have experienced a more profound decline in friendships than women over the past three decades. In 1990, 55 percent of men had six or more close friends, whereas in 2021, that figure dropped to 27 percent, with 15 percent of men indicating they have no close friends.

But when people feel connected, valued, and loved in their relationships, they are more likely to experience pleasant emotions, reduced stress, and increased self-esteem. This emotional security acts as a buffer against the challenges and adversities that life throws our way.

Lots of co-regulation happens implicitly: Some people just make us feel good! They elevate our moods and send signals that they value and respect us. We get a feeling of belonging and affection that nourishes us, builds our confidence, and buoys us not just in the moment but in times of difficulty.

Through interactions with others, we also learn important skills such as empathy, conflict resolution, and effective communication. As we navigate the complexities of different personalities and viewpoints within our social circles, we gain insight into our own emotional responses and coping mechanisms.

When I meet with groups, I always talk about Uncle Marvin and ask people if they have ever had someone like him in their lives—someone who created the conditions for them to talk about *all* emotions and to learn strategies to deal with them.

You may not be surprised to learn that most say no.

As part of an ongoing study, I have asked that question of more than ten thousand people all over the world. The responses are pretty much the same everywhere. Thus far, only about 35 percent of the adults say they have ever had someone in their lives with whom they can speak honestly about their feelings.

Of those who say yes, the majority say their Uncle Marvin was their mother (still only about 20 percent), and just 2 percent say it was their father.

Now, there are several reasons for that, and not all of them indicate bad parenting.

It could be that kids don't want to have that kind of relationship with their parents during their formative years. Most parents will tell you that they simply can't get their kids to talk. Perhaps it's part of the individuation process.

But I often hear from moms and dads who are honestly afraid of their kids' emotional lives. I've mentioned this before—they fear the knowledge that their children could be feeling difficult emotions and doing unhealthy things, and that if they found out they'd have to step in and take some action. And then what if they tried and were unsuccessful?

Not an appealing possibility.

There are also parents who are having trouble dealing with their own emotions and can't handle any extra burdens. Or parents who say they don't have the time or the tools to explore their kids' deepest feelings, especially considering that young people are notoriously close-mouthed about what's going on in their lives. And this is despite how much these parents love their children.

It's not always easy finding or being an Uncle Marvin. But it's important to try.

The first step in garnering good support is choosing the right person, with the right skills, to help us deal with our feelings. These are people who have a genuine interest in us and stop what they're doing to help. For children, in the ideal world, the right person will seek them out. The burden shouldn't be on the child to find their Uncle Marvin.

As I said, it's not necessarily the people closest to you, or the ones who love you most. In fact, they may find it difficult to assist you for the simple reason that they're *too* close. Here's another reason: Our loved ones are often the cause of our strongest emotions. If you're going through a rough patch in your marriage, your spouse might not be the perfect person to turn to for compassion.

The right person has three main attributes:

First, they're a good listener.

Second, they're nonjudgmental.

Third, they have empathy and compassion.

Let's look at those one by one.

Good listeners pay close attention to you without reading their texts or checking their Instagram likes. They don't multitask. Multitasking existed even before the internet, but today it happens on a much larger scale. Good listeners talk less and don't interrupt or rush you. They allow for silence. The quality of our listening shapes what people will share. As I described earlier with Uncle Marvin, good listeners are curious, have open body language, exhibit genuine interest in their facial expressions, want to hear and understand you, and have the patience and intelligence to do so. They don't steal the spotlight!

When we turn to a judgmental person for help, what do they sound like?

"That was a poor decision."

"That was the absolute wrong thing to do."

"Why would you let them treat you that way?"

How about someone who's nonjudgmental? They acknowledge that we all make mistakes, then ask open-ended questions:

"Is there another way to look at this situation?"

"How do you think they would describe what happened?"

"If you could do that moment over, would you do anything differently?"

"What would be the best way to begin moving forward from here?"

It's hard for anyone to be completely nonjudgmental. It seems like human nature to view what other people do through a lens of right or wrong, good or bad. Whatever the cause, it takes effort to stop ourselves from measuring other people against our own standards. Parents especially struggle with this. They say, "It's my job to tell my kids what they did right or wrong!" Or "How are they supposed to learn if I don't tell them?"

It's impossible not to form opinions, but it's important to put them on the back burner, not to place them front and center. It's a necessary skill for someone who wants to be supportive. Without it, we appear to lack goodwill, and worse, to consider ourselves morally superior. It can turn us into hypocrites who freely evaluate other people's actions without considering how our own might be viewed.

When we're struggling, we already feel judged by that arbiter inside our own heads. We're already aware of how weak or wicked we might look in the eyes of the world. The last thing we need is a person we trust affirming that view.

Empathy comes in many forms, each of which contributes to our ability to connect and relate to one another. The two primary types are cognitive and emotional empathy. They are joined by a third, which we'll call compassionate empathy.

*Cognitive empathy* is about simply getting another person's perspective—"I can imagine what you're going through is really rough."

*Emotional empathy* goes beyond intellectually understanding someone's experience and involves truly feeling what another person feels—"I've been there and can relate to what you're going through."

*Compassionate empathy* combines those two and adds in the motivation to take meaningful action—the desire to provide support and comfort to alleviate someone's suffering. As in, "Let's talk through this together. I'm here to help you build a plan."

I find that I have a lot of cognitive and emotional empathy. I can relate to other people's suffering, but I'm more cautious with the taking-action piece of the puzzle. My husband, on the other hand, excels at compassionate empathy. While I'm thinking about a friend who is suffering in the hospital and contemplating how best to support them, he's already gone shopping for gifts and scheduled a visit.

In today's world, it seems as though many of us are on emotional pause. We're afraid to approach one another too closely for fear of intruding or of getting overly involved. Or we get stuck thinking that the other person should take the initiative. Lately, I've been thinking it's time to "be the first." What are we waiting for? In the end, we all feel better when we have empathy *and* show compassion.

It's important to reinforce the key elements of empathy and compassion, which are often misunderstood.

Empathy is thoughtful and anticipates how our words might land. It requires us to be attuned to the other person's feelings and shift accordingly. We strive to offer validation, not pity.

Compassion doesn't mean we have to provide solutions. It's about working with the person to "co-construct" a response. It's about talking through the problem with the person, helping them to reflect and see different perspectives and options. Being compassionate also means following through. We tend to think the problem is solved once the other person feels better in the moment. But history repeats itself and people have setbacks. Follow-through is key.

There's a final consideration when searching for the right person to turn to—look for someone who *doesn't* automatically try to fix your problems. This trait is rarer than you might imagine, even though it requires *not* doing something. Desiring a compassionate listener or an outside perspective is not the same as wanting somebody to jump in and tackle our challenges for us. When we have compassion, we create the right opening: "Would you like some ideas for how to manage this? Or would you prefer me to just listen for now?"

Okay, we've narrowed down the people we can rely on. Now it's time to learn how to *be* those people—how to help. Here's the simple answer: by using the same strategies we've seen in previous chapters—except now with the goal of helping others, not ourselves.

We've already discussed the group of strategies we called "redirecting thoughts." This approach includes techniques and tactics that help us see a situation in a more positive light, such as *distanced self-talk*, which means we encourage others to stop referring to themselves with insults and uncharitable descriptions of things they've done, even when they weren't the wisest actions; *reappraising* negative experiences to take away their power to trigger difficult feelings, so that it's possible to find alternate ways of thinking about situations that are causing problems; or *visualizing* calming images (a "happy place") to counteract stress and anxiety by shifting attention away from what's doing the activating.

Again, these are all ways of managing how people respond to their emotions. We employ them on our own whenever needed. But we can also use them within our relationships.

Sometimes, even a simple "Do you need a hug?" or "Would you like to talk about what just happened?" is enough.

For all the forms of co-regulation that work wonders, there are three that tend not to be helpful. They arrive with the best intentions. But they don't help us deal positively with our own or others' feelings and can even have the opposite effect.

They are called *venting*, *tough love*, and *fixing*.

In the past, when I was feeling bad about how someone had treated me, I'd pick up the phone and call a friend to complain about it. And then another and another and another. These were kind, loving people who would take my side in everything and allow me to go on and on.

"Can you believe what they *said*?" I would rage. "How they *behaved*? I can't take it anymore!"

It was cathartic, or so I thought. But after the calls ended, I was left feeling the same horrible emotions as before. I'd go right back to my rumination and fury. And nothing in my life changed. Sound familiar?

Why was talking it out with a bunch of sympathetic friends so unhelpful?

Because I didn't get the support I actually needed. Nothing in those calls helped me regulate my emotions. All that talking did was further embed the bad vibes in my brain, without a hint about how to get past them. By the end of those calls, even my relatives and friends were furious at whoever had caused me such grief.

Or—even worse—the person I called would turn my complaint into *theirs*. This is when empathy quickly turns into the other person taking over the conversation.

"I had something just like that happen to *me*!" they'd say. "You're not going to believe this, but . . ." And then we'd spend the next half hour hashing over *their* terrible experience. By the end I'd feel unheard and unsupported, just the opposite of what I needed.

Venting doesn't work because it encourages us to dwell on our difficulties instead of searching for solutions. For example, research shows that teenage girls have the tendency to co-ruminate as a form of bonding, but it's actually not helpful. In fact, it can intensify the difficult emotions we feel. And at a certain point, even people who love us will grow weary of our complaining about the same things over and over and will tune us out.

Does venting *ever* work? According to my colleague Ethan Kross, it can—but only when it's followed by help in seeing our situation in a different way, reframing our experience.

Like maybe—instead of only listening—try asking:

"Is there another way to look at the situation?"

"Will this *really* matter to you in two weeks? Six months?"

"What advice would you give me if this were *my* problem?"

Here's another extremely tempting, nonhelpful form of co-regulation: tough love.

It's tempting because it's so easy to provide—it requires no great analysis of the other person's situation, let alone empathy or compassion. No wonder plenty of people believe it's an appropriate response to someone facing difficulty. Rather than offering a chance to deal differently with emotions, tough love usually does just the opposite—it's shaming and guaranteed to make the recipient think twice about opening up ever again.

It's an especially common tactic when dealing with a child who's struggling. When I was bullied as a kid, my father commanded, "Toughen up!" He was a tough guy himself, so maybe he thought that was a solution I could also adopt. It never occurred to him to find fault with the bullies who tortured me or to ensure my school was on top of it. It was a way for him to avoid dealing with who I was (and wasn't) and what I was going through. No way in hell was I a "toughen up" kind of kid, and he knew it.

One of my worst childhood memories was on a Christmas morning at a time when I was significantly overweight. My parents gave me a plastic "sweat outfit" and said I couldn't open the rest of my presents until I ran around the block three times in that nightmare getup to sweat off some weight.

That's tough love. Not to be confused with setting boundaries and establishing shared expectations if boundaries are not honored. Tough love says, "You're weak and soft and flawed and you better change." I needed help dealing with being overweight and the emotional damage that came with it. My parents' solution only made things worse.

One final nonhelpful form of co-regulation involves The Fixer. It sounds beneficial, in theory. But it's not.

A friend, Gloria, was going through some rough times with a colleague, Jenna. Both are clinical psychologists in the same large practice. Jenna was badmouthing Gloria to their colleagues, seemingly determined to get her fired.

Gloria called me late one night wanting only to rant and rave.

"This is so messed up!" she said. "Can you believe what she's saying? She's spreading lies and rumors about me!"

Now, at this point in the conversation, The Fixer would have said, "Okay, here's what you should do." And they would have spelled out, in great detail and with total confidence, the steps Gloria ought to take.

But here's what Uncle Marvin would ask, gently and patiently, always allowing the other person plenty of time to think before answering:

"What might make this situation better for you?"

"What do you think is going through that other person's head to make them do such a thing?"

"What outcome would make you happiest?"

And maybe the wisest question of them all:

"If this happened to your best friend, what would you tell her?"

Here's what I did, in my kindest Uncle Marvin way. I allowed her to go on complaining for ten minutes, to get it off her chest (we'll call that "short-term venting"!), and then I politely interrupted.

"Gloria," I said, "I agree, this really is messed up. It's understandable how angry and worried you are."

That was to show her support and empathy.

"Now let me ask you a few things," I continued, ready to redirect the conversation and begin helping.

"Okay, what do you want to know?"

"How much power does she *really* have over you?" I asked. "True, she did post that nasty comment on Glassdoor, but who follows her anyway? What will other people think of her posts?"

"Not much," Gloria said. "Not many people follow her."

"Have you reached out to her?" I asked.

"Yeah, like three times. She won't respond."

"That's odd," I said.

"It's disappointing that a psychologist doesn't have the courage to do what she tells other people to do," Gloria agreed.

"Tell me something," I said. "What's her reputation like with your other colleagues?"

"To be honest, she's the most negative person on the staff. Most people are uncomfortable around her."

"And what's your reputation with the others in your practice?"

"It's really solid, I think," Gloria said. "I've been there for twenty years and never had a problem with anyone."

"Okay, so according to what you're telling me, her reputation there isn't so hot, and she doesn't have a lot of followers reading what she wrote."

"All true."

"How often do you have to interact with her?"

"Almost never, that's the weirdest part."

"Okay," I said, "so Gloria, it doesn't look like you have much to worry about here. She's in a worse position than you are, by far."

Even over the phone I could feel the tension leaving my friend's body.

Notice, I didn't offer any advice for how to fix the situation. I didn't make any brilliant suggestions. I was a good listener. I asked open-ended questions. I didn't accuse my friend of overreacting. I was sympathetic without letting her vent to no good end. I repeated her words back to her, making them sound reasonable. I guided her to think about what was going on in different, less threatening ways.

Once she did that, she was able to downregulate her emotional response to being targeted by her coworker. My goal was not to tell Gloria how to solve her problem but to help her deal with her feelings better. It took some restraint on my part—we're all fixers at heart, which is why we need to practice this as much as possible.

Here's another example.

My friend Miguel was going through a rough divorce. On the one hand, he knew that living with his emotionally abusive wife was killing his spirit, and that he had to end the marriage. But he was also worried about what the split would do to his relationship with his children. He feared that his wife and in-laws would make things as ugly as possible to poison his kids' minds.

Knowing all that, I called him one night shortly after he moved out. He was in bad shape.

"I'm wondering if it's better to be back in the marriage," he said. "I'm lonely and don't want to be alone."

"Miguel, do you remember what you told me just before you filed for divorce?" I asked.

"Yes. I was miserable. She cheated on me with two different men. She would gaslight me. It was awful."

"So," I asked him, "what do you miss?"

"Being part of a family."

"That makes sense," I said. "What do you hope will happen next?"

"That she'll be in a healthy and happy relationship and so will I. And that we can co-parent the kids in a positive way."

"That sounds like a great future," I said.

"Yeah, but she already found someone, and I'm afraid I won't."

"What makes you think that?"

"All I hear about from my friends is dating disasters."

"How much effort have you put into finding someone new?"

"Not much yet."

"Okay, so you didn't put much effort into it but you're already sure it won't work out. Am I missing something?"

"No, you're right. I tend to ruminate a lot about bad stuff that never happens."

"You've got a great job, and you're an attractive, athletic, smart guy. You seem like a pretty good catch to me."

"Thanks. Maybe I just need some time."

"I agree," I said. "What's the rush? Get through this transition and if suddenly someone comes into your life, great. If not, I have a hunch that when you're ready, the right person will appear."

"I guess," he said. "Hey, thanks for calling."

"Miguel, I know it's a lot. Let's connect again next week. I'll text you later with some good times. Text or call if you want to talk."

I didn't offer any advice or tell him what I would do in his situation. I didn't encourage him to vent for very long or get anything off his chest. I tried to keep the focus on the future as a way of regulating how he was handling his emotions, which were still fixated on the past and the present.

I think he felt better after the call, which is a sign he had already begun dealing with his feelings in a healthy way. By saying we should reconnect in a week, I was making sure we took the important step of following up on what felt like a good beginning. It's a process, not a one-time intervention.

So now we're ready to begin using relationships to regulate our emotional responses.

Let's start by making a list of the people who fit the description of good co-regulators. Again, they are:

Good listeners.

Nonjudgmental.

Able to express empathy and compassion.

Not trying to fix anything.

Who's on your list? There might be some surprises. It's possible that the relatives and friends you're closest to don't possess those attributes. As we've said, those people could be a little *too* close. In that case, maybe they're not the best ones to call when you need a new perspective on your life. It's why my savior was an uncle and not a parent—just that slight remove made a difference in how Uncle Marvin was able to listen to me and not freak out.

It's entirely possible that you might not know someone who can understand your situation and help you navigate it in a positive way. Remember, only about one-third of the people we've surveyed from multiple countries said they have that kind of individual in their lives, which means two-thirds of us feel as though we've been on our own since childhood. As adults, we should be able to do that job to some degree on our own. Or we can imagine what an Uncle Marvin would say or do to help us out.

But there are also other steps we can take. Start by hanging around with like-minded people, perhaps taking part in some activity. Explore a passion. Try a new hobby. Take a class. Join a virtual group. If you have time, volunteer a few hours a week and do some good deeds. I found a second Uncle Marvin figure when I took up martial arts, and a third one in yoga a few years ago. It's also important to seek professional help with a psychiatrist, psychologist, counselor, or social worker when necessary. In the back of this book, I list a few resources to help you on that path.

Once you've decided who fits the bill as a good co-regulator, turn that list into a mental note: These are the people you will rely on when the need arises. It's like one of those forms we've all filled out: *In case of emergency, contact (fill in the blank)*. You might also wonder whose list you might be on.

Considering the richness and complexity of human relationships, and how important other people are to us, it's no surprise that there are still more techniques that use the power of connections to help us regulate our emotions. Here are five of my favorites.

### 1. Remember that time?

In stressful moments involving friends or loved ones, it's easy to forget that we've shared many happy times with them. This person may be hurting your feelings now, or driving you nuts, but you still possess memories of that summer when you had such great times together, or the surprise birthday party they threw for you, or when they got you through a bad breakup. Recalling how much they meant to you can be enough to defuse your anger and lower your emotional temperature, allowing you to deal more calmly with the current crisis. Research has found a strong link between intentionally revisiting meaningful memories and a whole range of mental health benefits. Just thinking about a shared positive experience activates parts of the brain involved in imagination and reward, which are related to decreases in the stress response. Reminiscing can inspire you, help you feel less alone, even guide you to your next step.

### 2. Who else needs a hand?

A counterintuitive but effective way of managing our own tough emotions is to help somebody else deal with theirs—especially when that person's troubles dwarf our own. It's a way of putting things into instant perspective. You're struggling to deal with a feeling? Call or text somebody who could use a friend and make an offer—a hike in the woods, a trip to the movies, a cup of coffee. Recently I was feeling triggered by a situation with a relative and decided to call an old friend whose husband is seriously ill. There was nothing I could do to ease her pain, but she was happy when I invited her to lunch. It gave her a break from worrying about her husband and it helped me, too: Just the feeling that I was being useful to somebody who truly needed a friend grounded me and brought me a bit of peace.

It may sound nonsensical, but research suggests that when we're in the thick of it and really struggling, reaching out to help someone who's also going through a hard time might actually improve our mood. We're all familiar with "retail therapy" as a method of emotion regulation when we're feeling down. Research shows that this actually works—but mostly when we buy gifts for other people, not ourselves!

Take a moment to scroll through your phone and look for a friend or family member who you know is struggling with something right now. Perhaps it's a friend going through a breakup, or a family member feuding with a coworker, or a loved one managing an illness.

Now, send a text to this person. Ask how they've been feeling. Validate their emotions, affirming that anyone in that situation would be struggling, and make a plan to connect. Think of something upbeat to add. Give them the type of support you would want in the same situation, with kindness and compassion.

Then, check in with yourself and ask, *Has my perspective on my own struggle shifted in any way?*

In psychological terms, this is called "helper's high." The reciprocal benefit comes from the social connection itself, which is associated with the release of dopamine and oxytocin, neurochemicals linked to pleasant emotions. When we bond with others, we feel part of something larger, contributing to our well-being and reducing anxiety, stress, and other unpleasant emotions. Research shows that helping others also enhances our sense of purpose and meaning in life. We often feel more gratitude and appreciation for what we have.

**3. Check in with someone who's not actually there.**

The person in the best position to help you won't always be present, but physical presence is unnecessary for this to work. As I've already suggested, when you're feeling emotionally activated, you can take a deep breath and then imagine what that particular person—a deceased grandparent or parent, or just someone important to you who's unavailable—might do or say or ask. If it helps, use photos or videos to evoke their spirit. I've actually created albums on my phone that serve specific purposes for regulation. For example, when I feel frustrated while writing, I'll pull up a picture of Uncle Marvin. There's one in particular that resonates deeply with me, from my teen years when I was really suffering. Uncle Marvin's expression reminds me how much he loved me. It also reinforces my reasons for doing this work. Another photo I have is of him giving a speech at Yale when I founded the Center for Emotional Intelligence there. It was near the end of his life, and whenever I see this photo, I'm reminded of his positive influence on me and the pride and satisfaction he felt at the end of his career. Or, when I'm traveling and feeling lonely, I'll look at photos of my two dogs, Tutti and Peque. Believe me, it helps.

**4. Initiate a spontaneous act of kindness.**

We all know the adage "It's better to give than to receive." When discussing how relationships help us deal with our feelings, the meaning is clear: Doing nice things for other people lifts our own mood as much as theirs. Naturally, psychologists have sought to test this proverb with lab experimentation and surveys and have all come to the same conclusion: Performing such actions—what we would call random acts of kindness—makes people feel happier and more satisfied with their lives regardless of sex or age. In fact, research shows that we underestimate the impact of our generosity; givers are often surprised by how moved recipients are by the gifts they've gotten.

My friend Sheila is amazing at how she spreads random acts of kindness. Sometimes it's a card sharing how much she values our friendship; other times it's a small package of my favorite mixed nuts that we discovered together on a trip. It's incredible how opening the card or package spreads warmth throughout my body, activates a feeling of connection, and motivates me to pay it forward by doing something kind for her or someone else.

So, especially when we're feeling down on ourselves, performing kind acts for people we know or total strangers has the effect of elevating our view of who we are, which in turn makes it easier to regulate how we respond to challenging emotions.

**5. Celebrate someone else's good mood.**

When it comes to empathy, we usually mean how we respond to another person's misfortune. The expression "walking in somebody else's shoes" comes to mind, and it's never on a happy occasion. But research shows that it's just as important to celebrate someone's joy as it is to comfort them in their pain.

It's called *positive empathy*, which is not the same as being positive or having an optimistic outlook. The psychology researcher Sylvia Morelli and her colleagues define it as understanding and vicariously sharing others' positive emotions.

How do we express this form of empathy? Same as any other—by learning about other people's situations.

Take a moment and think about a time when someone you know enjoyed a success or accomplished something important to them.

Now, think about how you responded. What did you say or do?

Most likely, you said something predictable, like:

"Great job!"

"Wow, that's incredible!"

"Awesome."

"Congratulations!"

And then you both moved on.

That's not positive empathy.

Think about how wonderful it could be to help the other person truly savor their experience. That means finding ways to embellish their story and help them stay with it. We express interest in all the details that brought them to this joyous moment. The process is similar to how we'd behave if the person had just had an unpleasant experience, but here we try to help them see how and why their efforts paid off.

Imagine a colleague who created a fantastic presentation at work. What might you say to this person after "Great job!"?

How about something like this?

"I want to hear everything. Walk me through the presentation."

"What do you think made this better than ones you've done in the past?"

"That must have been an incredible feeling. What was the high point?"

"What's your biggest takeaway?"

When somebody you know has achieved something, don't just give them a perfunctory congratulations. Really engage with what they did and what was so great about it. Ask them to describe how they did it, or to tell you in detail why it's such a big deal. They'll remember how you responded, and it will build a better bond between you two. And knowing that you enhanced their happy experience will also lift your spirits.

And so, to recap:

*Never worry alone.* That should be your motto, your guiding light in times when you are struggling with your emotions. Worrying has a way of isolating us, of turning us inward as we ponder what we could have done differently or whether we have the tools to overcome this difficulty. If we switch our approach, we may discover that a seemingly insurmountable challenge appears much more manageable when viewed from a different perspective.

Seek input from others about how they perceive your situation. Get perspectives other than your own, often. As the psychologist Angela

Duckworth shared with me on my podcast, "You don't always know you need it [perspective] when you are in the middle of not having it."

You can even "ask" people whom you trusted but who are no longer around to help out—like a wise elder, a parent, a grandparent, your own Uncle Marvin. The point is to see your experience through the eyes of someone else. It's possible they'll simply confirm your own sense of what you're going through, which is fine—it's worth knowing that even an outsider sees it the way you do. But maybe they'll notice something you've missed, or remind you of something you've forgotten, or ask an incisive question that will bring everything into focus.

Perhaps they'll say something that calms your anxieties and fears. Something like "Hey, you know what? In a month will you even remember it?"

Or "Will this matter to you in five years? Let's get a little perspective."

Or "This isn't the first time you've had to handle a problem like this."

Or "It sounds to me like you want to stick with your boyfriend. Am I right? Okay—is there anything you can do to lift, repair, or strengthen the relationship? If you did, how would that make you feel?"

*Try to be an Uncle Marvin to someone else.* It sounds counterintuitive, I realize, to deal with your own problem by helping someone else to deal with theirs. But it will give you a break from worrying about your own. It will remind you that you have the necessary skill to deal with feelings (even if they're someone else's). And it will bring you a little of the satisfaction that comes from helping other people—and lifting your spirits is never a bad idea.

Not long ago, I brought a close friend along to one of my presentations, a talk before a group of leaders. I had just finished presenting data from a large, ongoing study that found that as adults, those of us who had Uncle Marvins when we were children now have superior emotion regulation skills, enhanced problem-solving skills, higher-quality sleep, better mental and physical health, elevated life satisfaction, and greater purpose and meaning in life.

I finished my talk by urging my audience members to seek out their own Uncle Marvins, people who will give them permission to feel, and to try and be Uncle Marvins to others.

In the car on the way home, my friend said to me, "You know, I now realize why I have so much trouble dealing with my feelings, and why my life hasn't gone exactly in the direction I hoped—I never had an Uncle Marvin."

"It's never too late," I said. "And remember, you can be your own Uncle Marvin."

# 12.

# Optimizing Your Emotion Regulation Budget

*To keep the body in good health is a duty . . . otherwise we shall not be able to keep our mind strong and clear.*

—The Buddha

Here are three statistics you don't expect to find in a book about emotion regulation:

About a third of adults worldwide don't get enough physical activity. Among adolescents it's nearly two-thirds.

Forty-six percent of us don't eat a healthy diet.

Three-quarters of adults in the United States are either overweight or obese.

More than a third of us don't get sufficient sleep.

These stats matter a great deal in our discussion of dealing with feelings. It turns out those factors have a huge influence over our ability to manage how we respond to our emotions.

It's easy to see why that might be surprising: We trick ourselves into believing that the mind and the body are totally separate entities. After all, our minds can't be seen or touched, and they don't show up in X-rays or MRIs. The only evidence that the mind even exists is in . . . the mind.

But we locate our minds in our thinking organ, the brain—which *can* be seen, touched, and acted upon in all the same ways as the rest of our physical beings. Which means that those three lifestyle factors—activity, nutrition, and sleep—are critical to brain function and so also impact our emotional lives.

How could it be otherwise?

And yet, somehow, we fail to acknowledge the connection. Oh, we may recognize that weariness makes us vulnerable to mood swings. Or that hunger and discomfort can lower our tolerance for certain people. But we mostly think of our bodies and our emotions as occupying two completely different realms.

So let's fix that. We need to understand that if we don't look after how we move, eat, and sleep, then our ability to deal with feelings—our own and those of other people—will be impaired.

I like to think of those physiological factors as our emotion regulation budget. This idea has been inspired by Lisa Feldman Barrett's concept of the "body budget," which highlights how our brain constantly manages the resources our body needs to function, including our ability to regulate emotions. If we don't have sufficient brain income—which we earn with physical activity, good nutrition, and deep, restful sleep—we'll never have enough mental energy to spend on managing our emotions in positive, healthy ways.

Budget-wise, you might be broke and not even know it.

## PHYSICAL ACTIVITY

The exercise part of the budget equation holds special meaning for me.

As I've already shared, I grew up in a family that didn't know how to deal with emotions. I also witnessed relatives experiencing a lot of physical pain. My mom had terrible sciatica. My dad had back problems likely due to his work as a repairman. My grandmother could barely walk due to extreme obesity. My grandfather sat in a recliner all day smoking cigars.

Physical health wasn't even a subject to be discussed. My parents didn't exercise. We didn't talk about sports, and I was never encouraged to play them (mostly because my parents didn't want the inconvenience of bringing me to practice and attending games).

To toughen me up, my dad did eventually urge me into martial arts. I still remember the only time he and I played anything together. I had asked him to help me practice for my yellow belt test. And, if I remember correctly, it lasted thirty minutes before he got bored and went back to watching TV. It wasn't until I started working on this chapter that I thought about the relationship between my parents' aches and pains, their sedentary lifestyles, and their inability to deal with emotions—theirs, mine, anyone's.

It's hard to be present when you are unwell. It's difficult to experience joy when you can hardly walk. It's impossible to find inner strength when you feel physically lousy all the time.

For the first twenty-five years of my adult life, I was an active participant and instructor in martial arts. But over time, other responsibilities grew, and those commitments began to fade. As I aged, I wasn't feeling like myself anymore. My energy was low. My eating got bad. My activity level dropped.

Then the COVID pandemic hit, and I decided it was time to make some changes. I started to take long walks after work. When I returned home, my mood was better.

I found a coach, online of course, to help me get started. Marco required me to set goals for how I wanted to look and feel, take monthly photos, and track precisely both what I ate and my workout routine. He forced me to explain to him—and to myself—*why* I was exercising. What getting into shape meant to me at an emotional level. What my goals were.

Here's what I said:

"I want better posture. I want to feel good about how I look onstage while giving talks. I want more energy and to feel strong again."

We broke my self-reclamation project down into three phases, all based on Albert Bandura's concept of guided mastery—a method used to build self-efficacy, confidence, and competence by gradually increasing the difficulty of tasks as they're learned. The key is for the learner to experience success before moving onto more complex tasks.

The first step was just to get started. That meant taking small steps—cutting a few calories, working out at a moderate level, committing to tracking. Just enough to make a difference.

Next came phase two. By then I could actually see some results of phase one—the beginnings of a leaner, stronger me. Better cardio endurance. Noticeable differences in my daily moods. Still some distance from my long-term goals. But enough progress to keep me inspired and on track.

My road to physical fitness required a lot of emotional involvement—more than I ever imagined. There were times when work and other commitments got in the way of my exercise routine. Or when I felt too tired or distracted to hit the weights and treadmill and reach my activity targets.

In those moments, as you might imagine, my self-talk was deadly:

*Why didn't you pay attention to your body before you let yourself get so out of shape?*

*I'm exhausted. I was up until midnight working. I need to skip the gym today.*

*I did two sets of this exercise—it won't matter if I don't do the third.*

*You're a college professor—no one cares what you look like!*

*If you go to the gym so out of shape, you'll feel ashamed—everyone there will be staring and pitying you.*

When I confessed that last fear to Marco, he said, "Believe me, nobody is going to be looking at you. They're all completely obsessed with their own bodies and workouts. Why do you think there are mirrors everywhere?"

That made sense to me. I changed my self-talk.

*Marc, you're writing a book about emotion regulation. If you can't do this, no one can!*

*Marc, you're ready to lift this barbell, just do it!*

*Marc, what would you tell your best friend in this situation? You'd say, "Come on, you can make the time for a forty-five-minute workout! Focus on the results you are looking for. You've made so much progress already! And when you're finished, you'll have done something important for you!"*

The cognitive strategy of time travel also worked wonders for me: When I was low on motivation, I imagined how great I was going to feel and look six months down the road—as long as I kept exercising according to plan. That future vision of a stronger, leaner me was enough to keep me going.

And I used another great tool, one that we in education discuss all the time: SMART goals, meaning ones that are specific, measurable, attainable, relevant, and time-bound. You don't start out saying, "I want to lose twenty-five pounds and look like a Greek god." That's so ambitious it's discouraging. Instead, you say, "I'm going to work out three times a week and take a thirty-minute walk every other day. And I'm going to cut out a couple hundred calories per day." All of which are SMART.

I even began using physical activity as an emotion regulation skill. If I hit a block while writing and felt brainless, I'd take a walk. Or I'd do a ten-minute online yoga class. I might even drop everything and go to the gym to work out. I would joke to myself, *You might not finish your book, but you'll be in the best shape of your life!* Truth is, I always came back refreshed and ready to resume writing.

The third phase of my new regime (which took me two years to reach) involved just one change—a shift in my identity! By this point in the process, working out was no longer just something I did. It had become who I *was*—who I still *am*: a person who works out. I'm in better shape today than I was thirty years ago. That's how I see myself now, and I pray I always will.

Once you make that transition, you'll recognize how important self-identification is to how we behave. Working out no longer becomes a chore or a burden. You actually crave it. This is a key element of emotion regulation. Our ultimate goal is to identify as people who consistently, automatically deal with their feelings in healthy ways.

That person will be *you*.

Once you see yourself that way, managing how you respond to your emotions will be assured—*most* of the time, at least.

By now, I think, we're all aware of all the benefits that come from getting the right amount and kinds of physical activity. We've been hearing and reading for years about how exercise strengthens not just our muscles, bones, and cardiovascular and immune systems, but our brains, too. There's even evidence that working out can significantly reduce the risk of Alzheimer's and other kinds of dementia.

As an extra incentive, let's run through some of the more persuasive evidence on the direct links connecting physical activity, brain health, and emotion regulation.

A 2023 study analyzed the results from more than a thousand experiments with over 128,000 participants who engaged in a variety of activities, from yoga and tai chi to aerobics and dance to strength training. Results suggested that exercising helped reduce depression, anxiety, and distress. Working out was one and a half times more effective than counseling or medication. According to Michael Craig Miller, an assistant professor of psychiatry at Harvard Medical School, people who are depressed tend to have a smaller hippocampus—a region in the brain that helps regulate mood. The hippocampus helps to encode and retrieve emotional memories, supporting people in remembering past events and adapting their responses based on previous experiences. It also helps regulate the release of stress hormones like cortisol, which can exacerbate emotional responses. Exercising promotes the growth of nerve cells in the hippocampus and enhances the connections among cells. This process contributes to alleviating symptoms of depression by enhancing the brain's ability to regulate mood.

Other research suggests that exercise might affect brain circuitry involved in emotion regulation, including enhanced connections between the amygdala and prefrontal cortex.

There's a phenomenon most of us are familiar with called "runner's high"—the mental lift that athletes get from putting in serious mileage. But this phenomenon isn't restricted to the superjocks among us. Even moderate physical activity causes our bodies to release neurotransmitters—adrenaline, endorphins, serotonin, and dopamine. Each of these has a positive, uplifting effect on our mental state. Literally, it's like taking a drug that makes us feel good, and it's natural and produced (for free!) inside our own bodies. These substances create a kind of closed loop: Exercise causes their release, which makes us feel great, which reinforces our exercise habits.

In one study, sixty participants were randomly assigned to either a mind-body and aerobic exercise intervention or a wait-list control group (who would receive the intervention after the initial experiment was completed). Intervention sessions took place three times a week over the course of eight weeks. The aerobic component lasted for forty minutes and consisted of jogging for thirty minutes and stretching for ten. The mindfulness and yoga part lasted sixty minutes and included a mixture of breathing exercises, yoga postures, and a short meditation. After eight weeks, participants in the intervention group had improved their ability to downregulate unpleasant emotions, enhanced their mindfulness practice, and (as a bonus) increased their aerobic fitness levels. Additional analyses demonstrated that the combination of aerobic exercise and mindfulness led to healthier emotion regulation.

A separate but related study showed that when individuals who have difficulty managing their emotions are shown a sad film, they mentally recover faster after jogging for thirty minutes.

What about mini exercise breaks? Do they help? A significant body of research has investigated the effects of a single bout of physical activity on mood and mental functioning. The effect on our brains is almost instantaneous. After just five to ten minutes of exercise, there is a mood-enhancement effect that makes unpleasant emotions decrease, pleasant ones increase, and our ability to respond to stress improve. And these effects persist for up to twenty-four hours after we're done exercising.

Okay, so now you're ready to start your exercise routine, right? If you already engage in regular physical activity, you might wonder if it's enough and if you're exercising at the optimal times to reap the psychological benefits. But for those of us who are less active, it turns out that our predictions about how we'll feel during a workout matters.

Research shows that people who are not so active tend to underestimate how enjoyable exercise will be. Lower expectations for exercise enjoyment among less active people undermines motivation for regular physical activity. But once they start working out, research shows they experience levels of enjoyment similar to those active people report.

The takeaway? People who are trying to start regular exercise shouldn't allow their anticipated negative feelings to get in their way. Chances are you'll actually enjoy the experience!

Of course, not everyone is in a position to become a regular exerciser. Many people have physical limitations that prevent them from pursuing vigorous activity. At some point even age becomes a factor. Some of us are already juggling multiple responsibilities—work and family, to name but two—that leave little time or energy for anything more. It can be costly to join a gym or a workout studio.

But physical activity doesn't have to take place in gyms and health clubs. Walking and hiking, dancing, yoga, gardening, even mowing the lawn or cleaning the house all qualify as exercise—anything that keeps us moving energetically. Even stretching has been shown to increase blood flow to the brain and throughout the body, improve posture, and provide relief from back pain and tension—all of which are associated with enhanced mood. And you don't need to go all in. Even small doses of activity make a difference.

The research is clear: Physical activity—all kinds—plays a critical role in emotion regulation. Once we're more active, our physical and emotional lives will benefit. When we're feeling stressed or overwhelmed, taking an activity break can make a big difference and help us gain a fresh perspective. Even just going for a ten-minute walk, or doing some squats or push-ups, will alter your mood for the better. The rush of blood to your muscles and the release of endorphins will elevate your mind and clear away some of whatever's weighing you down. Physical activity is both a prevention strategy *and* an intervention strategy. Which means exercise helps us to become more psychologically fit; *at the same time* it's a tool we can use to help us manage emotions. Feeling frustrated or sleepy or unmotivated at work? Take a short walk. And for the workaholics among us, research shows that exercise promotes clearer thought and creativity, both of which have measurable influences on our emotional state and make it easier for our brains to help us deal with feelings.

**NUTRITION**

How's your relationship with food?

Mine is complex. I grew up in a family with two parents who were always dieting. And yet I was severely overweight as a child and even was taken to a "diet doctor" when I was eleven years old. Eating was my go-to strategy to deal with the feelings that resulted from the abuse and bullying I endured. I grew up in the era of canned vegetables, Cool Whip, instant mashed potatoes from a box, and frozen Hungry-Man dinners. On top of all that, mealtime was torture because of my father's constant complaining: "Shake 'N Bake chicken again, Diane?!"

They'd fight and often I'd eat alone. You can see how getting enough physical activity wasn't the only health-related challenge in my life.

Today, between the internet and the bookstore, you can find infinite advice on how to feed yourself in order to be well. I'm not going to burden you with any more of that, except to make one point: What we eat (and don't eat) exerts a great influence over how we regulate our emotions. Food is fuel for the brain.

The ancient wisdom says, "You are what you eat." Today, there's a huge body of scientific research proving it—your mental health, your moods, and your ability to manage your emotional responses all depend in part on your diet. We shouldn't be completely surprised. Throughout history, cultures have recognized that food may also be medicine, and for millennia we've treated disorders of the brain and the psyche with nutrition. The popular keto diet, for example, was developed in the 1920s to combat epilepsy. Studies have shown that more than half of children on the ketogenic diet experience at least a 50 percent reduction in seizures, and about 10 to 15 percent become seizure-free. Among adults, this diet is associated with fewer and less severe seizures, reduced medication dosages, and an overall better quality of life. While the underlying mechanisms are not fully understood, the diet may increase the production of neurotransmitters that stabilize brain activity.

Many studies demonstrate a lower incidence of depression in those who adhere to the dietary regimens followed in Norway, Japan, and the Mediterranean, all of which are based on the abundant consumption of vegetables, fruits, nuts, seeds, legumes, dairy, eggs, fish, moderate amounts of meat, and unsaturated fats. Meanwhile, so-called Western eating patterns with low levels of fruits and vegetables and high levels of refined grains, fried and processed foods, red meat, and high-fat dairy products have been linked to anxiety and depression.

Researchers have noted that barriers to healthful food choices can be geographic, economic, informational, and cultural. Underresourced groups tend to rely on foods that are inexpensive and convenient but often low in nutrients. For example, stores in poor neighborhoods are much less likely to offer healthy foods than those in wealthier parts of town. Fresh fruits and vegetables and other healthy items are often more expensive at small food markets than in chain supermarkets and big grocery stores. Where you live affects your diet.

In the realm of nutrition, there are five things that matter for your emotional health. I discussed these with Drew Ramsey, a nutritional psychiatrist and author of numerous books.

1. **Carbs matter.**

    The human brain is a greedy organ: Though it represents only 2 percent of our body weight, it accounts for 20 percent of our total energy consumption. And its main fuel is glucose—sugar. The best way to deliver that is definitely *not* by eating sugar itself, but instead by having complex carbohydrates—vegetables, legumes, fruit, and whole grains, the latter in moderation. Our bodies convert carbs into the glucose our brains demand. It's especially important to the prefrontal cortex and the amygdala, regions of the brain that play major roles in emotion regulation. The prefrontal cortex relies heavily on glucose metabolism to support the demanding processes required to employ strategies like cognitive reappraisal. When glucose levels are too low, our ability to come up with helpful responses to our emotions is impaired.

    Dietary science relies on the glycemic index, which measures the degree to which various foods increase blood sugar levels, as a guide to what constitutes a healthy diet. (You can google it.) The index is especially important, for obvious reasons, to those of us with diabetes. But we should all be familiar with it.

    We often hear about people—children especially—who experience that infamous "sugar high" when they've consumed too much of it. (Although we adults are not immune to that either, you might have noticed.) Others complain of feeling woozy due to too-low blood sugar, especially when they've gone a long time without eating. The goal for healthy brain function and emotion regulation is to maintain a stable level of glucose in the bloodstream, without spikes or dips.

    We can manage that only by eating wisely, and by avoiding too much sugar, refined grains, and ultra-processed foods.

2. **Fats matter.**

    Researchers have investigated why populations that eat a lot of fish experience low rates of depression. They learned that two of the so-called omega-3 fatty acids, eicosapentaenoic acid (EPA) and docosahexaenoic acid (DHA), both of which are found in oily fish such as sardines, mackerel, and salmon, may help people with mood disorders, depression, and postpartum depression. That's due to how these fats lower inflammation, a reminder that foods that increase inflammation make it harder for our brains to cope with intense emotions. Nuts and avocados also contain healthy fats. We need to avoid unhealthy fats, such as palm oil and hydrogenated oils, which are often found in packaged junk foods like sweets (cookies and cakes) and salty snacks (chips, etc.).

**3. Intestines matter.**

Not all emotion regulation happens in the brain. The microbiome—the trillions of microbes, found mostly in the gut, that influence and reflect our overall health—also plays a part. According to a study titled "The Gut-Brain Axis: Influence of Microbiota on Mood and Mental Health," which appeared in *Integrative Medicine: A Clinician's Journal*, "several mood disorders, such as anxiety, depression, and autism spectrum disorders now have well-established links to functional GI [gastro-intestinal] disruptions."

Scientists call the microbiome the "second brain" with good reason—by-products of the bacteria there interact with our nervous system and mental functions. In fact, those microbes produce a large percentage of the body's serotonin, the "feel-good" neurotransmitter heavily involved in regulating mood, emotions, and feelings of well-being. Serotonin helps promote feelings of happiness and contentment. It also regulates anxiety, aggression, appetite, and sleep. Imbalances in serotonin levels have been linked to depression, anxiety, and other mental illnesses.

The microbiome is also the source of half of the body's supply of dopamine, the "reward" neurotransmitter that induces feelings of pleasure and motivation, and reinforces fun behaviors like exercise, sex, and other physical activities—including eating things we love.

Clearly, it's important to maintain proper microbiome health. And how do we manage that? By following the diet we all know we should be eating—mostly whole, plant-based foods, fish, meat (but not to excess, and not processed kinds like cold cuts), eggs, and nothing loaded with sugar or other junk. High-fiber foods like beans, lentils, berries, and cruciferous vegetables (broccoli, brussels sprouts, cabbage) are great for our gut bacteria.

**4. Water matters.**

Dehydration affects emotion regulation in several ways. First, it impacts blood sugar levels, which leads to cognitive impairments such as difficulty concentrating, memory deficits, and reduced ability to process information effectively. This alone can make emotion regulation more challenging. Lack of hydration can also prompt a stress reaction within the body, leading to higher cortisol levels, which in turn hinder the ability to regulate emotions. Changes in mood, including increased irritability, anxiety, and fatigue, also are linked to dehydration—all of which interfere with emotion regulation. Finally, dehydration can cause headaches, dizziness, and increased heart rate—exacerbating emotional distress. If you are thirsty, you're likely dehydrated. Hydration needs vary significantly among individuals due to factors such as age, gender, body weight, climate, physical activity level, and overall health. Nevertheless, as a general guideline, many health authorities suggest aiming for about eight 8-ounce glasses of water a day.

**5. Feelings matter.**

We all are familiar with emotional eating—when anxiety, anger, worry, stress, and other negative feelings drive us to eat even when we're not hungry. And the things we're driven to consume are never the healthiest foods in the house. In a tense mood, nobody goes for the spinach. But gorging on sugary, fatty, or salty foods seems to quell the emotional storm.

A 2022 study showed that emotional eating often develops within childhood, persists into adulthood, and is linked to obesity. In the study, 244 mothers of three- to five-year-olds completed questionnaires about their own emotional eating, feeding practices, and their children's temperament and emotional eating. The researchers found that the way mothers manage their children's emotions—using food as a reward or restricting it (e.g., withholding sweets)—explains the link between emotional eating behaviors of parents and their children, irrespective of child temperament.

It isn't just your feelings that drive you to eat. When we're stressed or pressured, our brains release cortisol. This reduces our sensitivity to leptin, the satiety hormone, which under normal conditions would tell us that we're full. At these emotional moments, cortisol wins out. Higher cortisol also leads to higher insulin levels and dysregulation of blood sugar. This is why we crave comfort foods when we're stressed. But consuming high-calorie, sugary, or fatty foods also triggers the release of dopamine, which can temporarily alleviate feelings of stress and anxiety, creating a "conditioned response," meaning that we learn to associate eating junk food with decreased stress levels, reinforcing the cycle of emotional eating.

But the relief is short-lived. And once the initial pleasure wears off, we often feel disgust and shame, further exacerbating our stress, which only perpetuates the cycle. It gets even more complicated because stress eating is often accompanied by skewed thinking, like making excuses for poor dietary choices, downplaying the adverse effects of overeating, or adopting a defeatist viewpoint: *Since my diet is already off track, I may as well continue eating.*

Breaking this cycle often requires both addressing the underlying stressors and developing healthier regulation skills.

So, what can we do? This is a tough one to fix—when you're feeling vulnerable, self-control goes out the window. Can you use any of the strategies and skills we've been learning throughout this book? Take that deep breath and create the space to think.

Can you project yourself into the future and imagine how discouraged you'll feel after you polish off that bag of Doritos, and use that thought to stop yourself before you reach the kitchen?

In experiments, when obese participants experienced negative emotions such as anger, loneliness, boredom, or depression, they ate more than slimmer individuals did and reported that eating reduced the impact of those feelings.

How about if you simply stop buying the foods you crave during emotionally charged moments? If they're not in your kitchen, they won't be available during an impulsive moment. Research shows that just thinking about a favorite food kicks the motivation and reward circuitry into high gear. Think about it or see it, and the brain tells you a story about how you need to have it!

Research shows that cognitive reappraisal, a strategy we've discussed in detail, can help. In a 2020 study, Carmen Morawetz, a psychology professor at the University of Innsbruck in Austria, along with some colleagues, used functional MRI of the brain to examine the neural activity underlying the downregulation of so-called incidental emotions and its effects on subsequent food choices. (Imagine having an argument over breakfast at home and an hour later behaving badly toward a work colleague. The incidental emotion is your office anger caused by the argument at home, which made you lash out at your coworker.)

Results showed that the participants who used reappraisal to deal with incidental negative emotions showed a greater tendency to select tasty and healthy foods. Reappraisal also modulated activation in areas of the brain involved in decision-making, suggesting that increasing emotion regulation ability could effectively modulate food choices—thus improving our ability to eat healthier.

How often do you eat a relaxing meal with no distractions? I ask because there's another possible solution to poor nutritional habits, called "mindful eating." Like anything else that falls under the "mindful" rubric, it requires us to pay close attention and do only one thing at a time, slowly and with deliberate care and focus. A hard thing for a lot of us, but a skill worth cultivating.

Mindful eating means we don't read, watch TV, surf our social media apps, or take Zoom calls during meals. Instead, we create a peaceful space at mealtimes. It requires us to eat more slowly and really focus on what's at the end of our fork and savor it. It also means we attune ourselves to our body's signaling system—which includes the hunger hormone ghrelin, and the aforementioned satiety hormone, leptin. While dieticians once advised eating until we felt full, the recommendation now is to stop eating when we no longer feel hungry—a subtle but significant shift.

In one small study, ten obese volunteers enrolled in weekly mindfulness classes that focused on eating more slowly and listening to their feelings of hunger and fullness as they ate. They also paid close attention to their cravings and emotions. Not only did the participants drop an average of nine pounds each by the end of the three-month program, but they also reported less hunger, stress, anxiety, depression, and binge eating.

In another study, conducted in the Netherlands, researchers measured whether mindfulness could lead to less emotional eating. They found that acting with awareness—being more mindful of your feelings and deliberately choosing what to eat when faced with negative emotions—led to less emotional eating.

Research shows that mindful eating contributes to psychological and physical well-being:

- It fosters a more balanced approach to nutrition, empowering individuals to tune into their bodies' signals of hunger and satisfaction, fostering a healthier bond with food.
- It brings a greater appreciation for food, including enhanced pleasure during meals.
- It results in less tension and anxiety associated with eating.
- It improves digestive health and makes the digestive process

more comfortable and efficient. Slower eating is associated with more chewing, more saliva, and better metabolization of food.
- It increases overall mental well-being, which comes from nurturing self-compassion and fostering a positive and accepting relationship with one's body.

## SLEEP

Along with glucose, your brain requires one more form of nutrition: sleep. Sleep is absolutely necessary for proper cognitive function, and for emotion regulation, too.

Let's start with an abbreviated version of a quiz I created with Katharine Simon, a professor in pediatrics at the University of California, Irvine, who studies sleep. Answer each of these questions, a selection from the larger survey, to gain some insights about your sleep. Put a T or an F next to each statement.

TRUE OR FALSE:

- I have a relaxing nighttime ritual (stretching, meditation, reading) before going to sleep.
- I fall asleep easily at night.
- I get an average of seven to eight hours of sleep per night.
- I sleep through the night.
- I am consistent with the time I go to bed and wake up.
- I feel well rested when I wake up.
- There are "external factors" (e.g., bed partner, pet, children, environmental sounds) that interrupt my sleep.
- I put off falling asleep by working, ruminating, or talking about my day in bed.
- I use technology (social media, texting) in bed before going to sleep.
- I eat three hours or less before going to bed.

- I do rigorous exercise three hours or less before going to bed.
- I drink caffeinated beverages after 2 p.m.
- I drink alcoholic beverages three hours or less before going to bed.

We're not going to score this like a personality test. But the more Ts you have for the first six items, and the more Fs you have for the last seven, the better your sleep is likely to be. I just want you to build some awareness. If you are like a lot of people these days, you're not getting enough sleep, or enough high-quality sleep, in part due to the factors in the second half of that quiz. Data from multiple studies show that we don't get enough sleep. Thirty percent of adults have trouble falling or staying asleep. About 70 percent of high school students don't get enough sleep on school nights. Forty percent of adults report unintentionally falling asleep during the day at least once a month. Twenty-seven percent of adults say they are very sleepy during the day.

Your brain is recharged when you sleep. Metaphorically speaking, it takes a shower and flushes out all the waste and toxic by-products of the day. Sleep has been proven to reduce mental fatigue. When we sleep, our immune systems regenerate and recharge, allowing our bodies and brains to heal.

Sleep decreases inflammation, reducing risk for heart disease, stroke, high blood pressure, a weaker immune system, diabetes, and obesity. For example, adults aged twenty-seven and older who sleep less than six hours daily are 7.5 times more likely to have an elevated body mass index. Inadequate or poor sleep increases levels of ghrelin (a hunger hormone), decreases leptin (a hormone that tells us when we're full), and raises levels of cortisol (a stress hormone).

Individuals with good or great mental health are six times more likely to get proper sleep than people who report fair or poor mental health—which makes you wonder how much less therapy we might need if we were all well rested. And sleeplessness is often a symptom of mood disorders, such as depression and anxiety. When the National Sleep Foundation conducted a survey in 2022, half of those who said they slept less than seven hours each weekday also reported having depressive symptoms. It's also worth noting that studies investigating the treatment of depression and insomnia have shown that addressing sleep issues first can lead to improvements in depressive symptoms, while treating depression first does not necessarily lead to improved sleep.

The effects of limited sleep are cross-cultural. A June 2021 study analyzed the sleep habits of 85,000 people in the United Kingdom; those with misaligned sleep cycles were more likely to report depression, anxiety, and fewer feelings of well-being. In one study of nearly 2,000 Korean people with no history of medical or psychiatric diagnoses, researchers found that depressive symptoms and perceived stress were higher in those who slept less than four or five hours compared to those who slept seven or eight hours.

Insufficient sleep is also linked to a higher rate of job absenteeism, costing an estimated $44.6 billion in lost productivity annually, according to a 2022 Gallup survey conducted in the United States. It also creates worker stress and decreased job satisfaction. Employees who don't get enough sleep are 70 percent more likely to be involved in workplace accidents.

Sleep deprivation (the elimination of sleep for at least one night) can also degrade memory and cognition; studies have shown that driving on little sleep can be as dangerous as driving while intoxicated.

How does sleep affect our moods?

I work with a lot of parents who tell me they have difficulty regulating emotions in the morning. They say things like, "My kid is a disaster. He's never ready. My fuse is getting shorter."

I ask, "How much sleep do you get? How has the quality of your sleep been?"

Inevitably, they answer, "Not enough, and horrific!"

Sleep deprivation spurs system-wide biochemical changes that, over weeks, months, or years, can significantly impair our health, cognition, and mood.

Improper sleep hygiene causes the body to react as if it's constantly under stress. In fact, getting less than five hours of sleep a night has been linked to cortisol-related issues like high blood pressure. People who are sleep-deprived report increases in negative moods (anger, frustration, irritability, sadness) and decreases in positive moods. An analysis of nineteen studies found that while sleep deprivation worsens a person's ability to think clearly or perform certain tasks, it has an even greater negative effect on mood.

Among teens, poor sleep hygiene is associated with various mood disorders, conflict, driving accidents, and lower academic achievement.

Importantly, we usually evaluate our sleep by tallying the total number of hours spent asleep, but when we sleep also matters: If the timing of sleep fluctuates considerably, there's a mismatch with our internal body clock. As a result, we might still experience the mood consequences of poor sleep hygiene.

And just as sleep influences our ability to deal with our feelings, how we feel has an impact on how well we sleep. It's a feedback loop. A high-stress life nearly doubles a person's chances of poor sleep. And worrying about sleep triples your chances of not sleeping well. Around 81 percent of Americans say their sleep is affected by their minds racing or intense feelings.

After a difficult day at home or with the family, do you tend to lie in bed awake, hoping for some "me time"? If you answered yes, you likely have what's called "sleep procrastination." Some call this "revenge bedtime procrastination"—meaning you resent your busy daytime schedule and respond by taking chill time at the expense of solid sleep.

In a study published in 2023 in the *British Journal of Health Psychology*, researchers interviewed twenty-eight young people in the workforce about their bedtime habits. The majority said that when they got into bed, they experienced negative feelings and apprehension about the next day. They procrastinated going to sleep because of their need for me time. These feelings conflicted with their knowledge of the value of getting a good night's sleep. Often, when we delay our bedtime, we think we're prioritizing some much-needed personal time. But sleeping should be thought of as the ultimate form of me time. Research shows that using cognitive and behavioral strategies can decrease bedtime procrastination.

According to Matt Walker, a professor of neuroscience and psychology at the University of California, Berkeley, and founder and director of the Center for Human Sleep Science, sleep deprivation makes humans more emotionally reactive and more sensitive to stressful stimuli and events. He has shown in brain imaging studies that people who are sleep-deprived are about 60 percent more reactive to their emotions than those who get sufficient sleep. Our prefrontal cortex—known as the CEO of the brain—is the home of executive functioning, which is needed for effective emotion regulation. When we have a full night's sleep, the connection between the amygdala region and the prefrontal cortex is smooth. Deprivation causes poor communication between the two, which translates into emotional dysregulation. Adequate sleep, as I've shared, has been proven to drastically reduce feelings of anxiety by improving the ability to process stress and anxiety in helpful ways.

What about sleep's role in our ability to implement regulation strategies?

Iris Mauss and colleagues at the University of California, Berkeley, conducted an experiment to study the relationship between sleep quality and the ability to implement cognitive reappraisal. First, around 150 participants were shown a sad film. Then they were asked to regulate their emotional response to it and instructed, "Think about the situation you see in a more positive light." Those who reported poor sleep quality exhibited a lesser ability to implement cognitive reappraisal than those who slept better. These findings are consistent with the idea that sleep helps us use more helpful strategies to regulate emotions.

As I've shared, research shows that poor sleep can increase stress and even aggression, but it's unclear what explains this relationship. In a study with 740 participants, Olivia Demichelis, a researcher at the School of Psychology at the University of Queensland, and her colleagues investigated whether emotion regulation abilities may serve as a protective factor against the negative consequences of sleep disturbances. Results showed that difficulties in emotion regulation partially explained the relationship of sleep to stress, verbal aggression, anger, and hostility, and *fully* explained the relationship of sleep to physical aggression.

This research highlights that people who struggle with sleep and also have poor emotion regulation abilities might be particularly susceptible to the negative consequences of stress. Of course, improving sleep habits is critical, but educating ourselves in emotion regulation could help mitigate the impact of sleep disturbances. The research also shows that emotion regulation is important in reducing the likelihood of becoming physically aggressive after a poor night's sleep, particularly for those of us who struggle with sleep disturbances *and* aggressive tendencies.

As you might imagine, the experts offer a lot of good counsel on how to improve sleep hygiene. Our circadian rhythm is our body's natural, twenty-four-hour cycle that helps control when we sleep, wake up, eat, and release hormones. It's guided by light and darkness, helping our bodies to know the right times for these activities. Although everyone's circadian rhythms vary, most adults feel best going to bed around 11 p.m. and waking up at 7 a.m. If you need to be on an earlier or later schedule, say, for work, that's okay, as long as you're consistent with sleep and wake time.

Nevertheless, research shows that early risers are less likely than night owls to develop mental health problems. Routinely staying up late was associated with more emotional and behavioral difficulties, less emotional well-being, and being less "prosocial"—meaning less likely to help others.

For kids, being an early riser has the same impact and, interestingly, is unrelated to sleep duration and school start time. That said, there's a natural tendency for adolescents to stay up late and wake up late.

If you decide to make changes, do it slowly. If you now go to bed at midnight, start going at 11:45 for a few weeks, then at 11:30, and so on.

Safia Khan, a sleep medicine specialist at University of Texas Southwestern Medical Center in Dallas, says when you stay up past your natural bedtime, your body produces more wake-promoting hormones. These are supposed to be plentiful during the day and scarce at night. When your body has to produce more of them to keep you awake, that puts pressure on the adrenal glands (which produce stress hormones), cardiovascular system, and respiratory system. This can cause elevated blood pressure, increased blood sugar levels, and feelings of anxiety and depression, as well as muscle fatigue and discomfort in the joints.

Also, when we are sleep-deprived or restricted—like when we pull an all-nighter and miss our normal bedtime—we often get a second wind. But it catches up with us. When we are inconsistent, our sleep and circadian rhythms don't match. That means you might have less slow-wave sleep and fail to get enough REM sleep. Missing out on these stages disrupts both the body's physical restoration and the brain's emotional and cognitive processing, with far-reaching health consequences on physical health and emotion regulation ability.

Lynelle Schneeberg, a researcher in the Department of Psychiatry at the Yale School of Medicine, says it's a myth that we can "catch up" on sleep during the weekend. By pushing back our awakening time, we're confusing our bodies. As a result, we won't know when to trigger the production of cortisol to keep us awake, or of melatonin, the hormone that helps regulate sleep. Schneeberg suggests that when you start feeling drowsy, you typically have a twenty-minute window to fall asleep. If you don't manage to do so within that time frame, it often takes a couple of hours before you can fall asleep. That's when we get a second wind, which often leads us to pick up our phones!

Here are some tips to make bedtime something we can look forward to and benefit from.

What not to do:

- Don't drink caffeine after noon. If you feel drowsy in the afternoon, splash some cold water on your face or take a brief ten- to twenty-minute nap. Even if you don't experience negative effects of coffee at night, it's still good to monitor overall caffeine intake and consider any potential long-term impacts on your health.
- Don't look at any screens (phone, computer, TV) for an hour before bedtime.
- Don't eat three to five hours before bed.
- Don't drink alcohol three to five hours before bed. It messes with your brain and sleep.

What to do:

- Try to go to bed at the same time each night.
- Make sure your bedding is comfortable, that the room is neither too cool nor too warm—between sixty-five and sixty-eight degrees Fahrenheit is thought to be optimal—and that you sleep in the dark.
- Take care of your "me time" or worries before getting into bed. As we discussed, we can carry our worries to bed with us, which makes it hard to turn off our brains and get good rest. Instead, carve out time throughout the day to tend to your stress. Talk it out with a colleague, or journal about it earlier in the day. If you're likely to worry at night, keeping the journal next to your bed and jotting down your concerns with a plan to handle them (during the day!) can help. Often, you'll get to your planned "worry time" and realize it no longer concerns you.
- Practice slow, deep breathing exercises, like the ones I shared earlier, before bed. This initiates your relaxation response, so you fall asleep faster. It also improves sleep quality by synchro-

nizing your heart rate variability for restful sleep stages, and it increases melatonin production, too.
- Get your exercise early in the day or before dinner.
- Drink fluids earlier in the evening.
- When you wake up, get some sunlight as soon as you can. This can help you reset your internal clock and support a stable circadian rhythm.

A final thought about sleep:

Do you value it? I'm not asking if you want or need more sleep, but do you really *value* it? Or do you have that "sleep is for the weak" mindset? It might not even be conscious.

Where I work, all I hear from faculty and students is "I've got endless work to do," or "I had to pull an all-nighter," or "There's never enough time in the day."

This mindset conveys a message that you think you're being tough and resilient, and that people who prioritize sleep lack strength or dedication. In today's culture, many people associate sleep and rest with low productivity.

Here's an example that happened while I was writing this chapter. I was working on a project and got an email from someone at 11 p.m., after I had gone to bed. My colleague was asking for feedback on a document. By the time I had woken up and checked my email at 7 a.m., I had already received a follow-up email from that person saying, "Since I haven't heard back from you, I'm going ahead with it as is." This coworker actually expected me to edit their document and reply between 11 p.m. and 7 a.m.!

What's the message here? *You should be awake and working at all hours. Sleep is not important.* Now we know why so many of us are sleep-deprived.

Addressing your own sleep habits will also be helpful for your family and coworkers. Be a sleep role model—send messages to your team about the value of sleeping. After all, it makes you smarter, healthier, and better at dealing with life's ups and downs. Sounds like a win-win.

One concluding observation about the physiological "budget" component of emotion regulation: When we address the three aspects we've discussed here—activity, nutrition, and sleep—we create a powerful overall effect. They all reinforce one another. Eating right and exercising produce positive visible results that we all appreciate. They also contribute greatly to our body-wide feelings of well-being. Proper sleep has the same effect—it makes us feel better throughout our waking hours. When we address all three needs, we gain the knowledge that we're devoting our thoughts and energies to something that improves every part of our lives—including the emotional. That has a positive influence on our decisions and all our relationships, especially with the people we love.

PART FIVE

# PRACTICE MAKES PERMANENT

# 13.

# How Children Learn to Regulate Emotions

*Tell me and I forget. Teach me and I remember. Involve me and I learn.*
—Benjamin Franklin

Now the fun begins.

We've spent most of this book learning about the mindsets, skills, and strategies needed to deal with our own and other people's feelings in positive, helpful ways. Here, in this chapter and the next, we'll go from learning to doing.

It's like going from driver's ed to driving—a big leap. On the open road, on our own, the world looks very different than it did back in the classroom, with the instructor safely by our side. Things will move faster now. There are more factors to consider—more choices and higher stakes.

It's time to drive.

I tried to think of the best way to demonstrate exactly *how* we'll manage our emotional responses, the actual process of problem-solving about emotions and then putting all those strategies to good use. Then it dawned on me that I've been observing it in action for years now, decades even, on a regular basis.

It happens in classrooms.

Young children, by their very nature, are perfect examples to observe when it comes to feelings and how to deal with them. Emotionally, they are honest. They're full of feelings, and they haven't learned yet to deny them, or disguise them, or lock them away in mental compartments and pretend they don't exist. They haven't absorbed the sad lesson that, according to polite society, certain emotions are better left unexpressed.

Unfortunately, they'll learn those survival skills as they grow up, the way we all did. In fact, it appears that this is starting earlier than ever. During a recent classroom visit, a kindergarten boy said he didn't want to burden me with his feelings. His words stopped me in my tracks—I felt a wave of sadness that such a young child was already carrying the weight of self-censorship and worry about being a burden. But for now, thankfully, most young children are unguarded and uncensored. It's a beautiful thing to witness, as long as you can live with a certain level of intensity.

In a classroom full of kids, you'll hear all kinds of ideas about how to deal with feelings. Children are good at thinking outside the box because they're not aware there *is* a box. It's why classrooms are so useful as real-life laboratories of emotion regulation.

In school, children are facing new demands. They're expected to perform an important job there: to learn the things that will eventually turn them into high-functioning adults. Along the way they'll be constantly graded and judged. They'll have to adhere to a routine and follow rules for six to seven hours per day. They'll also want to make friends (and keep them), and they'll have to deal with peers (and adults) who can be mean and cruel. It would be a lot for anyone to handle—and it's especially challenging at an age when emotions are running hot and wild.

How would we adults fare under these conditions? Would we be exemplary role models for how to deal with feelings in beneficial ways that serve our long-term goals? Would we demonstrate the skills and strategies that also help the people around us manage their emotions properly?

Maybe. But maybe not.

Given my work in studying and teaching the skills of emotional intelligence, I get to see kids in schools all over the world who have advantages we adults didn't enjoy. They've been learning about the skills of emotion regulation for years, in many cases. That's because their schools recognized the vital role that emotions play in learning, relationships, well-being, and everyday life.

In the schools we've worked with, each student and teacher becomes an expert user of an invaluable tool we've already discussed, the Mood Meter—a grid of many boxes, each one signifying a different feeling, and each represented by a color. As I shared in chapter 6, using the Mood Meter gives a person the chance to locate their emotional state on a broad spectrum of possibilities, from peeved to enraged (red); sad to despondent (blue); joyful to elated (yellow); and calm to serene (green). Students also understand the role of what we call the Meta-Moment—the pause we take before we respond to a challenging feeling by first imagining our best selves. (We'll dive deeper into this tool in chapter 12.)

In schools where these tools are taught, students also partake in Feeling Words lessons that are integrated into the standard curriculum—all subject areas, actually. The lessons, which include *character analysis*—where students examine the thoughts, feelings, and motivations of characters in stories—and *social problem-solving activities*, span preschool through eighth grade. These experiences help children develop the vocabulary to describe their full range of emotions with precision while building the ability to think critically about their own and others' emotional experiences. Why? Naming what they feel and understanding why everyone feels the way they do makes it possible to address their own and others' emotions effectively.

As I've mentioned, this is a skill we adults are severely lacking. We use a paltry and inadequate handful of words to describe our most complex emotions. As a result, we have trouble pinpointing how we're really feeling and can't express our feelings in ways that others can understand. This makes it next to impossible to address them in helpful ways.

By high school, the curriculum encompasses a broad spectrum of topics pertinent to adolescents. Students learn how to build a vision for their academic, relationship, extracurricular, and well-being goals to help them make informed decisions. We teach high schoolers how to set these goals, understand their motivational needs and personality profiles, and apply emotion regulation skills to achieve what they want from their life in and out of school.

Many students in the schools that have adopted our approach live with these concepts for years, starting in preschool and going all the way through high school graduation. And, as we'll see soon, this prepares them to do the real work of emotion regulation—discovering, using, and refining the strategies and the skills that can work for them throughout their lives.

How do so many kids manage what still confounds us adults? The answer to that requires a brief history lesson.

My own education in dealing with feelings began, as I've shared, with Uncle Marvin. Marvin was a middle school teacher who consistently achieved extraordinary success with the students who moved through his sixth-grade classroom. Marvin figured out that it was his students' emotional state—not their intelligence or knowledge in any particular academic subject—that made the difference between flourishing and floundering. He saw that if kids grew up with the ability to understand their own and others' emotions and to regulate their emotional responses, they would become better learners, decision-makers, friends, parents, colleagues, and partners.

I was able to learn my uncle's lessons so well because they helped me to navigate the extreme bullying and loneliness I experienced in my childhood. Without his intervention, I never would have survived middle and high school.

Meanwhile, over three decades ago, when scientists were still debating whether emotions were a disruptive or adaptive force, two research psychologists proposed a concept they called "emotional intelligence." Peter Salovey and John Mayer held that there is "a set of skills contributing to the accurate appraisal of emotions in self and others and the effective regulation of emotion in self and others." They said that feelings could be channeled to motivate us and help us reach our goals. It was such an unorthodox notion that the article they wrote in 1990 could find a home only in an obscure journal. It wasn't until 1995 that the concept of emotional intelligence gained widespread recognition, thanks to psychologist Daniel Goleman's book *Emotional Intelligence: Why It Can Matter More Than IQ*.

At around the same time, a conference was held by psychologists and educators who had begun classroom instruction in what came to be known as social and emotional learning or SEL. They advocated for teaching children how to recognize and understand their emotions, how to label them precisely so they would be able to express them to others, and—most importantly—how to use the tactics and techniques required to deal in healthy ways with their feelings, including responsible decision-making.

That was the start of a widespread effort to develop evidence-based programs teaching social and emotional skills to students from preschool on up. As of 2022, 76 percent of principals across the United States reported that their schools used an SEL program. We also have abundant credible evidence showing that SEL works. A 2023 meta-analysis led by my colleague Christina Cipriano, an associate professor at the Yale Child Study Center, showed that SEL has a positive impact on students' problem-solving, work habits, and academics. Students have better relationships with their peers and teachers, earn higher grades, and report fewer instances of mental health issues, bullying, and other challenges. SEL teaches kids to acknowledge their emotions and then manage them, rather than allowing themselves to be controlled by their emotions. Even their teachers experience less stress and burnout. By any measure, it's a win for the children and also for the rest of us.

Given all that, most parents want their children to learn the skills of emotional intelligence. Yet SEL has its skeptics and detractors, people who believe that this kind of instruction doesn't belong in schools and is best left for parents to handle at home.

While it's true that SEL should ideally begin at home, the reality is that home alone isn't enough. All we need to do is look to the world around us to see why: Too many kids are struggling emotionally—with anxiety, depression, alienation, self-harm, suicidal ideation, and other forms of psychological distress and even mental illness, both in and out of school. Social media has taken normal adolescent angst and turned it viral and pathological. It's clear that most kids are not getting the help that SEL has been proven to provide in or out of school.

Recently an educator told me, "Parents say they don't want us to teach SEL because, as one mother put it, 'Empathy doesn't get your kid into an Ivy League college.'" I had to laugh—I am an Ivy League educator. What I really wanted to say was, "If your child can't manage the emotional roller coaster of adolescence, they won't have the emotional stamina to thrive in *any* college or career."

To prove the point, there's an exercise I sometimes perform with parents. It goes like this:

I tell them, "Right now I want you to live vicariously through your children during a typical school day, minute by minute. Literally imagine stepping into their shoes. Pay attention to what you're feeling as we go.

"Okay, so you wake up early, and the first thing that comes into your mind is that you need to hurry up and get ready for school.

"Are you excited? Happy? Eager to face the day? Or are you dreading it? Like you want to pull the covers over your head and go back to sleep?

"Now you're up, you're dressed, you're fed (hopefully), and you're on your way. What's on your mind? Are you anticipating what's going to happen today in math, or social studies? Who you'll sit with at lunch? Who you'll interact with in physical education? What team you'll be on? Or are you daydreaming about something else you'd rather be doing?

"You're now on the way to school, walking or in the car with a parent or on the bus. How are you feeling?

"Okay, now you're seated in your class, locked in, as ready as possible for whatever will come during the next six hours or so." And on and on, the normal school day unfolds, just as we all remember it, until the afternoon bell rings.

At this point, I'll ask the parents, "How was your day as your own child? What feelings did you have?"

Usually, they say it wasn't so great. The words they use to describe it are uniformly negative. The top ones always are *overwhelmed*, *exhausted*, *anxious*, *lonely*, and *busy*.

The first time I tried this exercise, that truth blew me away. We all know how discouraging the school experience can be for many of our children. A lot of our views are probably based on memories of what school was like for us. But they also reflect what we know about how our kids experience school today. For many, the prospect of twelve or more years in a classroom is a downer. But we accept it, like a prison sentence with no possibility of parole.

After one family workshop, a father came up to me and said, "Hasn't it always been this way? Haven't kids always been bored and hated school? There's nothing new about it."

"You're probably right," I said. "But let's put history aside for a moment and ask ourselves if it *has* to be this way. Let's ask if this is really what we want for our kids. Do we really want them to feel like they're trapped for six hours every day? Imagine what could be different if we took children's and adults' emotions more seriously in school? Perhaps it's time for us to rethink certain aspects of education that aren't serving our kids."

I'm constantly talking to school administrators and educators, and I ask them, "What is the biggest challenge you face today with your students?" The answers are always the same: kids who can't regulate their emotions. Kids who are fearful, resentful, depressed, worried, alienated, and angry, and who can't deal with these feelings. And kids who are unable to cope and don't know how to ask for help, or even what words to say to express how they're feeling. This results in tantrums, outbursts, fighting, and impulsive behavior, or shutting down and completely disengaging from the educational experience. As a result of these challenges and others, educator stress and burnout have escalated and are the leading reasons teachers report leaving the profession. A National Education Association survey in 2022 reported that 90 percent of educators felt that burnout was a serious problem, and 55 percent indicated they were planning to leave the profession earlier than anticipated due to the pressures of the COVID pandemic.

Not a great place for anyone to be. You can see why knowing how to regulate your emotions might be a useful skill, especially at a young age. During a conference we copresented at, my friend and colleague Stuart Ablon, a professor at Harvard Medical School and a leading expert in social problem-solving, emphasized, "When students and adults don't use effective regulation strategies, it's not because they don't want to, it's because they don't know how to."

The approach I've been working with for the past thirty years, beginning with Uncle Marvin, is called RULER—an acronym for the five key skills of emotional intelligence: recognize, understand, label, express, and regulate. It's a pre-K through high school approach developed by researchers and practitioners at the Yale Center for Emotional Intelligence. RULER has been adopted by over five thousand schools across the United States and in nearly three dozen other countries, reaching more than two hundred thousand educators and five million students.

A primary goal of RULER is to help students discover the full range of regulation strategies available to them. But that's just the starting point. They also have to practice these strategies and learn to evaluate them for their efficacy.

It's easy to tell a child to "Take a deep breath," or "Be positive," or "Think about your situation in a different way," or "Write about what happened in your journal," or "Talk to a friend." But what do those techniques accomplish? If you're feeling regretful about something you said or did, will taking a deep breath help solve the problem? How can you look at your situation in a different way? If you journal after a fight, what do you write, and why would that change anything? If you talk to a friend, what will you say, and how do you know their support will help you? These are the questions we deal with in classrooms. They're the same ones we adults must ask ourselves when we try to find helpful ways of dealing with our own intense emotions.

Observing how emotion regulation is practiced in classrooms can be highly instructive for any adult who wants to understand how the process should work.

In a RULER classroom, for example, it's common to see "strategy walls" where students showcase their top regulation strategies for various emotions and situations. This one is from a middle school classroom where students listed their specific strategies for managing anxiety and stress during tests:

- Notice the feeling and then let it go.
- Take a break and get a sip of water.
- Take a few deep breaths.
- Take a two-minute doodle break.
- Pause and say something to yourself like, "You can do this!"
- Skip the difficult question and come back.
- Close your eyes and think about your "calm place"... then return to the test.

Notice how students used a variety of strategies including mindfulness, breathing exercises, and cognitive techniques. This serves as a great reminder that we have a diverse range of approaches at our disposal and that different strategies work for different students. One day, a few deep breaths might be effective, while on another day, saying a few kind words to ourselves could do the trick.

Here's an abridged version of a thirty-minute RULER lesson from a roomful of fifth-grade students:

"I'm really curious," I said. "Is there something going on in your grade that's not cool? That makes people feel uncomfortable or unsafe?

I'd like you to partner with someone next to you to come up with a situation that could be handled better. I'm going to give you three minutes."

I let a little time pass, and then I said, "Okay, who's got something?"

One girl raised her hand immediately and said, "It's gossiping! There's always some kind of gossip and drama on the bus or the playground." (Coincidentally, that was a top concern in my meeting with the faculty and staff in the school.)

"Okay," I said. "Can you get more specific?"

"Yeah," a boy said. "Kids say mean things about other kids. They make fun of how someone looks or what they wear or who they're dating!" (I'm thinking, *Wait, you're eleven years old and you're dating?* But it's not for me to judge.)

I asked, "How many of you would agree that gossiping can be a problem sometimes?"

All hands went up.

"Let's just take a quiet moment—maybe soften your eyes or look down if that helps you focus," I said. "I have a few questions. I'm curious: How many of you have ever been gossiped about?"

All hands went up.

"Okay, you can put your hands down but keep your eye gaze down. Next question: How many of you have ever gossiped about someone else?"

All hands went up again.

"Okay, everyone, open your eyes and look around. What do you notice?"

Every face looked surprised.

"Wow!" one boy said.

"I guess we've learned something already," I said. "Now, let's come up with a scenario—no names, just a scenario where someone might gossip about someone else."

A girl said, "It's like people saying stuff behind your back. And they twist the story. They make stuff up."

"Okay, let's use that as our example. Let's imagine that someone is spreading a false rumor about you. First question: How might you feel?

Turn to your partner and take a minute to share the feelings you would have if you learned a classmate was spreading a rumor about you."

After a minute or two, I said, "Who would like to share?"

"I'd feel mad and angry!" a boy said.

"Depressed and rejected," said a girl.

"Confused."

"Humiliated and embarrassed."

"That's a lot of feelings," I said. "You all have great words to describe your feelings. So, what have we learned so far?"

"That we all feel different things," someone said.

"Right," I said. "Did you notice anything about the feelings people shared?"

A girl said, "Well, for me it would depend on what was being said and who said it. If they made fun of me, I might feel excluded or humiliated. If it was someone I was really close to, I might feel confused and angry. It really depends."

"That makes a lot of sense. Anything else come to mind about how people might feel when rumors are spread about them?"

"We can't assume we know," a boy said. "We have to ask!"

"Great insight!" I said. "We need to understand what exactly is going on. I'd like you now to break into groups of three or four. I want you to focus on how we might deal with the feelings we'd have when a rumor is being spread.

"Ask yourself and each other: What would you feel? Is there anything about that feeling that is helpful to the situation? If so, how can you channel it into something useful? If not, what feelings would be more helpful? How would you get there? I'd also like to know how we might *prevent* this from happening or *reduce* the strong emotions we might be feeling."

Once the students broke into small groups, I told them, "Let's brainstorm different strategies. Be creative. What might we do to prevent this from happening? What are the things we could think about or do to help a friend manage their feelings in a situation like this?" I phrased it that way because, as you may remember, we're better at coming up with helpful ideas for other people than when we're trying to regulate our own emotions.

Five minutes later I asked, "Which group wants to share first?" Lots of hands went up.

"I would give the person a hug and say I'm sorry this happened to you."

I asked, "How many of you think this would be helpful?"

Again, lots of hands.

"Okay," I said, "hold that thought. What's another idea?"

"I would ask if they'd like to take a walk and let them know I am there for them."

"Who thinks this would help?"

Again, lots of hands.

"I have a question," I said. "In this situation, if someone's feelings were hurt by gossip, what would hugging them or going for a walk accomplish?"

"It would show them you care. And taking a walk would give them a chance to calm down a little."

"Great! Comforting and calming helps a lot. Then what comes next?"

No easy answers to that one. Suddenly the room went silent.

I have good reasons for challenging their efforts to come up with useful strategies. This process is meant to be goal-directed, not merely feel-good. Sometimes it's not enough to help someone to calm down—being calm is useful in the heat of the moment, but it doesn't usually work as a way of regulating our response to a difficult interpersonal situation. In this case, calming down won't help us deal with the anger and humiliation of unkind gossip.

We'd need a different strategy, or perhaps a second one to use once we feel cared about and are calm enough to think and then act. This is an important principle of emotion regulation: Often, we need more than one strategy to complete the job. We can take a deep breath, walk away, reappraise, and ask for help!

"Instead of just talking about it," I said, "let's role-play the situation. I need two volunteers: one to be the person who had the rumors spread about them, and the other to be the support person. It's important to stay in character, and I want the first person to really imagine this is happening and let us know if the strategy is working or not."

"I'm really upset," the first student said. "Somebody is spreading a rumor about me, and I don't know what to do. I feel embarrassed."

"How about if we take a walk so you can calm down and we can talk about it?" the second student said.

I stepped in and asked the first kid, "Do you think this would help you?"

"Yes," she said, "it might."

I asked the rest of the students to share their ideas.

"I would give them a choice . . . like say, 'Would you like to take a walk—maybe you will feel calmer—or would you like to just stay here with me and talk it out?'"

It's a good idea to give someone a choice that immediately gives them a sense of control (albeit limited, of course).

"I would say that sometimes people do things that are stupid. This happens to everyone."

"I would tell a teacher and ask them to talk to the kid spreading the gossip."

This suggestion was interesting—it involved taking an action to defuse the emotional moment. But the group wasn't ready to absorb it quite yet, so I let it pass.

"I would offer to play with them."

"I would let them know their feelings are okay."

I asked, "What would validating or letting them know their feelings are okay look like?"

"I would say, 'I know that girl was mean to you. That wasn't nice. I'm your friend. Don't let it bother you.'"

"Any other thoughts?"

A student said, "You know, if it was me, I would just go out to the water fountain and drink some cold water. And that would soothe my body and help me with my anger."

Another said, "When I get angry, I like to play the piano. It helps me work through the problem."

Another said, "I would wait and write a letter to the person. Then I would read it and tear it up, because I would realize that I'm done with it already."

"It's possible the person spreading the rumor was just having a bad day. I'd want to know their motivation."

"I'd find out who it was and then tell my friend to tell them to stop spreading rumors."

We had circled back to the idea of doing something concrete to end the gossiping, rather than simply living with it.

"Okay," I said, "let's try that one out. What do we think?"

"I don't have enough confidence. I'd be too nervous to say something."

"So, what are some other options?"

"Let's think about this," a boy said. "Maybe if we get another friend and all three of us talk to the person it'll be easier. Or how about if we ask a teacher to do it with us?"

"That sounds like a good idea. What does anyone else think?"

During this part of the lesson, students were focused on dealing with the feelings after the incident had occurred. That's when I decided to pivot to *prevention*.

"Everyone, before we finish today's lesson, let's talk about what can be done to prevent or decrease the amount of gossiping happening in your classroom. What did you come up with in your groups?"

One boy said, "This is why we have our classroom charter! If people would follow it, there would be less rumors!"

The charter, constructed by the students, is a poster that summarizes conversations students have about their needs and hoped-for emotions in school. It creates a sense of shared accountability for everyone to realize agreed-upon goals and norms.

"Tell us more," I said.

While pointing to the charter, he said, "We all agreed that we want to feel safe, valued, supported, optimistic, and united. Spreading rumors breaks the charter!"

"Make sense to me. How about everyone else? Raise your hand if you agree."

All hands went up.

Another girl shared, "Letting the person know they broke the charter would at least get them to reflect on their behavior!"

"But then they might start spreading rumors about *you*," a boy said.

"It's possible. Any thoughts?"

A girl raised her hand and said, "I wouldn't care if the person started spreading rumors about me. Actually, I like the idea of someone spreading rumors that I care about my friends!"

That conversation had the potential to keep flowing.

I observe and conduct sessions like this one all the time. I learn a lot every time, and they're fun for me, too. Kids have a great gift for turning things into games—they make the search for effective emotion regulation strategies into a form of creative play. And what I've learned is that kids are incredible if given respect and a road map. Think about the long-term academic payoff a thirty-minute investment in teaching emotion regulation can make.

Early education in emotion regulation allows students to develop a strong foundation for navigating challenges both inside and outside the classroom. It cultivates important skills like empathy, perspective-taking, critical thinking, real-world problem-solving, and cultural competence. As students progress through different grade levels, continued reinforcement of these skills ensures that they build upon their abilities and apply them in increasingly complex situations.

This method for teaching emotion regulation could take place in all classrooms, but many teachers lack confidence in their ability to do it properly. Not because they can't do it, but because they haven't had any formal training in it. That's why our approach to working with schools starts first with supporting all adults in cultivating their mindsets about emotion and building their own emotion skills. Once they possess a more nuanced feelings vocabulary and learn and practice research-based regulation strategies like the ones in this book, their confidence and desire for relaying this information to kids goes up.

One of the best things about our approach, I believe, is that the instructor doesn't have to be the knower of all things for all children. They just have to ask the right questions and create the space to help students think critically about their regulation choices. That's important because it tells kids that the process depends on simply suggesting and then sifting through the many possibilities. We can't just stop once we've identified one strategy that might work—it's important to go deeper.

The same is true for us adults. But we won't have a classroom full of smart and creative students to help us with that. So we must learn to do it on our own, inside our own heads.

Kids recognize that age doesn't necessarily bring mastery at dealing with intense feelings. They bring their emotion educations home with them. After a talk I gave, a mother came up to me and said, "You know, I was yelling at my son over something he did and he said to me, 'Mom, you're in the red, you need to take a Meta-Moment.' And I was like, 'What the heck is this kid talking about?'"

The point of all this is that we adults must learn to respond to emotions using helpful strategies, just as our children do. Like I've said all along, it's work. It's not easy. It's not foolproof. But it's necessary.

14.

# Becoming the Best Version of Yourself

*We are what we repeatedly do. Excellence, then, is not an act but a habit.*

—Aristotle

Back when I was teaching my very first psych course at Yale, a student journalist wrote an article about me and my work for the school newspaper. He titled the story "The Feelings Master," which—as you can imagine—prompted lots of mocking from friends and colleagues, who would call and ask, "May I please speak with the Feelings Master?"

It was a little embarrassing, but I also thought there was something cool about the concept. It created an *identity*—I was being depicted as someone who knew how to master the emotional side of life, which usually resists our attempts at mastery. "Feelings Master" felt like a status that could be earned, like a peak position of emotional intelligence not unlike becoming a master in the martial arts (I hold a fifth-degree black belt in hapkido, a Korean martial art). We admire those people who unfailingly behave calmly and intentionally even at moments that would severely challenge the rest of us.

I'm still intrigued by the idea that regulating our emotional responses in healthy, positive ways can turn into a form of self-identification—into how we see ourselves and how others might see us. For the most part, we deal with our unruly feelings as they arise—something triggers us and, if we're able, we pause for a deep breath and then decide how to act. Once the moment passes, though, we go back to how we were before, until the next trying interaction comes along.

But what if the ability to manage our feelings went from being something that we did to someone who we *are*? Would seeing the emotion regulation skill as an intrinsic, defining part of ourselves, as something powerful at our core, make a difference in how well we do it?

What if, I wonder, we could *all* become Feelings Masters?

Of course, you might not want to go through life with a title befitting a comic book superhero. But there's another, more realistic term for basing an identity on how we manage our emotions.

All along in this book, from the start, we've discussed the ultimate goal for dealing with our feelings: achieving the outcomes we desire—the results that will best serve whatever it is we want from life. If we accept that, then regulating our emotions—in beneficial, purposeful ways—will allow us to become something even better than Feelings Masters: our *best selves*.

With that as our aim, perhaps we'll consistently make better decisions about how to respond to emotions. And if we manage that, everything in our lives will benefit. Loved ones, colleagues, total strangers, all will witness how we navigate even the most challenging moments without losing our cool. When that happens, we'll become role models—that's how human beings operate; we observe someone else behaving in positive ways, and it registers. We carry that experience forward with us, and it begins to influence how we respond in similar situations.

Our best selves:

- Engage in all aspects of life—at home, work, and school
- Make better and more informed decisions
- Build and maintain closer, more honest relationships
- Find our purpose and meaning in life

- Enjoy greater well-being and mental health
- Achieve personal and professional goals

The concept of *best self* has taken many forms over time. In the recent past, Oprah Winfrey advised us to "Surround yourself with only people who are going to lift you higher. Life is already filled with those who want to bring you down. Make the choice to focus on your best self." Michelle Obama said, "History has shown us that courage can be contagious and hope can take on a life of its own. Become the best version of yourself and bring out the best in others." Tony Robbins, the famous motivational speaker, asserted, "If you want to be truly fulfilled, you have to know that you're constantly improving, that you're growing, and that you're contributing to others in a way that's meaningful. That's how you find your best self."

For centuries, philosophers from Socrates and Plato to John Locke and psychologists like Carl Jung pondered the idea of the self as a being we can know and embody. Positive psychology, as pioneered by Martin Seligman, focused on the strengths and virtues we can use to create fulfilling lives. Hazel Markus, a professor of psychology at Stanford, was the first to study what she called "possible selves." According to Markus, these represent individuals' ideas of what they might become, what they would like to become, and even what they are afraid of becoming (the feared self). E. Tory Higgins, a professor of psychology at Columbia, has distinguished between one's ought self (the attributes you believe you should or ought to possess) and your ideal self (the attributes of the self you want to become). Higgins found that a discrepancy between the ought and actual self can engender anxiety, and a discrepancy between actual self and ideal self can lead to disappointment or even depression. His research elucidates the potential threats to our well-being when our ideal conceptions of ourselves do not line up with our present ones.

But researchers have found that—for the most part—we benefit by envisioning and articulating our ideal selves. According to one study, doing this is "likely to improve self-regulation because it allows an opportunity to learn about oneself, to illuminate and restructure one's priorities, and to gain better insight into one's motives and emotions." A recent analysis of twenty-nine studies involving nearly three thousand participants showed that imagining our best selves can increase optimism and decrease depressive symptoms.

Psychologists have even studied how children relate to the best self concept by using what's known as the Batman effect. Based on fictional characters' beliefs and values, kids begin to grasp why superheroes act in certain ways, such as saving lives or fighting villains. This allows children to appreciate the complexities of decisions based on fairness and empathy. Research shows that pretending to be a superhero can significantly enhance a child's perseverance and executive function skills. In studies where children were asked to complete challenging tasks, those who pretended to be superheroes persevered longer than those who didn't pretend.

Recall, when we're regulating emotions—consciously or not—we have PRIME goals (e.g., to prevent anxiety, reduce anger, initiate happiness, maintain contentment, or enhance excitement) that serve higher-order goals (e.g., to be a better partner, to have greater well-being, to make a sound decision). And we achieve these aims by using the specific regulation strategies taught in this book, such as mindfulness, reappraisal, or social support.

Nearly twenty years ago, Robin Stern and I stumbled upon an important insight. We both observed that people didn't make connections between their values, goals, and success or failure at regulating their emotions. Robin, through her clinical work, and I, through research and teaching emotion regulation skills in schools, were perplexed by a common pattern: Many individuals were open to learning how to better manage their emotions and even experienced the benefits, but eventually they would revert to their old habits.

Robin and I thought that incorporating the concept of best self into the emotion regulation process might help. To get us there, we created a tool called the Meta-Moment. We used the term *meta* because it was about taking a moment *within* the moment to activate our best selves. The goal was to help people move from mostly automatic, unhelpful ways of dealing with their feelings to conscious and deliberate ways.

Here is how you can start practicing the Meta-Moment:

1. *Sense.* You're aware that you're activated. A feeling has surfaced—something happened (or you anticipate that something will happen) and you're about to react on autopilot. You have the impulse to say or do something you'll likely regret. Your habitual, deeply ingrained way of dealing with your feelings is surfacing. So you …
2. *Stop.* You create a space. You take a breath. Another one. Maybe another one to lower your emotional temperature. You might even pinch yourself. You don't say or do what's on your mind. If there's time, you might identify your feeling. As we've learned, emotion regulation strategy selection is best informed when we're calm and know *what* we're feeling. Then the magic happens.
3. *See your best self.* You imagine your best self—the person you want to be, the one you want others to see. You ask yourself, *How would my best self respond in this moment?* Visualizing an ideal, positive version of oneself while managing emotions helps us reconnect with our values and goals, and it also blocks negative thoughts.
4. *Strategize and act.* Now you delve into your emotion regulation tool kit and select the strategies that will help bridge the gap between your current state and your emerging best self. As a result, your behavior aligns with your highest potential.

Importantly, we need to be an emotion scientist around the success (or not) of our Meta-Moment. We need to ask ourselves: *Was my response true to my best self? Did it help me achieve my relationship goals? Or do I need more practice with this strategy? Perhaps I need to replace the strategy with a more helpful one?*

If you were successful, acknowledge it and savor the feeling of accomplishment. Research shows that we often abandon our goals because we don't enjoy pursuing them. What could be more enjoyable than successfully regulating your emotions?

Regular practice of the Meta-Moment trains us to implement more adaptive versus maladaptive strategies and to build neural pathways for healthy emotion regulation over time.

Now it's important to define this: Who is *your* best self?

Here's a simple, universal definition to start with—it's the self you've envisioned yourself becoming. Now the question is, what steps do you need to take to make that vision of yourself a reality?

Here's one way to begin.

Make a list of the five people with whom you spend the most time and who matter to you most. Probably your partner, if you have one, will be at the top. If you have children they'll be up there, too. Your coworkers and boss. Parents? Siblings? Workout buddy? Bridge partner? Close old friends you've known forever?

Next to each name, use a few words to say how you think that person would describe you or experience you. There will no doubt be some variety. Your friends from high school probably see you differently than your children do.

Now look at the list of descriptions—those add up to your collective reputation. Some of the descriptions, I hope, are pleasing to you. There are (hopefully) people who view you in the way you wish to be viewed.

But all of them? If we're being totally honest, there are probably a few descriptions in there that sting a little. Maybe to our kids we're a good parent but also a killjoy. Perhaps our partner sees us as loving but controlling, or not empathic, or impatient. It's possible that even at work or on the golf course we're not universally beloved and admired.

We play many roles in life—parent, partner, provider, employee, sibling, friend, child. Each has its own context that determines the best ways to interact. Our emotional response to a cranky four-year-old can't be the same as our reaction to our cranky supervisor at work, or to our grandmother, or to the driver in the Jeep trying to sneak into our lane.

The final step toward best selfhood requires us to examine how our decisive emotional moments have played out with the people in our lives. Did how I regulate my emotions bring me closer to my goals? Make my relationships stronger? If it did, I learned a useful lesson. If it didn't, the lesson may have been even more valuable. Was my execution flawed, or was my choice of response the wrong one?

Okay, now it's time to close the gap—the gap between your two selves.

Take a minute to picture your best self. What do you see? Which adjectives would you use to describe the best version of yourself?

If you struggle with finding those adjectives, pick a role (friend, parent, boss, colleague) and think about the characteristics of people you admire and would like to emulate. Take advantage of what you've observed and learned from your role models.

Fill in these blanks:

Role _____

I want to see myself as someone who is _____, _____, _____.

I want other people to know me as someone who is _____, _____, _____.

In the course of my research, I've posed these questions to tens of thousands of people.

Here are some of the most common answers:

| | | |
|---|---|---|
| Accepting | Cheerful | Empathic |
| Approachable | Compassionate | Encouraging |
| Balanced | Confident | Flexible |
| Calm | Creative | Honest |
| Caring | Durable | Hopeful |

| | | |
|---|---|---|
| Inspiring | Persistent | Thoughtful |
| Kind | Positive | Understanding |
| Loving | Present | Wise |
| Open | Relaxed | |
| Patient | Supportive | |

I have my own list.

Earlier in this book, I wrote about a rather shameful moment during the pandemic when I spoke rudely to my mother-in-law. I was chastened and tried to make up for it the next morning.

Then I went further in my quest to become my best son-in-law self. I decided that each day, before coming down for breakfast, I would pause and remind myself about the son-in-law I hope always to be: Patient. Kind. Compassionate. Respectful. I also resolved to be more curious about my mother-in-law—to ask questions about her life and engage in friendly banter with her.

My best self is evolving, just like yours, just like everyone's. As a husband, I'm trying to be more patient. As a public speaker, more inspiring. As a mentor, more present.

Finally, our best selves are context dependent. For example, a teenage boy who sees his best self as nonviolent may find it challenging to maintain this ideal if he lives in a neighborhood with high levels of violence and crime. In such an environment, his safety could be at risk, making it difficult for him to adhere to his nonviolent values while trying to protect himself. Our best selves are also deeply influenced by our cultural backgrounds. If our culture values harmony and we have a strong need for affiliation, we are more likely to prioritize our relationships. Conversely, if our culture values achievement, we are more likely to develop strategies to motivate ourselves and others to excel academically.

What gets in the way of being our best selves? Research conducted by Gabriele Oettingen, a psychology professor at New York University, suggests that comparing our envisioned best self with our current reality is crucial. This comparison allows us to identify obstacles that stand in the way of achieving our best self and to create realistic plans to overcome them.

We've spent a lot of this book talking about emotional triggers as though they're one-size-fits-all, but the truth is that they're highly individualized. What sets me off might not bother you in the slightest. So we each need to recognize our personal barriers to best selfhood. It could be anything—the presence of certain people, or how we feel at specific times of day, or our existing emotional state, or issues we've been carrying around since childhood. Understanding what cues your particular emotional challenges, or what activates your worst self, is essential to addressing root causes.

In our research at the Center, we've asked thousands of people to name the obstacles they face on the path to becoming their best selves.

Some are personal, such as anxiety, weariness, distractibility, procrastination, unrealistically high expectations, or the need for control and the drive for perfection.

Others are relational, like a life partner with dramatically differing views, work demands, childcare responsibilities, or family obligations.

And some are larger, impersonal forces, including financial matters, health issues, or the general state of national and global politics, which affect us no matter who we are or what we do.

These aren't any excuses for why we can't embody our best selves. They are simply factors we all need to anticipate and overcome. Obstacles can either stop us or inspire us. It's our decision to make.

Here's a major obstacle we often fail to consider: plain old exhaustion. You've identified that you want to be kinder and felt great when you left the house this morning. All day at work, you had plenty of physical, cognitive, and emotional energy to handle whatever came your way. But those powers became depleted as you used them up. After a full day of operating at the top of your game, you return to the place where you matter most—home, surrounded by loved ones, some of whom might be children, all of whom are full of their own expectations and needs.

By now, though, you're not up for whatever emotional demands might arise here. Your fuse is shorter, and you're more easily triggered. It's hard for you to actualize your best self. You need a strategy to deal with this obstacle. You can't bank mental energy for the evening's demands, but perhaps if you build in a little break between work and home, you'll be better able to deal with your feelings. Even just fifteen minutes sitting quietly in the car might be enough, or a short mindfulness exercise, or a half hour on the treadmill at the gym. Maybe anticipating what the post-work hours will bring can help you plan how best to respond.

Anything is better than snapping at a child or a significant other and then spending the rest of the night thinking, *Why did I say that? Why can't I be better at this?*

I talk to a lot of educators, and this is an especially big problem for them. They spend all day surrounded by children, dealing with their needs and desires, and then they go home to the same kinds of challenges. And when their ability to deal is stretched a little too thin, they feel guilty about it—somebody else's kids are getting their best efforts, while their own children are faced with exhausted, depleted moms and dads.

Another obstacle is our failure to take care of our physical health. As we've already discussed, this means good nutrition, physical activity, and sufficient sleep. Our brains require huge amounts of energy to function at their peak. They are fueled by the same things that the rest of our bodies depend on. Neglect your health and you'll never have the mental powers you need to be your best self.

We also must keep up our breathing and mindfulness exercises and check in on our emotional state from time to time. These habits are necessary so that when the moment arrives to deactivate a strong emotion, we can manage without too much struggle. Over the course of each day, we need to pause and turn inward—to breathe in and out slowly, to allow our brains a few moments of calming thought.

Realizing the best version of ourselves requires time, energy, and focus. For many of us, these are often in short supply. Our intentions are good, but we lack the ability to make changes stick. That sends us spiraling into frustration, fatigue, and failure.

And when we do falter, we need to create "if-then" plans. For example, if I start feeling the urge to be impatient with my mother-in-law, then I will take a break, step outside, and do a five-minute mindfulness exercise centered on compassion. Be creative in imagining specific moments that might stop you from becoming your best self, and then plan ways to transcend them.

Perhaps the biggest obstacle to achieving our best selves is the hardest one to observe: a lack of care and compassion for ourselves.

Kristin Neff, a psychologist at the University of Texas at Austin, identifies three components to self-compassion: self-kindness, understanding that we're not alone in facing challenges, and mindfulness of our experience without being overwhelmed by it. She finds that people have much greater compassion for others than for themselves.

At a recent conference where we both presented, she shared that for many people, self-compassion feels "soft." But her view is that it actually makes us stronger. It does not involve letting yourself off the hook when you make mistakes; it simply means learning from your failures instead of beating yourself up with them.

A related false belief, Neff says, is the idea that self-compassion decreases our motivation to improve. Instead, she says, it lessens our fear of failure and instills grit and a growth mindset. In a study, she found that people with higher self-compassion used as many negative terms to describe themselves as did people with low self-compassion. But the higher self-compassion group experienced far less anxiety. Self-compassion makes us resilient regardless of the praise or criticism we receive.

The simplest form of self-compassion, Neff has found, is thinking about how you would advise a friend who's suffering from whatever's troubling you. This distancing, as we've discussed, seems to help us come up with views that are kind rather than mean-spirited.

Her research shows that individuals with higher levels of self-compassion experience reduced anxiety and depression, increased life satisfaction, improved emotional resilience, and a greater ability to cope with stress. Neff says that practicing self-compassion also results in positive outcomes: less depression, stress, shame, anxiety, and disordered eating; fewer symptoms of post-traumatic stress disorder; and decreases in suicidal ideation. It also increases life satisfaction, happiness, optimism, body appreciation, hope, and gratitude—all of which strengthen our ability to regulate our emotions.

How can we manifest compassion for ourselves? In a number of ways.

Start by asking yourself how exactly you spend your days. The answer will tell you what's getting favorable treatment and what's being neglected. Do we pack our lives with more tasks and activities than we can comfortably manage? Do we fritter time away scrolling on social media or binge-watching mindless TV? Minute by minute, we declare our priorities.

For example, if we don't fit shopping for groceries and cooking into our schedules, we wind up dining in a rush on fast food rather than eating something healthy. If we overwork ourselves and allow no space to wind down from the day, we end up sleep-deprived. It all shows how extremely important time management is to our physical health, which enables our emotion skills and abilities.

The other day a woman said to me, "Well, my best time for myself, because of my kids and everything, is from 8:30 at night until 2:30 in the morning. That's when I do my best thinking—it's when I'm most productive."

"Hang on," I said, "what time do you get up in the morning?"

"I have to be up by six to get the kids to school so I can get to work."

"So, you're getting three and a half or four hours of sleep a night?"

"Yeah," she said.

"How's that going for you?" I asked.

"I'm a mess!"

We need to carve out space for ourselves in our lives. Let's say we spend seven or eight hours sleeping. Another eight or so working. Maybe two hours getting to and from our job. There's eighteen hours gone, and we haven't yet taken a moment for ourselves. What will we do with those six remaining hours? Cook dinner and clean up? Hang out with the family? Scroll through our Instagram feed? Walk the dog? Pay some bills? Help with homework? Not a lot of time in there just for you, is there? Nothing to give your brain a rest and a chance to regroup. We'll never find that time unless we schedule it—like an appointment we can't miss.

I recently reached the point in my own life where I took that lifesaving step and scheduled time on most days to just stop everything and see what happens. Sometimes I'll have a rush of creative ideas related to work. At other times I daydream, or drift in and out of meditation. It's all restorative. It gives me a reliable and much-needed mental vacation. In the end, that bit of respite makes me better able to regulate my emotions and deal with challenging feelings when the time comes—and it always comes, sooner or later.

Use these breaks to do things you love that you don't manage often enough. Make a list. Could be anything—watching old movies, reading, walking in nature, listening to your favorite music, having dinner with friends, going to a sports bar, playing with your pets. Research indicates that pets can help regulate your nervous system. When you lie next to them or watch them in a calm state, your nervous system responds by relaxing and feeling more secure. Some of us like to journal, to commit to paper our thoughts and wishes in moments of quiet solitude. Many of us are part of religious or spiritual communities. That can be another form of mental and emotional self-care. It allows us to turn inward without the distractions of the worlds we inhabit. It gives us a chance to reconnect to who we are and to bond with other like-minded people.

But without setting time aside, we'll never get around to doing any of these.

Now, look at your own schedule and begin to fit those breaks in. We have to find space every day, even if we need to steal from the other demands on our time. If you think of this as indulging yourself, you're missing the point: Satisfying your wishes this way makes it more likely that you'll rise to the moment when the people in your life—loved ones, colleagues, everyone else—need you to be your best self.

Think of a lifeguard saving someone from drowning. The lifeguard must ensure they are strong and secure in their own position before attempting to rescue others, especially when the water is turbulent. Only when the lifeguard is composed can they provide unwavering support to another person. It's the same principle here—if you want to be your best self for the people in your life, you first must focus on *you*. Otherwise, you won't have the emotional wherewithal or the mental strength to achieve your goals.

Here's an exercise I often perform when I address business leaders and parents: I ask them to take out their phones, go to their calendars, and see if their schedules support or prevent them from living the lives they desire. I ask if they've included any opportunities for joy, purpose, meaning, and passion in their plans.

"Did you build in any fun?" I ask them. "Have you scheduled dinners with family and friends, or long walks, or time to daydream? How about yoga? Ping-Pong? Sitcoms? Did you block out some time to go outside and stare at clouds?"

You can imagine the looks I get.

I've always loved this quote by Benjamin Franklin: "Dost thou love life? Then do not squander Time; for that's the Stuff Life is made of." We need to realize that when we spend time, what we're really spending is our lives.

I'm the kind of person who needs a little solitude every day, so I started taking post-work walks on trails near our home. Those walks calm my brain after a long day of cogitating and make it easier for me to live up to my own best-self ideals.

Here's another, not so obvious way of being nicer to ourselves. Just as it's better to prevent sickness than to treat it, it's better to avoid a triggering emotional moment than to wrestle with it. James Gross calls this "situation selection." It's about intentionally cultivating our best selves—preparing to show up as the person we aspire to be, even before we arrive. We discussed this earlier: Situation selection means not sitting next to a colleague who gossips, and not driving by the ice cream shop that has irresistible hot fudge, and not going on vacation with a relative who doesn't know when to stop talking, and realizing ahead of time that you'll be anxious in a meeting with a disgruntled client. Watching your spouse cook makes you nervous? Take a walk and come back when it's time to eat.

I work with schools where kids are being taught how to handle being bullied, which is useful, but it's not a replacement preventing it from happening altogether. The more we address the problems that cause bullying, the less time we'll have to spend supporting children (or adults) who have been its victims.

Of course, no matter how hard we try, we're all works in progress. We can set wonderful emotion regulation goals, but sometimes we'll fail. You'll be so tired you forget to take that breath and remain still for a moment. Or you'll be so activated that your worst self will leap out before your best self can stop it.

Now what? Do we ignore what we said or did, deny it, or attempt to excuse it? We've tried all three in the past.

There's a better option: Apologize for it. Own it.

Like Elton John sang, sorry seems to be the hardest word. It's an admission of a failure that might have wounded someone else, and who wants to own that? But if to be human is to fail, what exactly are we owning when we apologize? And what does it say when we seem incapable of admitting that we were wrong? That deep down we don't believe we did or said anything deserving of apology? Or that the rest of the human race must embrace us, right or wrong? Either way, it probably doesn't reflect your idea of your best self.

It's the job of our best self to acknowledge the existence of our worst self, but not to accept it.

An apology is a sign of fearlessness. It's an admission that we can be both wrong and strong. But the inability to acknowledge our missteps says we can't accept our humanity or the fallibility that comes with it.

As we apologize, we must also be willing to forgive ourselves and others. And, as Harriet Lerner, author of *Why Won't You Apologize?*, reminds us, it's not about accepting that what happened was okay, or even about continuing a relationship. Rather, it's an acknowledgment of what did happen rather than what should have happened—the latter being a recipe for a lifetime of bitter rumination.

People who report higher levels of forgiveness have better health habits and decreased depression, anxiety, and anger levels. They even feel "lighter"—both mentally and physically.

Even in couples working through a betrayal, greater levels of forgiveness are associated with more satisfied relationships, a stronger parenting alliance, and children's perceptions of parents being capable of functioning properly. Physiologically, higher reported levels of forgiveness are even associated with a lower white blood cell count, a sign of low inflammation.

Even for someone who has been dubbed a Feelings Master, finding my best self on every occasion is not always easy or simple.

I'm much better at this than I once was. But when I'm triggered, there are still times when I want to react immediately and say exactly what's on my mind. I have to remind myself to pause and take the Meta-Moment, because that's what my best self would do. I think, *Marc, you don't need to say what's on your mind. It's not going to have a positive effect. You want this person to be on your side. You don't want to alienate him or put him on the defensive. How do you want this moment to turn out? Your best self needs to step up and make that happen.*

As you can see, there's a fair amount of convincing I have to do in those moments. Whenever we're triggered and about to say or do something rash, we need to ask ourselves, *Is it worth it?* Chances are the answer will be *No*.

Let's go back now to your list of the things your best self is all about. Make sure it reflects your life and your needs.

This is a place to start.

How will you become that person? Not just by making lists, of course, or by vowing to fulfill some vision of who you might be.

You'll become that person in small acts, by dealing wisely with your feelings, one by one. Those small acts will add up to a new version of you. Not perfect, of course. But better.

# Epilogue
## A VISION REALIZED

I started this book by asking you to imagine a world where parents, kids, bosses, CEOs, artists, and policymakers alike have learned and applied the skills of emotion regulation.

That dream is starting to take shape. You've discovered what's needed to make that vision a reality, though there's still a path ahead.

Imagine it's a year from now, and you've embraced and consistently applied the strategies outlined in this book. Pause for a moment and ask yourself: *How has my life transformed?* Consider your relationships, your work, and even how you approach challenges. What's different for you now? How have these changes impacted your sense of well-being, your decisions, and your connections with others? Take some time to envision this future self and the ripple effects of mastering emotion regulation. How does this version of you show up in the world? Please write your response in the space provided below.

_____

_____

_____

_____

_____

_____

At the end of my seminars, I often ask people to imagine a world where everyone has learned the skills involved in regulating emotions. Here's what they say:

- We would experience lower levels of anxiety, stress, and depression, and have better mental well-being.
- We would have more harmonious relationships—we'd be more considerate, empathic, and kind.
- There would be less bullying and conflict and more collaboration and healthy dialogue.
- People would feel less lonely and more connected.
- Children would perform better at school because they and their teachers would have improved focus and resilience; there would be less stress in schools.
- Workplaces would benefit from higher morale and increased productivity because managers and leaders would be better role models.
- We'd enjoy greater social cohesion, less division, and more cooperation among diverse groups.
- We would harness our emotions to fuel creativity and innovative thinking, leading to technological advancements.
- Parents would be more patient and understanding.
- Parent-child relationships would be healthier and happier.
- People would be in better physical health—we'd be taking care of our minds and bodies because we'd recognize the connection between physical and emotional health.
- Society as a whole would function better—a more compassionate culture fosters supportive and connected communities.

To coincide with the writing of this book, I launched a YouTube series and podcast, *Dealing with Feeling*, where I interview an eclectic group of prominent scientists, actors, authors, musicians, and some of the world's leading experts in emotion regulation, including MacArthur Fellows (the genius-award winners), psychologists, Grammy-nominated artists, US Navy SEALs, and others.

I've asked them all the same question—what differences they think we'll see once the world learns to regulate emotions in healthy, positive ways.

Here's what they shared.

> People would cause less self-inflicted drama and be less likely to stir the pot. You might notice when you are actually insecure and jealous of a workmate and you can stop and say to yourself, *That's interesting—that's a me problem that's not so and so's problem.* People will behave in a way that attracts what they want. If you can get in a state where people are doing that, that's real power.
> —Jewel, Grammy-nominated singer-songwriter and mental health advocate

> I would love to be in that world and want to work as hard as I can to get us a little closer. I see a world in which there are real connections between people. There are difficult moments, but they don't derail people or relationships. People are able to pursue valued goals, be their true selves, and channel their real passions into making changes in the world. There'll be fewer barriers and digging yourself into ditches.
> —James Gross, professor of psychology, Stanford University

> I see so much compassion and grace between people. I see healthy resolution of conflict that actually brings people deeper into a relationship with each other. I see a lot more

peace in the world. I see a path toward solving world problems.

—Jenny Wang, clinical psychologist and
founder of Asians for Mental Health

What wouldn't be different? It would not be a world of robots. It would be a world full of people experiencing emotions, but under their own terms to some degree. There would be a lot fewer instances of cardiovascular disease and cancer. Depression, anxiety, and other societal ills that cause massive suffering would come down. We'd also have more productive intergroup relationships. We would have a much more skilled and efficient workforce and better performance at work, on the sports field, and at school.

—Ethan Kross, author of *Chatter* and professor of psychology,
University of Michigan

I really do think it would be a world with more peace and less war. I think people would be much more productive. It would be greener. Food would be more equitably distributed. I'm optimistic that the future could hold exactly that vision.

—Angela Duckworth, author of *Grit* and
professor of psychology, University of Pennsylvania

I see less conflict. I see less war. I see more compassion. I see that school of nonjudgment. I see differences of opinion, but they're more easily managed to some kind of compromise or resolution. I especially think about marginalized kids. They'll have the freedom to express the full range of their emotions and not worry about being judged or vilified for having them.

—Alfiee Breland-Noble, psychologist and
founder of the AAKOMA Project

I have chills all over. Mother Nature is responding to us with her arms wide open and saying, *I was waiting for this moment.* When we are able to swim, navigate, love, fall, get back up in this beautiful chaos we call the universe, there will be a sense of liberation and respect, a bow toward life that reflects a feeling of oneness.

—Sophie Grégoire Trudeau, mental health advocate

Start this in your own little backyard. Of course, I hope those small worlds start connecting. If we can take care of what's going on in the four walls of our homes and our immediate surroundings, like in my case my band and my family . . . that should spread.

—Duff McKagan, bassist for Guns N' Roses

People are actually happier in the sense that they're content with life. People are physically and emotionally healthier. They're kinder to each other. The results: more equity and better treatment of people. That's why I want to bring this work to a billion people.

—Rich Hua, global head of EPIC Leadership at Amazon

I think it will be a more peaceful place. People will be more productive. I imagine a lot more creativity from lots of different people.

—Emily Kinney, actress, singer, and mental health advocate

I see us highly technologically advanced, completing interstellar travel. It's an actualization of the fuel that is emotion. I see hyper development and evolution.

—Rich Diviney, retired Navy SEAL and founder of the Attributes

With the right kind of emotion education we won't have the crises of meaning that is dominating young people. People feel that way because they are not listening to their emotions. We also would have much less sexism, homophobia, and racism. We'd have a sense that our economic inequality is not fair and we would change that.

—Dacher Keltner, author of *Awe* and professor of psychology, University of California, Berkeley

I have a lot of hope! If we can raise kids who can manage how they feel, they won't be threatened by how other people feel. I can hold one opinion and feel one way and someone else can hold another opinion and feel another way. We can negotiate and understand each other. I can picture a world where there is a lot less polarization, a lot more communication and negotiation, better leaders, and a lot more peace.

—Becky Kennedy, clinical psychologist and founder and CEO of Good Inside

I think work would be more fun and playful. We'd see being fallible as a strength because we've normalized appropriate failure. I see our workplaces as more courageous communities where we are much wiser about feeling and learning together, where failing is actually fun and enlivening and elevating. I see workplaces where our aspirations and our hopes are at the center rather than our fears and worries.

—Heidi Brooks, leadership expert at the Yale School of Management

I think we would have less crisis and hospitalizations. We don't have enough beds and haven't for a very long time. ER nurses and doctors would not be burned out having to take care of so many psych patients and trying to manage a broken system.

—Jessi Gold, author of *How Do You Feel?* and
chief wellness officer of the University of Tennessee System

I see a restoration of a sense of community and trust with our neighbors. A world where children aren't sequestered behind walls and screens—they are living life again.
—Jonathan Haidt, author of *The Anxious Generation* and professor, New York University Stern School of Business

I think there would be a lot more compassion. When I see how mean and cruel people can sometimes be, part of me is appalled and part of me thinks about who did not take care of you in the way you deserved. I wonder, Who didn't hear you and let you feel something? Who wasn't tender with you? For me this work has major societal implications for how we conduct a civil society.
—Lisa Damour, clinical psychologist and author
of *The Emotional Lives of Teenagers*

What's the theme that connects what I've heard from all the people I've studied and interviewed? It's that dealing with feelings is the new marker of success. It's not just a set of skills, but a universal goal capable of creating a more harmonious, productive, and compassionate world.

As a scientist, I don't make bold promises or offer magic pills. What I *do* offer is a foundation built on decades of research, practice, and human experience.

This book is your guide to cultivating the knowledge, mindsets, and skills to become the best version of yourself—and to empower others to do the same.

My hope is that you now see emotion regulation not as a quick fix but as a lifelong practice that honors your inner world and helps shape the future you want to live. After all, how you feel and how you deal with your feelings influence the quality of your decisions, relationships, health, performance, and overall well-being.

I can't promise this book will change your life. But if you put its ideas into action, it just might.

# Your Practical Guide to Building Emotion Regulation Skills

This section is designed to be a practical guide to help you build your emotion regulation skills and enhance your well-being. Use this regularly to set goals, evaluate your progress, overcome barriers, and set new actionable steps to ensure you stay on track.

Research shows it takes at least two months to form a new habit. When it comes to emotion regulation, not all emotions and strategies are created equal. Some strategies might be easier to learn and apply than others. But when you think about how long you've lived with some of your unhelpful techniques, a few months or even a year of practice to change your life should be inspiring.

Here are a few tips to help you succeed.

1. **Set clear and specific goals.** According to Ayelet Fishbach, a researcher in motivation, specificity in goal setting provides direction and a clear end point to strive toward. This also increases the likelihood that you will achieve your aims. Once we set our emotion regulation goals, it matters how we think about them.

*Approach vs. avoidance goals.* Approach goals help us move toward desired outcomes, while avoidance goals steer us away from unwanted outcomes. In the approach, we say to ourselves, *I'm going to take a Meta-Moment and think about my best self before I respond to my colleague.* In the avoidance, we think, *I'm not going to overreact.* Approach goals, which involve taking action rather than avoiding it, are associated with greater psychological well-being.

It's best to avoid using general terms like *improve, reduce,* or *increase.* The more specific goals are, the better. For example, in order to bring more gratitude into her life, the psychologist Angela Duckworth set a very concrete goal: She would look at a painting by her mother each morning and say three specific things she's grateful for.

When we set goals that are too easy or vague, we don't need to think very much about them. Specificity requires effort and thought and is incompatible with easy generalizations.

*Performance vs. mastery goals.* Performance goals focus on judging and evaluating existing abilities (e.g., I want to lose twenty pounds). Mastery goals emphasize increasing existing abilities and learning new skills (e.g., I want to learn to prepare nutritious meals). Mastery goals encourage problem-solving and active engagement, and they are associated with improving self-efficacy, knowledge, and accomplishment. When we fail with a mastery goal, it feels like a natural part of learning. When we fail with a performance goal, it feels like a personal failure.

2. **Make emotion regulation fun and enjoyable!** We like to be the person who did something, not the person who is working on something. Our minds go directly to, *Once I reach my goal, I'll be happy.* We don't like to work on the means to the end, which often includes struggle and failure.

As you're building healthy emotion regulation habits, focus on the process, not the outcome. This increases intrinsic motivation and persistence. Don't fixate on the gap between where you are and where you'd like to be. We get immobilized when all we think about is the ultimate goal.

I struggle with this when writing scholarly articles. I often think, *I know the results of the study and just want to get the ideas out already!* It takes a long time to summarize research, analyze data, and explain it all, and I'm impatient. But once I let go of the outcome and allow myself to enjoy the process of learning more about a topic and writing creatively about it, producing these articles becomes more enjoyable. For example, if you find the breathing and mindfulness exercises relaxing, focus on the immediate benefits, not the long-term health effects, which are hard to track.

When you struggle or fail, give yourself permission to feel and get curious, not judgmental, about what happened. Research shows that when people are invited to feel uncomfortable, they focus twice as long on their goals.

Most goals are abandoned not because they are unimportant but because people don't enjoy pursuing them. When we look forward to performing the behavior associated with our goals, we become more intrinsically motivated to do it. In my instance, now that working out has become part of my regulation repertoire, I feel off when I don't work out.

3. **Combine strategies you want to cultivate with those you must.** Pair tasks you wish to develop with activities you enjoy or existing habits, which can make the unappealing ones easier to stick with. For example, listen to your favorite podcast while walking. Set up environmental cues and reminders to keep you focused on your goals (e.g., set an alarm for a mindfulness session at a particular time of day, or place motivational quotes around on your desk). I've benefited from something called "habit stacking," which is a form of

productive multitasking. Like many people who have desk jobs, I did a lot of sitting while writing and attending meetings. While writing this book I started to use a walking desk. That change resulted in an extra five thousand to ten thousand more steps per day. Now it's hard for me to be in a meeting and *not* walk!

4. **Share your goals.** People naturally keep their goals to themselves for fear of sounding flawed to others or failing where everyone can see. But declaring your aims helps you to articulate them. It also keeps you from setting unrealistic goals. It creates an accountability system, putting the law of reciprocity into effect. If the people around you know your goals, they will likely help you attain them. This is why a buddy system can help with mutual accountability.

5. **Pay attention to obstacles and apply "go-to" or "if-then" strategies.** When I'm working out and get the urge to quit, I remind myself of the progress I've made and the feelings of accomplishment I'll enjoy during my last set. I have a few go-to phrases like *Marc, you know how much you love that post-workout feeling!* I also have a group of friends I refer to as my "feelings mentors." They are my go-to people when I want to share a success story or need social support.

6. **Celebrate your progress and its immediate benefits.** As I've shared, emotion regulation is our life's work. There will be many successes and many failures. Take time to celebrate even small wins. *This week while walking into my home, I caught my negative talk three times and switched to more positive talk to be more present for my family.* That's an achievement: Take a bow! Also, consider the reciprocal benefits of using your strategies. Notice that when you do better at work, your homelife improves, and vice versa. That can increase motivation.

## THE DEALING WITH FEELING WHEEL

The Dealing with Feeling Wheel represents the seven broad areas of healthy emotion regulation discussed in this book. The reflections under the wheel can guide you in developing specific strategies within each area. The worksheet on page 275 can then help you to set goals and make a concrete plan for implementing the strategies. Visit my website (marcbrackett.com) to take the *Dealing with Feeling* survey and gain insights into your emotional strengths and areas for growth.

## THE HIDDEN DRIVER OF REGULATION: YOUR BELIEFS ABOUT EMOTIONS

Your mindset about emotions significantly influences how you experience and respond to them. Adopting a growth mindset can lead to healthier emotion regulation.

**Reflections:**

- I allow myself to experience the full range of emotions, both pleasant and unpleasant, without shame or resistance.
- I believe that all emotions serve a purpose, even the unpleasant ones.
- I have taken steps to reshape any unhelpful beliefs I have about emotions.
- I approach emotions with openness and curiosity, seeking to understand them rather than judge them as good, bad, positive, or negative.

## FROM CHAOS TO CLARITY: LABELING YOUR EMOTIONS PRECISELY

Labeling emotions accurately is a powerful tool for understanding and managing your feelings. It improves emotional awareness and clarity and helps in regulating. Developing a more precise feelings vocabulary can lead to improved emotion regulation.

**Reflections:**

- I pause to identify how I'm feeling before responding.
- I accurately label the emotions I'm experiencing.
- I explore my emotions to discover their underlying causes.
- I am able to distinguish between similar emotions (e.g., anger vs. frustration or happiness vs. contentment).

- I practice labeling emotions in real time during challenging situations.
- I notice a difference in how I feel after I label my emotions.

## QUIETING YOUR MIND AND BODY

Breathing exercises can help us to deactivate and feel calm. Mindfulness involves being present and fully engaged in the current moment without judgment. These practices can enhance your emotion regulation skills and overall well-being.

**Reflections:**

- I have a routine or practice to calm my mind, such as deep breathing or mindfulness.
- I am not easily swept away by emotions.
- I consciously relax my body when I notice tension building.
- I am present with others.
- I incorporate mindfulness exercises into everyday activities like eating or walking.

## REDIRECTING YOUR THOUGHTS

Redirecting your thinking involves shifting from negative, unproductive thoughts to positive, constructive ones, using strategies like positive self-talk, reappraisal, and distancing. These regulation strategies are highly beneficial to your overall well-being.

**Reflections:**

- I speak to myself with kindness and encouragement.
- I consciously redirect my focus to more constructive thoughts during stressful situations.
- I have a habit of using cognitive strategies like reappraisal and psychological distancing.

- I am less critical of myself and blame myself less than before.
- When I experience pleasant emotions, I make an effort to savor and extend them.
- I take a few moments each day to reflect on things I am grateful for.

## CULTIVATING YOUR EMOTIONAL STRENGTH THROUGH RELATIONSHIPS

Healthy relationships are the cornerstone of healthy emotion regulation and emotional well-being. Strong, supportive connections with others help us navigate life's challenges and celebrate its joys.

**Reflections:**

- I communicate my emotions effectively within my relationships.
- I seek advice or emotional support from trusted people when needed.
- I find ways to acknowledge and highlight other people's positive experiences.
- I set boundaries to limit contact with people who drain my energy or cause me stress.
- I am empathic and listen to people, especially those who are having a difficult time.
- I find moments of humor, even in challenging situations, to stay positive.
- I feel emotionally strong and resilient because of my connections with others.

## OPTIMIZING YOUR EMOTION REGULATION BUDGET

Physical health directly affects emotional well-being. Regular exercise, balanced nutrition, and sufficient sleep are essential for maintaining healthy emotion regulation.

Reflections:

- I prioritize eating nutritious meals as often as possible.
- I am physically active for twenty to thirty minutes per day.
- I get sufficient sleep and feel restored each morning.
- I avoid drinking excessive alcohol as a way to deal with my feelings.
- I drink enough water daily to stay hydrated.
- I feel emotionally balanced, energized, and stable.

## BECOMING THE BEST VERSION OF YOURSELF

Being your best self involves living authentically and striving for personal growth. It's about aligning your actions with your values and aspirations. It means prioritizing tasks and making time for activities that nourish your emotional health.

Reflections:

- I create daily routines or rituals that are fulfilling and support my well-being (e.g., spending time in nature, engaging in spiritual or religious practices, listening to music, spending time with others, having hobbies).
- I avoid situations that I know will trigger unpleasant emotions.
- I stay informed but avoid getting overwhelmed by world events.
- I am consistent in applying the strategies from this book to my daily life.
- When I fail at dealing with my feelings, I reflect and problem-solve about how I could have been a better version of myself.
- I show compassion toward myself.
- I am living in alignment with my values and feel closer to becoming the best version of myself.

My hope is that this practical framework can help you enhance your emotion regulation skills and boost your well-being. By setting clear, specific goals and focusing on approach and mastery goals, you'll find more effective and satisfying ways to deal with your feelings.

I want to highlight the importance of enjoying the process, combining emotion regulation with activities you love, and sharing your goals to create accountability. Overcoming obstacles with if-then plans and celebrating your progress are crucial steps. This guide also emphasizes the roles of healthy relationships, physical health, and a growth mindset in achieving your emotion-related goals. With the Dealing with Feelings Wheel, you can assess and target specific areas for improvement. By practicing these strategies and aligning your actions with your values, you'll be well equipped to achieve your goals and become the best version of yourself.

## DEALING WITH FEELING WORKSHEET

1. Rank each of the seven areas in terms of your current level of agreement from 1 (strongly disagree) to 10 (strongly agree).

    \_\_\_\_ I am giving myself and others permission to feel all emotions.

    \_\_\_\_ I am accurately labeling my emotions.

    \_\_\_\_ I am effective at calming my mind and body and am more present.

    \_\_\_\_ I am successful at shifting from unhelpful thoughts to more constructive ones.

    \_\_\_\_ I am emotionally fortified by the supportive relationships in my life.

    \_\_\_\_ I am getting enough sleep, eating nutritious meals, and staying physically active.

    \_\_\_\_ I am making progress toward becoming the best version of myself.

2. Based on your ratings, which one or two areas of emotion regulation would you like to work on?

    Area 1:_____    Area 2:_____

3. Imagine what will be different after you've enhanced these areas of regulation. How will you feel? What do you imagine others will see? How will you have benefited from cultivating this strategy? Be detailed.

_____
_____
_____
_____

4. What specific things will you do to strengthen these areas? Remember to frame these as approach and mastery goals. Who might support you? Who might help you stay accountable?

_____
_____
_____
_____

5. What obstacles will you face in implementing this strategy? What's your if-then plan when things get in the way of you achieving your emotion regulation goals?

_____
_____
_____
_____

Downloadable PDF copies of this worksheet are available at marcbrackett.com.

# Resources

Marc's website: marcbrackett.com

Follow Marc on Instagram (@marcbrackett), X (@marc.brackett), Facebook (@drmarcbrackett), and LinkedIn.

*Dealing with Feeling* podcast on Spotify, Apple, and YouTube (@MarcBrackett): youtube.com/watch?v=YJPb_SFCplo

How We Feel app: howwefeel.org

Yale Center for Emotional Intelligence: ycei.org

RULER approach to cultivating emotional intelligence in schools: rulerapproach.org

### MENTAL HEALTH RESOURCES

The Mental Health Coalition: thementalhealthcoalition.org

Mental Health First Aid: mentalhealthfirstaid.org/mental-health-resources

National Alliance on Mental Illness: nami.org

# Acknowledgments

I am deeply grateful to the many incredible people and organizations whose wisdom, support, and inspiration have shaped my personal journey, professional growth, and the ideas brought to life in this book.

I would first like to thank my wonderful agent, Richard Pine, and the team at InkWell Management, especially Eliza Rothstein and Lyndsey Blessing, for all their guidance and care.

I'm profoundly thankful to Bill Tonelli for his unwavering support throughout the writing of this book. His invaluable guidance helped transform my own and others' academic research into something both engaging and accessible for a wide audience.

I cannot say thank you enough times to the dedicated and talented people at Celadon, the publisher of my first book, *Permission to Feel*, and this book, including Jamie Raab, my editor and publisher, and so many others on the team: Deb Futter, Rachel Chou, Margaux Kanamori, Ryan Doherty, Anne Twomey, Chloe Dorgan, Christine Mykityshyn, Anna Belle Hindenlang, Jaime Noven, Jane Haxby, Sara Carminati, and Frances Sayers. Their suggestions, support, and enthusiasm have made my dream of writing this book a reality.

I have tremendous gratitude for the creative and dedicated members of the Yale Center for Emotional Intelligence who have contributed to my thinking and made our Center what it is today, including Karen Niemi, our executive director; Robin Stern, cofounder and senior advisor to the director; our center's executive team, including Nikki Elbertson, Jessica Hoffmann, Danica Kelly, and Katy McGrath; and our senior researchers: Zorana Ivcevic, Craig Bailey, and James Floman. These talented individuals lead teams of other talented people, including: Alexandra Brizuela, Sebert Brooks, Erin Brough, Jacqueline Campoli, Sandy Chang, Aakash Chowkase, Aidan Doyle, Megan Happ, Jennifer Hay, Tangular Irby, Stella Jackman-Ryan, Mariam Korangy, Olivia Martinez, Julie McGarry, Katy McGrath, Susan Morales, Amy Norback, Rebecca Ouellette, Yifei Pei, Nathan Perez, Joanne Richardson, Amanda Roberts, Rebekah Rodriguez-Boerwinkle, Whitney Sanders, Jennifer Seibyl, Sophia Selino, and Valerie Zielinski. Lastly, I have to thank Michelle Lugo, my executive assistant and daily partner, who provided her unconditional support every step of the way. I would not have been able to write this book without her!

At Yale, I have many people to thank, including Linda Mayes, chair of the Child Study Center and Peter Salovey, past president of Yale.

I am deeply grateful to everyone who generously shared their time and expertise, offering invaluable feedback that enriched this entire manuscript, including: Lyndsey Blessing, Diana Divecha, Ron Elson, Andrea Hoban, Kathryn Lee, Alexandra Marks, Andrew Morrison, Matt Kursh, Karen Niemi, and Robin Stern. Robin, Diana, and I have spent countless hours discussing the science and practice of emotion regulation. These friends and colleagues read specific chapters and provided critical feedback: Diane Archer, Nikki Elbertson, James Floman, Jessica Hoffmann, Katharine Simon, and Sheila Ohlsson Walker. And a special thank-you to Sophia Selino who provided extensive support in pulling together the scholarly references.

I owe my physical health and stamina throughout the writing of this book to Marco Jimenez. And I'm forever grateful to my executive coach,

Diana Dill, who kept me on track and encouraged me throughout my writing journey.

While crafting this book, I launched the *Dealing with Feeling* podcast and YouTube series. Each guest influenced my thinking and taught me something about emotion regulation that I've included in this book. My guests have been Alfiee Breland-Noble, Heidi Brooks, Lisa Damour, Tracy Dennis-Tiwary, Rich Diviney, Angela Duckworth, Jessi Gold, James Gross, Sophie Grégoire Trudeau, John Haidt, Marco Jimenez, Becky Kennedy, Irene Keilback, Dacher Keltner, Emily Kinney, Ethan Kross, Rich Hua, Duff McKagan, Jenny Wang, and Jewel. I also want to thank the team who have helped to produce and manage the YouTube series, including Mike Lenz, Logan Rando, Ellyn Solis, and Kirill Myltsev. A special thank-you to Suzen Pettit and Marcus Estevez, who have provided invaluable solutions to marketing and communications.

I want to express my gratitude to the incredible team at the How-WeFeel project who have been instrumental in my thinking about how to teach emotion regulation, including Ben Silbermann, cofounder; James Regan, our lead; and the team: Marc Anders, Meredith Arthur, David Cheng, Camille Emig, Ankita Kodavoor, Ari Simon, Andreas Shelin, Sara Strand, Ryan Probasco, and Ben Weissman.

I am privileged to serve as an adviser and board member for several remarkable organizations dedicated to advancing social and emotional well-being, including Narrative 4, CASEL(Collaborative for Academic, Social, and Emotional Learning), the Rare Beauty Mental Health Council founded by Selena Gomez, and the Mental Health Coalition founded by Kenneth Cole. I am deeply grateful to the visionary leaders and dedicated individuals who inspire and support this important work, including Aaliyah Samuels, Elyse Cohen, Katie Welch, Judith Martinez, Raquel Mata, Jennifer Moore, Nicole Moriarty, and Amanda Roston.

Over the last twenty-five years, I have had the unique privilege of working with talented educators in thousands of schools across the United States and in other countries. I learned something from each person and school with whom I've interacted. I am especially grateful to a number of schools that influenced my thinking while writing this book: Girton Grammar in Australia (Vanessa Juergens, Prue Milner, Georgiana Rice, Paul Flanagan, and Donald Thompson); Harlem Community District 5 (Dawn Brooks-DeCosta); Highview Elementary School, Nanuet, New York (Matthew Lutz, Myrtelle Mehu, and Melissa Lipson); Horace Mann School, Bronx, New York (Deena Neuwirth, Javaid Khan, and Tom Kelly); John Cooper School, The Woodlands, Texas (Juan-Diego Estrada, Stephen Popp); John Philip Sousa Elementary School, Port Washington, New York (Jen Biblowitz, Meg Sheehan, Dave Meoli); NY PS/IS 226K (Evan Klein); NY PS13 (Paul Martucci); PrepaTec/Tecnológico de Monterrey, Mexico (Rafael Ábrego Hinojosa); Shepherd Glen School, Hamden, Connecticut (Valerie LaRosa-Sousa); The Willows Community School, Culver City, California (Lisa Rosenstein, Susan Sleeper, Lily Solomon).

Above all, I thank my parents, William and Diane Brackett; my uncle Marvin Maurer and aunt Phyllis Maurer; my brother Steven Nadler and my sister-in-law, Leticia Fraga Nadler, and their children, Benjamin and Sofia; my brother David Nadler; my cousin Ellyn Solis and her daughter, Esme; and my cousins Richard and Lisa Maurer and their children, Jared, Jacob, and Megan. I also have tremendous gratitude for my mother-in-law, Irene Crespo, who taught me invaluable lessons about healthy emotion regulation—far more than I could have ever imagined.

I am profoundly grateful to my husband, Horacio Marquínez, whose love and unwavering support over the past thirty years have exceeded anything I could ever hope for in a life partner. His patience and encouragement, especially as I've learned and continue to refine the strategies shared in this book, have been nothing short of extraordinary.

This book is about personal growth and transformation, powered by the science and practice of emotion regulation. Writing it has deepened my understanding of my own emotional world and strengthened my commitment to refining these skills in everyday life. My hope is that it has offered you similar insights and inspiration. Thank you for allowing me—and this book—to be a companion on your journey.

# References

## 2. SEVEN REASONS WE CAN'T DEAL WITH OUR FEELINGS

American Psychological Association. *Stress in America: Generation Z*. Stress in America Survey, American Psychological Association, 2018. https://www.apa.org/news/press/releases/stress/2018/stress-gen-z.pdf.

Brackett, Marc. "Social and Emotional Learning: Pathway to Healthy, Caring, and Successful Students." Presentation, New York State Youth Mental Health Summit, New York, NY, June 15, 2023.

Brackett, Marc, and Robin Stern. "The Truth About Emotional Intelligence: Part 1, A Brief History of Emotional Intelligence." *Psychology Today*, March 5, 2024. https://www.psychologytoday.com/us/articles/202403/the-truth-about-emotional-intelligence.

Centers for Disease Control and Prevention. "Children's Mental Health: Data and Statistics." Centers for Disease Control and Prevention, March 8, 2023. https://www.cdc.gov/childrensmentalhealth/data.html.

Christian, Sonya. "We Can't Afford Not To: All Colleges and Universities Should Have a Prison Education Program." *Liberal Education*, Spring 2023. https://www.aacu.org/liberaleducation/articles/we-cant-afford-not-to.

Chzhen, Yekaterina, Anna Gromada, and Gwyther Rees. *Are the World's Richest Countries Family Friendly? Policy in the OECD and EU*. UNICEF Office of Research,

June 2019. https://www.unicef.org/media/55696/file/Family-friendlypolicies research2019.pdf.

Crone, Eveline A., and Elly A. Konijn. "Media Use and Brain Development During Adolescence." *Nature Communications* 9, no. 1 (2018): 588. https://doi.org/10.1038/s41467-018-03126-x.

Davis, Lois M., Jennifer L. Steele, Robert Bozick, et al. *How Effective Is Correctional Education, and Where Do We Go from Here? The Results of a Comprehensive Evaluation.* RAND Corporation, March 18, 2014. https://www.rand.org/pubs/research_reports/RR564.html.

Durose, Matthew R., Alexia D. Cooper, and Howard N. Snyder. *Recidivism of Prisoners Released in 30 States in 2005: Patterns from 2005 to 2010.* US Department of Justice Bureau of Justice Statistics, April 2014. https://bjs.ojp.gov/content/pub/pdf/rprts05p0510.pdf.

Gallup. *State of the Global Workplace: 2024.* Gallup, 2024. https://www.gallup.com/workplace/349484/state-of-the-global-workplace.aspx.

Grose, Jessica. "Teachers Can't Hold Students Accountable. It's Making the Job Miserable." *The New York Times*, October 4, 2023. https://www.nytimes.com/2023/10/04/opinion/teachers-grades-students-parents.html.

Haidt, Jonathan. *The Anxious Generation: How the Great Rewiring of Children Is Causing an Epidemic of Mental Illness.* Penguin, 2024.

Harvard Business Review Analytic Services. *The Battle Against Workplace Stress: How Smart Organizations Are Creating Healthier Environments.* Harvard Business School Publishing, 2023. https://hbr.org/resources/pdfs/comm/calmbusiness/TheBattleAgainstWorkplaceStress.pdf.

Lally, Phillippa, Cornelia H. M. van Jaarsveld, Henry W. W. Potts, and Jane Wardle. "How Are Habits Formed: Modelling Habit Formation in the Real World." *European Journal of Social Psychology* 40, no. 6 (2010): 998–1009. https://doi.org/10.1002/ejsp.674.

Murthy, Vivek. "Surgeon General Discusses Health Risks of Loneliness and Steps to Help Connect with Others." Interview by Amna Nawaz and Cybele Mayes-Osterman. *PBS News Hour*, PBS, May 2, 2023. https://www.pbs.org/newshour/show/surgeon-general-discusses-health-risks-of-loneliness-and-steps-to-help-connect-with-others.

Office of the Surgeon General. *Protecting Youth Mental Health: The U.S. Surgeon General's Advisory.* US Department of Health and Human Services, 2021. https://www.hhs.gov/sites/default/files/surgeon-general-youth-mental-health-advisory.pdf.

Pearson, Catherine. "Health Panel Recommends Screening All Kids 8 and Up for Anxiety." *The New York Times*, October 11, 2022. https://www.nytimes.com/2022/10/11/well/family/anxiety-screening-recommendation-children.html.

Perry, Nicole B., Jessica M. Dollar, Susan D. Calkins, Susan P. Keane, and Lilly Shanahan. "Childhood Self-Regulation as a Mechanism Through Which Early Overcontrolling Parenting Is Associated with Adjustment in Preadolescence." *Developmental Psychology* 54, no. 8 (2018): 1542–54. https://doi.org/10.1037/dev0000536.

Santomauro, Damian F., Ana M. Mantilla Herrera, Jamileh Shadid, et al. "Global Prevalence and Burden of Depressive and Anxiety Disorders in 204 Countries and Territories in 2020 Due to the COVID-19 Pandemic." *The Lancet* 398, no. 10312 (2021): 1700–12. https://doi.org/10.1016/S0140-6736(21)02143-7.

## 3. WHAT IS EMOTION REGULATION?

Aldao, Amelia. "The Future of Emotion Regulation Research: Capturing Context." *Perspectives on Psychological Science* 8, no. 2 (2013): 155–72. https://doi.org/10.1177/1745691612459518.

Ask, K., and P. A. Granhag. "Hot Cognition in Investigative Judgments: The Differential Influence of Anger and Sadness." *Law and Human Behavior* 31, no. 6 (2007): 537–51. https://doi.org/10.1007/s10979-006-9075-3.

Baumeister, Roy F., Ellen Bratslavsky, Catrin Finkenauer, and Kathleen D. Vohs. "Bad Is Stronger Than Good." *Review of General Psychology* 5, no. 4 (2001): 323–70. https://doi.org/10.1037/1089–2680.5.4.323.

Bonanno, George A., and Charles L. Burton. "Regulatory Flexibility: An Individual Differences Perspective on Coping and Emotion Regulation." *Perspectives on Psychological Science* 8, no. 6 (2013): 591–612. https://dx.doi.org/10.1177/1745691613504116.

Brackett, Marc. *Permission to Feel: Unlocking the Power of Emotions to Help Our Kids, Ourselves, and Our Society Thrive.* Celadon, 2019.

Brackett, Marc A., and Diana Divecha. "Emotion Regulation Through the Lens of Emotional Intelligence." In *Handbook of Emotion Regulation*, 3rd ed., edited by James J. Gross and Brett Q. Ford. Guilford Press, 2024.

Braunstein, Laura Martin, James J. Gross, and Kevin N. Ochsner. "Explicit and Implicit Emotion Regulation: A Multi-Level Framework." *Social Cognitive and Affective Neuroscience* 12, no. 10 (2017): 1545–57. https://doi.org/10.1093/scan/nsx096.

Ford, Brett Q., and James J. Gross. "Why Beliefs About Emotion Matter: An Emotion-Regulation Perspective." *Current Directions in Psychological Science* 28, no. 1 (2019): 74–81. https://doi.org/10.1177/0963721418806697.

Ford, Brett Q., James J. Gross, and June Gruber. "Broadening Our Field of View: The Role of Emotion Polyregulation." *Emotion Review* 11, no. 3 (2019): 197–208. https://doi.org/10.1177/1754073919850314.

Fredrickson, Barbara L. "Positive Emotions Broaden and Build." In *Advances in Experimental Social Psychology*, vol. 47, edited by Patricia Devine and Ashby Plant. Academic Press, 2013.

Gross, James J. "The Emerging Field of Emotion Regulation: An Integrative Review." *Review of General Psychology* 2, no. 3 (1998): 271–99. https://doi.org/10.1037/1089-2680.2.3.271.

Gross, James J. "The Extended Process Model of Emotion Regulation: Elaborations, Applications, and Future Directions." *Psychological Inquiry* 26, no. 1 (2015): 130–37. https://dx.doi.org/10.1080/1047840X.2015.989751.

Gyurak, Anett, James J. Gross, and Amit Etkin. "Explicit and Implicit Emotion Regulation: A Dual-Process Framework." *Cognition and Emotion* 25, no. 3 (2011): 400–12. https://doi.org/10.1080/02699931.2010.544160.

Ivcevic, Zorana, and Marc Brackett. "Predicting School Success: Comparing Conscientiousness, Grit, and Emotion Regulation Ability." *Journal of Research in Personality* 52 (2014): 29–36. https://dx.doi.org/10.1016/j.jrp.2014.06.005.

Kam, Katherine. "How Anger Can Hurt Your Heart." WebMD, April 26, 2015. https://www.webmd.com/balance/stress-management/features/how-anger-hurts-your-heart.

Koole, Sander L., and Klaus Rothermund. "'I Feel Better but I Don't Know Why': The Psychology of Implicit Emotion Regulation." *Cognition and Emotion* 25, no. 3 (2011): 389–99. https://doi.org/10.1080/02699931.2010.550505.

Metcalfe, Janet, and Walter Mischel. "A Hot/Cool-System Analysis of Delay of Gratification: Dynamics of Willpower." *Psychological Review* 106, no. 1 (1999): 3–19. https://doi.org/10.1037/0033-295X.106.1.3.

Parkinson, Brian, and Peter Totterdell. "Classifying Affect-Regulation Strategies." *Cognition and Emotion* 13, no. 3 (1999): 277–303. https://doi.org/10.1080/026999399379285.

Salovey, Peter, and John D. Mayer. "Emotional Intelligence." *Imagination, Cognition and Personality* 9, no. 3 (1990): 185–211. https://doi.org/10.2190/DUGG-P24E-52WK-6CDG.

Scherer, Klaus R., and Grazia Ceschi. "Lost Luggage: A Field Study of Emotion-Antecedent Appraisal." *Motivation and Emotion* 21, no. 3 (1997): 211–35.

Tamir, Maya. "Effortful Emotion Regulation as a Unique Form of Cybernetic Control." *Perspectives on Psychological Science* 16, no. 1 (2021): 94–117. https://doi.org/10.1177/1745691620922199.

Tamir, Maya. "Why Do People Regulate Their Emotions? A Taxonomy of Motives in Emotion Regulation." *Personality and Social Psychology Review* 20, no. 3 (2016): 199–222. https://doi.org/10.1177/1088868315586325.

## 4. EMOTION REGULATION IN ACTION

Brackett, Marc. *Permission to Feel: Unlocking the Power of Emotions to Help Our Kids, Ourselves, and Our Society Thrive.* Celadon, 2019.

Brackett, Marc A., and Diana Divecha. "Emotion Regulation Through the Lens of Emotional Intelligence." *Handbook of Emotion Regulation*, 3rd ed., edited by James J. Gross and Brett Q. Ford. Guilford Press, 2024.

Gross, James J. "The Emerging Field of Emotion Regulation: An Integrative Review." *Review of General Psychology* 2, no. 3 (1998): 271–99. https://doi.org/10.1037/1089-2680.2.3.271.

Gross, James J. "The Extended Process Model of Emotion Regulation: Elaborations, Applications, and Future Directions." *Psychological Inquiry* 26, no. 1 (2015): 130–37. https://dx.doi.org/10.1080/1047840X.2015.989751.

## 5. WHAT IS CO-REGULATION?

Ainsworth, Mary D. Salter, Mary C. Blehar, Everett Waters, and Sally Wall. *Patterns of Attachment: A Psychological Study of the Strange Situation.* Lawrence Erlbaum Associates, 1978.

Bowlby, John. *A Secure Base: Parent-Child Attachment and Healthy Human Development.* Basic Books, 1988.

Calkins, Susan D., and Esther M. Leerkes. "Early Attachment Processes and the Development of Emotional Self-Regulation." In *Handbook of Self-Regulation: Research, Theory, and Applications*, 2nd ed., edited by Kathleen D. Vohs and Roy F. Baumeister. Guilford Press, 2011.

Cukor, George, director. *Gaslight.* Metro-Goldwyn-Mayer, 1944.

Feldman, Ruth. "Mutual Influences Between Child Emotion Regulation and Parent-Child Reciprocity Support Development Across the First 10 Years of Life: Implications for Developmental Psychopathology." *Development and Psychopathology* 27, no. 4, pt. 1 (2015): 1007–23. https://doi.org/10.1017/S0954579415000656.

Folkman, Susan, and Judith T. Moskowitz. "Positive Affect and the Other Side of Coping." *American Psychologist* 55, no. 6 (2000): 647–54. https://doi.org/10.1037/0003-066X.55.6.647.

Kaplan, Lauren A., Lynn Evans, and Catherine Monk. "Effects of Mothers' Prenatal Psychiatric Status and Postnatal Caregiving on Infant Biobehavioral Regulation: Can Prenatal Programming Be Modified?" *Early Human Development* 84, no. 4 (2008): 249–56. https://doi.org/10.1016/j.earlhumdev.2007.06.004.

Kundakovic, Marija, and Frances A. Champagne. "Early-Life Experience, Epigenetics, and the Developing Brain." *Neuropsychopharmacology* 40, no. 1 (2015): 141–53. https://doi.org/10.1038/npp.2014.140.

Liska, DeAnn, Eunice Mah, Tristin Brisbois, Pamela L. Barrios, Lindsay B. Baker, and Lawrence L. Spriet. "Narrative Review of Hydration and Selected Health Outcomes in the General Population." *Nutrients* 11, no. 1 (2019): 70. https://doi.org/10.3390/nu11010070.

Nelson, Charles A., Nathan A. Fox, and Charles H. Zeanah. *Romania's Abandoned Children: Deprivation, Brain Development, and the Struggle for Recovery*. Harvard University Press, 2014.

Niven, Karen. "Interpersonal Emotion Regulation." In *Handbook of Emotional Regulation*, 3rd ed., edited by James J. Gross and Brett Q. Ford. Guilford Press, 2024.

Niven, Karen, Peter Totterdell, and David Holman. "A Classification of Controlled Interpersonal Affect Regulation Strategies." *Emotion* 9, no. 4 (2009): 498–509. https://doi.org/10.1037/A0015962.

Ozbay, Fatih, Douglas C. Johnson, Eleni Dimoulas, C. A. Morgan III, Dennis Charney, and Steven Southwick. "Social Support and Resilience to Stress: From Neurobiology to Clinical Practice." *Psychiatry* 4, no. 5 (2007): 35–40.

Schore, Allan N. "Plenary Address, Australian Childhood Foundation Conference Childhood Trauma: Understanding the Basis of Change and Recovery Early Right Brain Regulation and the Relational Origins of Emotional Wellbeing." *Children Australia* 40, no. 2 (2015): 104–13. https://doi.org/10.1017/cha.2015.13.

Silkenbeumer, Judith, Eva-Marie Schiller, Manfred Holodynski, and Joscha Kärtner. "The Role of Co-Regulation for the Development of Social-Emotional Competence." *Journal of Self-Regulation and Regulation* 2 (2016): 17–32. https://doi.org/10.11588/josar.2016.2.34351.

Sroufe, L. Alan. *Emotional Development: The Organization of Emotional Life in the Early Years*. Cambridge University Press, 1997.

Stern, Robin. *The Gaslight Effect: How to Spot and Survive the Hidden Manipulation Others Use to Control Your Life*. Harmony Books, 2007.

Tronick, Ed. "Developmental Sciences at UMass Boston." Zero to Three, 2007, posted March 12, 2010, by UMass Boston. YouTube, 8 min., 33 sec. https://youtu.be/vmE3NfB_HhE.

Weir, Kirsten. "The Lasting Impact of Neglect." *Monitor on Psychology* 45, no. 6 (2014): 36. https://www.apa.org/monitor/2014/06/neglect.

## 6. CO-REGULATION IN ACTION

Butler, E. A., and A. K. Randall. "Emotional Coregulation in Close Relationships." *Emotion Review*, 5 no. 2 (2013): 202–210. https://doi.org/10.1177/1754073912451630.

Coan, J. A., H. S. Schaefer, and R. J. Davidson. "Lending a Hand: Social Regulation of the Neural Response to Threat." *Psychological Science*, 17, no. 12 2006: 1032–39. https://doi.org/10.1111/j.1467-9280.2006.01708.x.

Gottman, J. M., and R. W. Levenson. "Assessing the Role of Emotion in Marriage." *Behavioral Assessment* 8, no. 1 (1986): 31–48.

Niven, Karen, Peter Totterdell, and David Holman. "A Classification of Controlled Interpersonal Affect Regulation Strategies." *Emotion* 9, no. 4 (2009): 498–509. https://doi.org/10.1037/A0015962.

## 7. THE HIDDEN DRIVER OF REGULATION: YOUR BELIEFS ABOUT EMOTIONS

Burnette, Jeni L., Laura E. Knouse, Dylan T. Vavra, Ernest O'Boyle, and Milan A. Brooks. "Growth Mindsets and Psychological Distress: A Meta-Analysis." *Clinical Psychology Review* 77 (2020): 101816. https://doi.org/10.1016/j.cpr.2020.101816.

De France, Kalee. "The Power of Emotion Mindsets." *Psychology Today*, October 26, 2020. https://www.psychologytoday.com/us/blog/the-science-feeling/202010/the-power-emotion-mindsets.

De France, Kalee, and Tom Hollenstein. "Implicit Theories of Emotion and Mental Health During Adolescence: The Mediating Role of Emotion Regulation." *Cognition and Emotion* 35, no. 2 (2021): 367–74. https://doi.org/10.1080/02699931.2020.1817727.

Dweck, Carol S. "Growth Mindset and the Future of Our Children." *Parents League of New York* (blog), September 26, 2017. https://www.parentsleague.org/blog/growth-mindset-and-future-our-children.

Dweck, Carol S. *Mindset: The New Psychology of Success*. Ballantine Books, 2007.

Dweck, Carol S. "The Power of Yet." TEDx Talk, Norrköping, Sweden, September 12, 2014. YouTube, 11 min., 18 sec. https://youtu.be/J-swZaKN2Ic.

Floman, J. L., M. A. Kirk Chang, and M. Brackett. "The Effects of Compassion Cultivation Training (CCT) Vs. Mindfulness-Based Stress Reduction (MBSR) on Social Well-Being and Mental Health: A Randomized Controlled Trial." Presentation, Association for Psychological Science Convention, Washington, DC. May 2023.

Ford, Brett Q., Sandy J. Lwi, Amy L. Gentzler, Benjamin Hankin, and Iris B. Mauss. "The Cost of Believing Emotions Are Uncontrollable: Youths' Beliefs About Emotion Predict Emotion Regulation and Depressive Symptoms." *Journal of Experimental Psychology: General* 147, no. 8 (2018): 1170–90. https://doi.org/10.1037/xge0000396.

Gunderson, Elizabeth A., Sarah J. Gripshover, Carissa Romero, Carol S. Dweck, Susan Goldin-Meadow, and Susan C. Levine. "Parent Praise to 1- to 3-Year-Olds Predicts Children's Motivational Frameworks 5 Years Later." *Child Development* 84, no. 5 (2013): 1526–41. https://doi.org/10.1111/cdev.12064.

Gunderson, Elizabeth A., Nicole S. Sorhagen, Sarah J. Gripshover, Carol S. Dweck, Susan Goldin-Meadow, and Susan C. Levine. "Parent Praise to Toddlers Predicts Fourth Grade Academic Achievement via Children's Incremental Mindsets." *Developmental Psychology* 54, no. 3 (2018): 397–409. https://doi.org/10.1037/dev0000444.

Harmon-Jones, Eddie, Cindy Harmon-Jones, David M. Amodio, and Philip A. Gable. "Attitudes Toward Emotions." *Journal of Personality and Social Psychology* 101, no. 6 (2011): 1332–50. https://doi.org/10.1037/a0024951.

Lipson, Sarah Ketchen, Emily G. Lattie, and Daniel Eisenberg. "Increased Rates of Mental Health Service Utilization by U.S. College Students: 10-Year Population-Level Trends (2007–2017)." *Psychiatric Services* 70, no. 1 (2019): 60–63. https://doi.org/10.1176/appi.ps.201800332.

Mangels, Jennifer A., Brady Butterfield, Justin Lamb, Catherine Good, and Carol S. Dweck. "Why Do Beliefs About Intelligence Influence Learning Success? A Social Cognitive Neuroscience Model." *Social Cognitive and Affective Neuroscience* 1, no. 2 (2006): 75–86. https://doi.org/10.1093/scan/nsl013.

Mueller, Claudia M., and Carol S. Dweck. "Praise for Intelligence Can Undermine Children's Motivation and Performance." *Journal of Personality and Social Psychology* 75, no. 1 (1998): 33–52.

Tamir, Maya. "What Do People Want to Feel and Why? Pleasure and Utility in Emotion Regulation." *Current Directions in Psychological Science* 18, no. 2 (2009): 101–5. https://doi.org/10.1111/j.1467-8721.2009.01617.x.

Tamir, Maya, and Brett Q. Ford. "Should People Pursue Feelings That Feel Good or Feelings That Do Good? Emotional Preferences and Well-Being." *Emotion* 12, no. 5 (2012): 1061–70. https://doi.org/10.1037/a0027223.

Tamir, Maya, Oliver P. John, Sanjay Srivastava, and James J. Gross. "Implicit Theories of Emotion: Affective and Social Outcomes Across a Major Life Transition." *Journal of Personality and Social Psychology* 92, no. 4 (2007): 731–44. https://doi.org/10.1037/0022-3514.92.4.731.

Tullett, Alexa M., and Jason E. Plaks. "Testing the Link Between Empathy and Lay Theories of Happiness." *Personality and Social Psychology Bulletin* 42, no. 11 (2016): 1505–21. https://doi.org/10.1177/0146167216665092.

Weigensberg, Marc J., Cheng K. Fred Wen, Donna Spruijt, and Christianne Joy Lane. "Effects of Group-Delivered Stress-Reduction Guided Imagery on Salivary Cortisol, Salivary Amylase, and Stress Mood in Urban, Predominantly Latino Adolescents." *Global Advances in Health and Medicine* (February 2022): https://doi.org/10.1177/21649561211067443.

## 8. FROM CHAOS TO CLARITY: LABELING YOUR EMOTIONS PRECISELY

Aldao, Amelia. "Why Labeling Emotions Matters." *Psychology Today*, August 4, 2014. https://www.psychologytoday.com/us/blog/sweet-emotion/201408/why-labeling-emotions-matters.

Barrett, Lisa Feldman. "Are You in Despair? That's Good." *The New York Times*, June 3, 2016. https://www.nytimes.com/2016/06/05/opinion/sunday/are-you-in-despair-thats-good.html.

Barrett, Lisa Feldman. *How Emotions Are Made: The Secret Life of the Brain*. Houghton Mifflin Harcourt, 2017.

Barrett, Lisa Feldman, James Gross, Tamlin Conner Christensen, and Michael Benvenuto. "Knowing What You're Feeling and Knowing What to Do About It: Mapping the Relation Between Emotion Differentiation and Emotion Regulation." *Cognition and Emotion* 15, no. 6 (2001): 713–24. https://doi.org/10.1080/02699930143000239.

Brooks, David. "The Benefits of Emodiversity." *The Atlantic*, November 26, 2021. https://www.theatlantic.com/ideas/archive/2021/11/benefits-emotional-diversity/620629/.

Brown, Brené, host. *Unlocking Us with Brené Brown*, podcast. "Dr. Marc Brackett and Brené on *Permission to Feel*." Vox Media, April 14, 2020. 57 min., 53 sec. https://brenebrown.com/podcast/dr-marc-brackett-and-brene-on-permission-to-feel/.

Cordaro, Daneil T., Marc Brackett, Lauren Glass, and Craig L. Anderson. "Contentment: Perceived Completeness Across Cultures and Traditions." *Re-

*view of General Psychology* 20, no. 3 (2016): 221–35. https://doi.org/10.1037/gpr0000082.

David, Susan. *Emotional Agility: Get Unstuck, Embrace Change, and Thrive in Work and Life.* Avery Publishing, 2016.

Fan, Rui, Onur Varol, Ali Varamesh, et al. "The Minute-Scale Dynamics of Online Emotions Reveal the Effects of Affect Labeling." *Nature Human Behaviour* 3, no. 1 (2019): 92–100. https://doi.org/10.1038/s41562-018-0490-5.

Floman, James L., Marc A. Brackett, Matthew L. LaPalme, Annette Ponnock, Sigal G. Barsade, and Aidan Doyle. "Development and Validation of an Ability Measure of Emotion Understanding: The Core Relational Themes of Emotion (CORE) Test." *Journal of Intelligence* 11, no. 10 (2023): 195. https://doi.org/10.3390/jintelligence11100195.

Izard, Carroll, Sarah Fine, David Schultz, Allison Mostow, Brian Ackerman, and Eric Youngstrom. "Emotion Knowledge as a Predictor of Social Behavior and Academic Competence in Children at Risk." *Psychological Science* 12, no. 1 (2001): 18–23. https://doi.org/10.1111/1467-9280.00304.

Kashdan, Todd B., Lisa Feldman Barrett, and Patrick E. McKnight. "Unpacking Emotion Differentiation: Transforming Unpleasant Experience by Perceiving Distinctions in Negativity." *Current Directions in Psychological Science* 24, no. 1 (2015): 10–16. https://doi.org/10.1177/0963721414550708.

Kircanski, Katharina, Matthew D. Lieberman, and Michelle G. Craske. "Feelings into Words: Contributions of Language to Exposure Therapy." *Psychological Science* 23, no. 10 (2012): 1086–91. https://doi.org/10.1177/0956797612443830.

Lazarus, Richard S. *Emotion and Adaptation.* Oxford University Press, 1991.

Lee, Kent M., and Ajay B. Satpute. "More Than Labels: Neural Representations of Emotion Words Are Widely Distributed Across the Brain." *Social Cognitive and Affective Neuroscience* 19, no. 1 (2024): nsae043. https://doi.org/10.1093/scan/nsae043.

Lichtman, Judith H., Erica C. Leifheit, Basmah Safdar, et al. "Sex Differences in the Presentation and Perception of Symptoms Among Young Patients with Myocardial Infarction: Evidence from the VIRGO Study (Variation in Recovery: Role of Gender on Outcomes of Young AMI Patients)." *Circulation* 137, no. 8 (2018): 781–90. https://doi.org/10.1161/CIRCULATIONAHA.117.031650.

Lieberman, Matthew D., Naomi I. Eisenberger, Molly J. Crockett, Sabrina M. Tom, Jennifer H. Pfeifer, and Baldwin M. Way. "Putting Feelings into Words: Affect Labeling Disrupts Amygdala Activity in Response to Affective Stimuli." *Psychological Science* 18, no. 5 (2007): 421–28. https://doi.org/10.1111/j.1467-9280.2007.01916.x.

Lindquist, Kristen A., Maria Gendron, and Ajay B. Satpute. "Language and Emotion: Putting Words into Feelings and Feelings into Words." In *Handbook of Emotions*, 4th ed., edited by Lisa Feldman Barrett, Michael Lewis, and Jeannette M. Haviland-Jones. Guilford Publications, 2016.

Moors, Agnes, Phoebe C. Ellsworth, Klaus R. Scherer, and Nico H. Frijda. "Appraisal Theories of Emotion: State of the Art and Future Development." *Emotion Review* 5, no. 2 (2013): 119–24. https://doi.org/10.1177/1754073912468165.

Pennebaker, James W. "Putting Stress into Words: Health, Linguistic, and Therapeutic Implications." *Behaviour Research and Therapy* 31, no. 6 (1993): 539–48. https://doi.org/10.1016/0005-7967(93)90105-4.

Plato. *The Apology of Socrates*. Cambridge University Press, 1969.

Roseman, Ira J. "Appraisal Determinants of Discrete Emotions." *Cognition and Emotion* 5, no. 3 (1991): 161–200. https://doi.org/10.1080/02699939108411034.

Roseman, Ira J. "Appraisal in the Emotion System: Coherence in Strategies for Coping." *Emotion Review* 5, no. 2 (2013): 141–49. https://doi.org/10.1177/1754073912469591.

Russell, James A. "A Circumplex Model of Affect." *Journal of Personality and Social Psychology* 39, no. 6 (1980): 1161–78. https://doi.org/10.1037/h0077714.

Scherer, Klaus R., Angela Schorr, and Tom Johnstone, eds. *Appraisal Processes in Emotion: Theory, Methods, Research*. Oxford University Press, 2001.

Schrauf, Robert W., and Julia Sanchez. "The Preponderance of Negative Emotion Words in the Emotion Lexicon: A Cross-Generational and Cross-Linguistic Study." *Journal of Multilingual and Multicultural Development* 25, nos. 2–3 (2004): 266–84. https://doi.org/10.1080/01434630408666532.

Stern, Robin, and Marc Brackett. "Traumatized? Gaslit? How to Know If You're Misusing Therapy Words." *The Washington Post*, January 26, 2023. https://www.washingtonpost.com/wellness/2023/01/10/misuse-gaslighting-trauma-narcissism.

Torre, Jared B., and Matthew D. Lieberman. "Putting Feelings into Words: Affect Labeling as Implicit Emotion Regulation." *Emotion Review* 10, no. 2 (2018): 116–24. https://doi.org/10.1177/1754073917742706.

Tugade, Michele M., Barbara L. Fredrickson, and Lisa Feldman Barrett. "Psychological Resilience and Positive Emotional Granularity: Examining the Benefits of Positive Emotions on Coping and Health." *Journal of Personality* 72, no. 6 (2004): 1161–90. https://doi.org/10.1111/j.1467-6494.2004.00294.x.

## 9. QUIETING YOUR MIND AND BODY

Anderson, Ian A., and Wendy Wood. "Social Motivations' Limited Influence on Habitual Behavior: Tests from Social Media Engagement." *Motivation Science* 9, no. 2 (2023): 107. https://doi.org/10.1037/mot0000292.

Aurelius, Marcus. *Meditations*. General Press, 2018.

Balban, Melis Yilmaz, Eric Neri, Manuela M. Kogon, et al. "Brief Structured Respiration Practices Enhance Mood and Reduce Physiological Arousal." *Cell Reports Medicine* 4, no. 1 (2023): 100895. https://doi.org/10.1016/j.xcrm.2022.100895.

Elliot, Stephen. "An Introduction to Coherent Breathing." *BMED Report*, November 29, 2009. https://www.bmedreport.com/archives/7303.

Fincham, Guy W., Clara Strauss, and Kate Cavanagh. "Effect of Coherent Breathing on Mental Health and Wellbeing: A Randomised Placebo-Controlled Trial." *Scientific Reports* 13, no. 1 (2023): 22141. https://doi.org/10.1038/s41598-023-49279-8.

Goldberg, Simon B., Kevin M. Riordan, Shufang Sun, and Richard J. Davidson. "The Empirical Status of Mindfulness-Based Interventions: A Systematic Review of 44 Meta-Analyses of Randomized Controlled Trials." *Perspectives on Psychological Science* 17, no. 1 (2022): 108–30. https://doi.org/10.1177/1745691620968771.

Hafenbrack, Andrew C., Lindsey D. Cameron, Gretchen M. Spreitzer, Chen Zhang, Laura J. Noval, and Samah Shaffakat. "Helping People by Being in the Present: Mindfulness Increases Prosocial Behavior." *Organizational Behavior and Human Decision Processes* 159 (2020): 21–38. https://doi.org/10.1016/j.obhdp.2019.08.005.

Hafenbrack, Andrew C., Matthew L. LaPalme, and Isabelle Solal. "Mindfulness Meditation Reduces Guilt and Prosocial Reparation." *Journal of Personality and Social Psychology* 123, no. 1 (2022): 28–54. https://doi.org/10.1037/pspa0000298.

Ma, Xiao, Zi-Qi Yue, Zhu-Qing Gong, et al. "The Effect of Diaphragmatic Breathing on Attention, Negative Affect and Stress in Healthy Adults." *Frontiers in Psychology* 8 (2017): 874. https://doi.org/10.3389/fpsyg.2017.00874.

Mark, Gloria. *Attention Span: A Groundbreaking Way to Restore Balance, Happiness and Productivity*. Hanover Square Press, 2023.

Metz, Stacie M., Jennifer L. Frank, Diane Reibel, Todd Cantrell, Richard Sanders, and Patricia C. Broderick. "The Effectiveness of the Learning to BREATHE Program on Adolescent Emotion Regulation." *Research in Human Devel-*

*opment* 10, no. 3 (2013): 252–72. https://doi.org/10.1080/15427609.2013.818488.

Russo, Marc A., Danielle M. Santarelli, and Dean O'Rourke. "The Physiological Effects of Slow Breathing in the Healthy Human." *Breathe* 13, no. 4 (2017): 298–309. https://doi.org/10.1183/20734735.009817.

Salzberg, Sharon. *Lovingkindness: The Revolutionary Art of Happiness*. With a foreword by Jon Kabat-Zinn. Shambhala Publications, 2004.

Sedlmeier, Peter, Caroline Loße, and Lisa Christin Quasten. "Psychological Effects of Meditation for Healthy Practitioners: An Update." *Mindfulness* 9, no. 2 (2018): 371–87. https://doi.org/10.1007/s12671-017-0780-4.

Tang, Yi-Yuan, Britta K. Hölzel, and Michael I. Posner. "The Neuroscience of Mindfulness Meditation." *Nature Reviews Neuroscience* 16 (2015): 213–25. https://doi.org/10.1038/nrn3916.

Zaccaro, Andrea, Andrea Piarulli, Marco Laurino, et al. "How Breath-Control Can Change Your Life: A Systematic Review on Psycho-Physiological Correlates of Slow Breathing." *Frontiers in Human Neuroscience* 12 (2018). https://doi.org/10.3389/fnhum.2018.00353.

## 10. REDIRECTING YOUR THOUGHTS

American Psychological Association. "What Is Cognitive Behavioral Therapy?" *Clinical Practice Guideline for the Treatment of Posttraumatic Stress Disorder*. APA Div. 12, Society of Clinical Psychology, 2017. https://www.apa.org/ptsd-guideline/patients-and-families/cognitive-behavioral.

Berboth, Stella, and Carmen Morawetz. "Amygdala-Prefrontal Connectivity During Emotion Regulation: A Meta-Analysis of Psychophysiological Interactions." *Neuropsychologia* 153 (2021): 107767. https://doi.org/10.1016/j.neuropsychologia.2021.107767.

Blackwell, Simon E. "Mental Imagery in the Science and Practice of Cognitive Behaviour Therapy: Past, Present, and Future Perspectives." *International Journal of Cognitive Therapy* 14, no. 1 (2021): 160–81. https://doi.org/10.1007/s41811-021-00102-0.

Brackett, Marc, host. *Dealing with Feelings*, webcast. "Jewel Talks Overcoming Anxiety & Embracing Emotional Impermanence." Premiered February 21, 2024. YouTube, 53 min., 9 sec. https://youtu.be/6scYwkJGtws.

Brackett, Marc, host. *Dealing with Feelings*, webcast. "Can We Control the Voice in Our Heads? Harnessing Your Inner Chatter." Premiered March 20, 2024. YouTube, 58 min., 2 sec. https://youtu.be/d_CtjEYIaKs.

Brackett, Marc, host. *Dealing with Feelings*, webcast. "The *Walking Dead* Star Emily Kinney Talks Hollywood Rejection & Mental Health." Premiered June 26, 2024. YouTube, 46 min., 23 sec. https://youtu.be/6aneMhZ4JIc.

Bruehlman-Senecal, Emma, and Ozlem Ayduk. "This Too Shall Pass: Temporal Distance and the Regulation of Emotional Distress." *Journal of Personality and Social Psychology* 108, no. 2 (2015): 356–75. https://doi.org/10.1037/a0038324.

Burnett, Paul C. "Children's Self-Talk and Significant Others' Positive and Negative Statements." *Educational Psychology* 16, no. 1 (1996): 57–67. https://doi.org/10.1080/0144341960160105.

Crum, Alia J., Peter Salovey, and Shawn Achor. "Rethinking Stress: The Role of Mindsets in Determining the Stress Response." *Journal of Personality and Social Psychology* 104, no. 4 (2013): 716–33. https://doi.org/10.1037/a0031201.

Dobson, Keith S., and David J. A. Dozois, eds. *Handbook of Cognitive-Behavioral Therapies*. Guilford, 2019.

Driskell, James E., Carolyn Copper, and Aidan Moran. "Does Mental Practice Enhance Performance?" *Journal of Applied Psychology* 79, no. 4 (1994): 481–92. https://doi.org/10.1037//0021-9010.79.4.481.

Ellis, Albert. "Rational-Emotive Therapy and Cognitive Behavior Therapy: Similarities and Differences." *Cognitive Therapy and Research* 4 (1980): 325–40.

Garfield, Charles A., and Hal Zina Bennett. *Peak Performance: Mental Training Techniques of the World's Greatest Athletes*. Grand Central Publishing, 1985.

Grossmann, Igor, and Ethan Kross. "Exploring Solomon's Paradox: Self-Distancing Eliminates the Self-Other Asymmetry in Wise Reasoning About Close Relationships in Younger and Older Adults." *Psychological Science* 25, no. 8 (2014): 1571–80. https://doi.org/10.1177/0956797614535400.

Hoffmann, Jessica D., Kalee De France, Jennifer Seibyl, Raphael Orleck-Jetter, Ruth Castillo Gualda, and Marc A. Brackett. "The Role of Originality, Distancing, and Tentative Language in Effective Cognitive Reappraisal Among Adolescents." *Thinking Skills and Creativity* 49 (2023): 101377. https://doi.org/10.1016/j.tsc.2023.101377.

Kim, Junhyung, Joon Hee Kwon, Joohan Kim, et al. "The Effects of Positive or Negative Self-Talk on the Alteration of Brain Functional Connectivity by Performing Cognitive Tasks." *Scientific Reports* 11, no. 1 (2021): 14873. https://doi.org/10.1038/s41598-021-94328-9.

Kross, Ethan. *Chatter: The Voice in Our Head, Why It Matters, and How to Harness It*. Crown Publishing Group, 2021.

Lyubomirsky, Sonja, Laura King, and Ed Diener. "The Benefits of Frequent Positive Affect: Does Happiness Lead to Success?" *Psychological Bulletin* 131, no. 6 (2005): 803–55. https://doi.org/10.1037/0033-2909.131.6.803.

Mannix, Lisa K., Rohit S. Chandurkar, Lisa A. Rybicki, Diane L. Tusek, and Glen D. Solomon. "Effect of Guided Imagery on Quality of Life for Patients with Chronic Tension-Type Headache." *Headache: The Journal of Head and Face Pain* 39, no. 5 (1999): 326–34. https://doi.org/10.1046/j.1526-4610.1999.3905326.x.

Martin, Kathleen A., Sandra E. Moritz, and Craig R. Hall. "Imagery Use in Sport: A Literature Review and Applied Model." *The Sport Psychologist* 13, no. 3 (1999): 245–68. https://doi.org/10.1123/tsp.13.3.245.

McRae, Kateri, Bethany Ciesielski, and James J. Gross. "Unpacking Cognitive Reappraisal: Goals, Tactics, and Outcomes." *Emotion* 12, no. 2 (2012): 250–55. https://doi.org/10.1037/a0026351.

Rozin, Paul, and Edward D. Royzman. "Negativity Bias, Negativity Dominance, and Contagion." *Personality and Social Psychology Review* 5, no. 4 (2001): 296–320. https://doi.org/10.1207/S15327957PSPR0504_2.

Stern, Robin, and Marc A. Brackett. "Gaslighting Is Emotional Abuse. Here's How to Recognize and Stop It." *The Washington Post*, June 2, 2023. https://www.washingtonpost.com/wellness/2023/06/02/gaslighting-signs-strategies/.

Stern, Robin, and Marc A. Brackett. "How to Deal with the 3 Levels of Gaslighting." *The Washington Post*, April 26, 2024. https://www.washingtonpost.com/wellness/2024/04/26/gaslighting-emerging-moderate-severe-coping-strategies/.

Suksasilp, Chatrin, Sarah Griffiths, Catherine L. Sebastian, and Courtenay Norbury. "Reliability and Validity of a Temporal Distancing Emotion Regulation Task in Adolescence." *Emotion* 21, no. 4 (2021): 830–41. https://doi.org/10.1037/emo0000744.

Vaish, Amrisha, Tobias Grossmann, and Amanda Woodward. "Not All Emotions Are Created Equal: The Negativity Bias in Social-Emotional Development." *Psychological Bulletin* 134, no. 3 (2008): 383–403. https://doi.org/10.1037/0033-2909.134.3.383.

Winch, Guy. "Why You Should Start Talking to Yourself." *Psychology Today*, May 29, 2014. https://www.psychologytoday.com/us/blog/the-squeaky-wheel/201405/why-you-should-start-talking-to-yourself.

Wood, Alex M., Jeffrey J. Froh, and Adam W. A. Geraghty. "Gratitude and Well-Being: A Review and Theoretical Integration." *Clinical Psychology Review* 30, no. 7 (2010): 890–905. https://doi.org/10.1016/j.cpr.2010.03.005.

Wray, Herbert. "The (Paradoxical) Wisdom of Solomon." Association for Psychological Science, March 14, 2015. https://www.psychologicalscience.org/news/were-only-human/the-paradoxical-wisdom-of-solomon.html.

## 11. CULTIVATING YOUR EMOTIONAL STRENGTH THROUGH RELATIONSHIPS

Brackett, Marc, host. *Dealing with Feelings*, webcast. "Did Angela Duckworth Lose Her Grit?" Premiered March 6, 2024. YouTube, 42 min., 4 sec. https://youtu.be/UD8OzWZjoEc.

Butler, Emily A., and Ashley K. Randall. "Emotional Coregulation in Close Relationships." *Emotion Review* 5, no. 2 (2013): 202–10. https://doi.org/10.1177/1754073912451630.

Cacioppo, John T., and William Patrick. *Loneliness: Human Nature and the Need for Social Connection*. W. W. Norton, 2009.

Cedars Sinai. "The Science of Kindness." *Cedars-Sinai Blog*, February 13, 2019. https://www.cedars-sinai.org/blog/science-of-kindness.html.

Cox, Daniel A. "Men's Social Circles Are Shrinking." Survey Center on American Life, June 29, 2021. https://www.americansurveycenter.org/why-mens-social-circles-are-shrinking/.

Curry, Oliver Scott, Lee A. Rowland, Caspar J. Van Lissa, Sally Zlotowitz, John McAlaney, and Harvey Whitehouse. "Happy to Help? A Systematic Review and Meta-Analysis of the Effects of Performing Acts of Kindness on the Well-Being of the Actor." *Journal of Experimental Social Psychology* 76 (2018): 320–29. https://doi.org/10.1016/j.jesp.2018.02.014.

Dahl, Melissa. "Why You Should Never Worry Alone." *The Cut*, January 21, 2015. https://www.thecut.com/2015/01/why-you-should-never-worry-alone.html.

Dunn, Elizabeth W., Lara B. Aknin, and Michael I. Norton. "Spending Money on Others Promotes Happiness." *Science* 319, no. 5870 (2008): 1687–88. https://doi.org/10.1126/science.1150952.

Holt-Lunstad, Julianne, Timothy B. Smith, and J. Bradley Layton. "Social Relationships and Mortality Risk: A Meta-Analytic Review." *PLoS Medicine* 7, no. 7 (2010): e1000316. https://doi.org/10.1371/journal.pmed.1000316.

Inagaki, Tristen K., and Edward Orehek. "On the Benefits of Giving Social Support: When, Why, and How Support Providers Gain by Caring for Others." *Current Directions in Psychological Science* 26, no. 2 (2017): 109–13. https://doi.org/10.1177/0963721416686212.

Kross, Ethan. *Chatter: The Voice in Our Head, Why It Matters, and How to Harness It*. Crown Publishing Group, 2021.

Martino, Jessica, Jennifer Pegg, and Elizabeth Pegg Frates. "The Connection Prescription: Using the Power of Social Interactions and the Deep Desire for Connectedness to Empower Health and Wellness." *American Journal of Lifestyle Medicine* 11, no. 6 (2015): 466–75. https://doi.org/10.1177/1559827615608788.

Morelli, Sylvia A., Matthew D. Lieberman, and Jamil Zaki. "The Emerging Study of Positive Empathy." *Social and Personality Psychology Compass* 9, no. 2 (2015): 57–68. https://doi.org/10.1111/spc3.12157.

Office of the Surgeon General. *Our Epidemic of Loneliness and Isolation: The U.S. Surgeon General's Advisory on the Healing Effects of Social Connection and Community.* US Department of Health and Human Services, 2023. https://www.hhs.gov/sites/default/files/surgeon-general-social-connection-advisory.pdf.

Poulin, Michael J., Stephanie L. Brown, Amanda J. Dillard, and Dylan M. Smith. "Giving to Others and the Association Between Stress and Mortality." *American Journal of Public Health* 103, no. 9 (2013): 1649–55. https://doi.org/10.2105/AJPH.2012.300876.

Reed, Paul. "Coming Together to Address Loneliness and Isolation." *Health and Well-Being Matter* (blog), Office of Disease Prevention and Health Promotion, US Department of Health and Human Services, May 29, 2024. https://health.gov/news/202405/coming-together-address-loneliness-and-isolation.

Rose, Amanda J., Wendy Carlson, and Erika M. Waller. "Prospective Associations of Co-Rumination with Friendship and Emotional Adjustment: Considering the Socioemotional Trade-Offs of Co-Rumination." *Developmental Psychology* 43, no. 4 (2007): 1019–31. https://doi.org/10.1037/0012-1649.43.4.1019.

Schwartz, Carolyn, Janice Bell Meisenhelder, Yunsheng Ma, and George Reed. "Altruistic Social Interest Behaviors Are Associated with Better Mental Health." *Psychosomatic Medicine* 65, no. 5 (2003): 778–85. https://doi.org/10.1097/01.PSY.0000079378.39062.D4.

Speer, Megan E., and Mauricio R. Delgado. "Reminiscing About Positive Memories Buffers Acute Stress Responses." *Nature Human Behaviour* 1, no. 5 (2017): 0093. https://doi.org/10.1038/s41562-017-0093.

Stern, Robin, and Marc A. Brackett. "Are You Exercising Good Judgment or Being Judgy?" *The Washington Post*, June 7, 2024. https://www.washingtonpost.com/wellness/2024/06/07/good-judgment-judgmental-judgy/.

Sturgeon, John A., and Alex J. Zautra. "Social Pain and Physical Pain: Shared Paths to Resilience." *Pain Management* 6, no. 1 (2016): 63–74. https://doi.org/10.2217/pmt.15.56.

## 12. OPTIMIZING YOUR EMOTION REGULATION BUDGET

Akbaraly, Tasnime N., Eric J. Brunner, Jane E. Ferrie, Michael G. Marmot, Mika Kivimaki, and Archana Singh-Manoux. "Dietary Pattern and Depressive Symptoms in Middle Age." *British Journal of Psychiatry* 195, no. 5 (2009): 408–13. https://doi.org/10.1192/bjp.bp.108.058925.

Almondes, Katie Moraes de, Hernán Andrés Marín Agudelo, and Ulises Jiménez-Correa. "Impact of Sleep Deprivation on Emotional Regulation and the Immune System of Healthcare Workers as a Risk Factor for COVID 19: Practical Recommendations from a Task Force of the Latin American Association of Sleep Psychology." *Frontiers in Psychology* 12 (2021): 564227. https://doi.org/10.3389/fpsyg.2021.564227.

Alvaro, Pasquale K., Rachel M. Roberts, and Jodie K. Harris. "A Systematic Review Assessing Bidirectionality Between Sleep Disturbances, Anxiety, and Depression." *Sleep* 36, no. 7 (2013): 1059–68. https://doi.org/10.5665/sleep.2810.

Appleton, Jeremy. "The Gut-Brain Axis: Influence of Microbiota on Mood and Mental Health." *Integrative Medicine: A Clinician's Journal* 17, no. 4 (2018): 28–32.

Ashton, Jennifer E., Marcus O. Harrington, Diane Langthorne, Hong-Viet V. Ngo, and Scott A. Cairney. "Sleep Deprivation Induces Fragmented Memory Loss." *Learning & Memory* 27, no. 4 (2020): 130–35. https://doi.org/10.1101/lm.050757.119.

Basso, Julia C., and Wendy A. Suzuki. "The Effects of Acute Exercise on Mood, Cognition, Neurophysiology, and Neurochemical Pathways: A Review." *Brain Plasticity* 2, no. 2 (2017): 127–52. https://doi.org/10.3233/BPL-160040.

Bernstein, Emily E., and Richard J. McNally. "Acute Aerobic Exercise Helps Overcome Emotion Regulation Deficits." *Cognition and Emotion* 31, no. 4 (2016): 834–43. https://doi.org/10.1080/02699931.2016.1168284.

Carter, Kiera. "Why Do I Feel More Anxious at Night?" *The New York Times*, March 23, 2023. https://www.nytimes.com/2023/03/23/well/mind/anxiety-night-sleep.html.

Centers for Disease Control and Prevention. "Chronic Disease Indicators: Sleep." Centers for Disease Control and Prevention. June 3, 2024. https://www.cdc.gov/cdi/indicator-definitions/sleep.html.

Centers for Disease Control and Prevention. "Sleep in Middle and High School Students." Centers for Disease Control and Prevention, September 10, 2020. https://www.cdc.gov/healthyschools/features/students-sleep.htm.

Dalen, Jeanne, Bruce W. Smith, Brian M. Shelley, Anita Lee Sloan, Lisa Leahigh, and Debbie Begay. "Pilot Study: Mindful Eating and Living (MEAL): Weight,

Eating Behavior, and Psychological Outcomes Associated with a Mindfulness-Based Intervention for People with Obesity." *Complementary Therapies in Medicine* 18, no. 6 (2010): 260–64. https://doi.org/10.1016/j.ctim.2010.09.008.

Demichelis, Olivia P., Sarah A. Grainger, Lucy Burr, and Julie D. Henry. "Emotion Regulation Mediates the Effects of Sleep on Stress and Aggression." *Journal of Sleep Research* 32, no. 3 (2023): e13787. https://doi.org/10.1111/jsr.13787.

Ducharme, Jamie. "Can You Really Catch Up on Lost Sleep? Here's What the Science Says." *Time*, March 4, 2019. https://time.com/5541101/how-to-catch-up-on-sleep/.

Duckworth, Angela. "Guided Mastery." *Character Lab* (blog), *Psychology Today*, October 18, 2021. https://www.psychologytoday.com/us/blog/actionable-advice-to-help-kids-thrive/202110/guided-mastery.

"Exercise Is an All-Natural Treatment to Fight Depression." Harvard Health Publishing, February 2, 2021. https://www.health.harvard.edu/mind-and-mood/exercise-is-an-all-natural-treatment-to-fight-depression.

Gallup. *Casper-Gallup State of Sleep in America 2022 Report.* Gallup, 2022. https://www.gallup.com/analytics/390536/sleep-in-america-2022.aspx.

Ganley, Richard M. "Emotion and Eating in Obesity: A Review of the Literature." *International Journal of Eating Disorders* 8, no. 3 (1989): 343–61. https://doi.org/10.1002/1098-108X(198905)8:3<343::AID-EAT2260080310>3.0.CO;2-C.

Gariépy, Geneviève, Kira E. Riehm, Ross D. Whitehead, Isabelle Doré, and Frank J. Elgar. "Teenage Night Owls or Early Birds? Chronotype and the Mental Health of Adolescents." *Journal of Sleep Research* 28, no. 3 (2019): e12723. https://doi.org/10.1111/jsr.12723.

Graham, Sarah. "Sleep Deprivation Tied to Shifts in Hunger Hormones." *Scientific American*, December 7, 2004. https://www.scientificamerican.com/article/sleep-deprivation-tied-to/.

Gross, James J., and Ricardo F. Muñoz. "Emotion Regulation and Mental Health." *Clinical Psychology: Science and Practice* 2, no. 2 (1995): 151–64. https://doi.org/10.1111/j.1468-2850.1995.tb00036.x.

Guthold, Regina, Gretchen A. Stevens, Leanne M. Riley, and Fiona C. Bull. "Global Trends in Insufficient Physical Activity Among Adolescents: A Pooled Analysis of 298 Population-Based Surveys with 1.6 Million Participants." *The Lancet Child & Adolescent Health* 4, no. 1 (2020): 23–35. https://doi.org/10.1016/S2352-4642(19)30323-2.

Heid, Markham. "Is Melatonin Safe to Take Every Night?" *Time*, October 1, 2019. https://time.com/5672106/melatonin-safety.

Hill, Vanessa M., Sally A. Ferguson, Grace E. Vincent, and Amanda L. Rebar. "'It's

Satisfying but Destructive': A Qualitative Study on the Experience of Bedtime Procrastination in New Career Starters." *British Journal of Health Psychology* 29, no. 1 (2024): 185–203. https://doi.org/10.1111/bjhp.12694.

Höppener, Marthe M., Junilla K. Larsen, Tatjana van Strien, Machteld A. Ouwens, Laura H. H. Winkens, and Rob Eisinga. "Depressive Symptoms and Emotional Eating: Mediated by Mindfulness?" *Mindfulness*, 10 (2019): 670–78. https://doi.org/10.1007/s12671-018-1002-4.

Institute of Medicine (US) Committee on Sleep Medicine and Research. "Extent and Health Consequences of Chronic Sleep Loss and Sleep Disorders." In *Sleep Disorders and Sleep Deprivation: An Unmet Public Health Problem*, edited by Harvey R. Colten and Bruce M. Altvogt. National Academies Press, 2006.

Irwin, Michael R. "Why Sleep Is Important for Health: A Psychoneuroimmunology Perspective." *Annual Review of Psychology* 66, no. 1 (2015): 143–72. https://doi.org/10.1146/annurev-psych-010213-115205.

Kim, Hyo-Min, and Sang Won Lee. "Beneficial Effects of Appropriate Sleep Duration on Depressive Symptoms and Perceived Stress Severity in a Healthy Population in Korea." *Korean Journal of Family Medicine* 39, no. 1 (2018): 57–61. https://doi.org/10.4082/kjfm.2018.39.1.57.

Kumar, Akash, Jhilam Pramanik, Nandani Goyal, et al. "Gut Microbiota in Anxiety and Depression: Unveiling the Relationships and Management Options." *Pharmaceuticals* 16, no. 4 (2023): 565. https://doi.org/10.3390/ph16040565.

Lai, Jun S., Sarah Hiles, Alessandro Bisquera, Alexis J. Hure, Mark McEvoy, and John Attia. "A Systematic Review and Meta-Analysis of Dietary Patterns and Depression in Community-Dwelling Adults." *American Journal of Clinical Nutrition* 99, no. 1 (2014): 181–97. https://doi.org/10.3945/ajcn.113.069880.

Lefevre, Frank, and Naomi Aronson. "Ketogenic Diet for the Treatment of Refractory Epilepsy in Children: A Systematic Review of Efficacy." *Pediatrics* 105, no. 4 (2000): e46. https://doi.org/10.1542/peds.105.4.e46.

Leproult, Rachel, Georges Copinschi, Orfeu Buxton, and Eve Van Cauter. "Sleep Loss Results in an Elevation of Cortisol Levels the Next Evening." *Sleep* 20, no. 10 (1997): 865–70. https://doi.org/10.1093/sleep/20.10.865.

Liu, Hongyan, Yi Yang, Yunbing Wang, et al. "Ketogenic Diet for Treatment of Intractable Epilepsy in Adults: A Meta-Analysis of Observational Studies." *Epilepsia Open* 3, no. 1 (2018): 9–17. https://doi.org/10.1002/cpi4.12098.

Liu, Yong, Anne G. Wheaton, Daniel P. Chapman, Timothy J. Cunningham, Hua Lu, and Janet B. Croft. "Prevalence of Healthy Sleep Duration Among

Adults—United States, 2014." *Morbidity and Mortality Weekly Report* 65, no. 6 (2016): 137–41. http://doi.org/10.15585/mmwr.mm6506a1.

Loehr, Valerie G., and Austin S. Baldwin. "Affective Forecasting Error in Exercise: Differences Between Physically Active and Inactive Individuals." *Sport, Exercise, and Performance Psychology* 3, no. 3 (2014): 177–83. https://doi.org/10.1037/spy0000006.

Lollies, Friederika, Marisa Schnatschmidt, Isabell Bihlmeier, et al. "Associations of Sleep and Emotion Regulation Processes in Childhood and Adolescence—A Systematic Review, Report of Methodological Challenges and Future Directions." *Sleep Science* 15, no. 4 (2022): 490–514. https://doi.org/10.5935/1984-0063.20220082.

Mandolesi, Laura, Arianna Polverino, Simone Montuori, et al. "Effects of Physical Exercise on Cognitive Functioning and Wellbeing: Biological and Psychological Benefits." *Frontiers in Psychology* 9 (2018): 509. https://doi.org/10.3389/fpsyg.2018.00509.

Mauss, Iris B., Allison S. Troy, and Monique K. LeBourgeois. "Poorer Sleep Quality Is Associated with Lower Emotion-Regulation Ability in a Laboratory Paradigm." *Cognition & Emotion* 27, no. 3 (2012): 567–76. https://doi.org/10.1080/02699931.2012.727783.

McEntee, Jesse, and Julian Agyeman. "Towards the Development of a GIS Method for Identifying Rural Food Deserts: Geographic Access in Vermont, USA." *Applied Geography* 30, no. 1 (2010): 165–76. https://doi.org/10.1016/j.apgeog.2009.05.004.

Mergenthaler, Philipp, Ute Lindauer, Gerald A. Dienel, and Andreas Meisel. "Sugar for the Brain: The Role of Glucose in Physiological and Pathological Brain Function." *Trends in Neurosciences* 36, no. 10 (2013): 587–97. https://doi.org/10.1016/j.tins.2013.07.001.

Morawetz, Carmen, David Steyrl, Stella Berboth, Hauke R. Heekeren, and Stefan Bode. "Emotion Regulation Modulates Dietary Decision-Making via Activity in the Prefrontal–Striatal Valuation System." *Cerebral Cortex* 30, no. 11 (2020): 5731–49. https://doi.org/10.1093/cercor/bhaa147.

National Institute for Occupational Safety and Health (NIOSH). "Impairments Due to Sleep Deprivation Are Similar to Impairments Due to Alcohol Intoxication!" NIOSH Training for Nurses on Shift Work and Long Work Hours, Centers for Disease Control and Prevention, March 31, 2020. https://www.cdc.gov/niosh/work-hour-training-for-nurses/longhours/mod3/08.html.

National Sleep Foundation. *National Sleep Foundation's Sleep in America Poll: Amer-*

*icans Can Do More During the Day to Help Their Sleep at Night.* National Sleep Foundation, 2022. https://www.thensf.org/wp-content/uploads/2022/03/NSF-2022-Sleep-in-America-Poll-Report.pdf.

National Sleep Foundation. *National Sleep Foundation's 2023 Sleep in America Poll: The Nation's Sleep Health Is Strongly Associated with the Nation's Mental Health.* National Sleep Foundation, 2023. https://www.thensf.org/wp-content/uploads/2023/03/NSF-2023-Sleep-in-America-Poll-Report.pdf.

O'Loughlin, Jessica, Francesco Casanova, Samuel E. Jones, et al. "Using Mendelian Randomisation Methods to Understand Whether Diurnal Preference Is Causally Related to Mental Health." *Molecular Psychiatry* 26, no. 11 (2021): 6305–16. https://doi.org/10.1038/s41380-021-01157-3.

Pacheco, Danielle, and Abhinav Singh. "Lack of Sleep and Diabetes." Sleep Foundation, October 26, 2023. https://www.sleepfoundation.org/physical-health/lack-of-sleep-and-diabetes.

Pan, Weihong, and Abba J. Kastin. "Leptin: A Biomarker for Sleep Disorders?" *Sleep Medicine Reviews* 18, no. 3 (2014): 283–90. https://doi.org/10.1016/j.smrv.2013.07.003.

Pilcher, June J., and Allen I. Huffcutt. "Effects of Sleep Deprivation on Performance: A Meta-Analysis." *Sleep* 19, no. 4 (1996): 318–26. https://doi.org/10.1093/sleep/19.4.318.

Ramsey, Drew. *Eat to Beat Depression and Anxiety: Nourish Your Way to Better Mental Health in Six Weeks.* HarperCollins, 2021.

Ravi, Dave. "13 Tips on Getting the Sleep You Need for Good Mental Health." Anxiety, March 1, 2024. https://www.anxiety.org/sleep-a-fundamental-cure-for-anxiety, archived at https://web.archive.org/web/20240425112515/https://www.anxiety.org/sleep-a-fundamental-cure-for-anxiety.

Rehm, Colin D., José L. Peñalvo, Ashkan Afshin, and Dariush Mozaffarian. "Dietary Intake Among US Adults, 1999–2012." *JAMA* 315, no. 23 (2016): 2542–53. https://doi.org/10.1001/jama.2016.7491.

Ruder, Debra Bradley. "The Gut and the Brain." On the Brain, Harvard Medical School, 2017. https://hms.harvard.edu/news-events/publications-archive/brain/gut-brain.

Ruusunen, Anu, Soili M. Lehto, Jaakko Mursu, et al. "Dietary Patterns Are Associated with the Prevalence of Elevated Depressive Symptoms and the Risk of Getting a Hospital Discharge Diagnosis of Depression in Middle-Aged or Older Finnish Men." *Journal of Affective Disorders* 159 (2014): 1–6. https://doi.org/10.1016/j.jad.2014.01.020.

Serrano, Jamie Friedlander. "How to Stop Procrastinating at Bedtime and Actually Go to Sleep." *Time*, March 18, 2024. https://time.com/6957353/bedtime-procrastination-how-to-go-to-sleep.

Singh, Ben, Timothy Olds, Rachel Curtis, et al. "Effectiveness of Physical Activity Interventions for Improving Depression, Anxiety and Distress: An Overview of Systematic Reviews." *British Journal of Sports Medicine* 57, no. 18 (2023): 1203–9. https://doi.org/10.1136/bjsports-2022-106195.

Smith, Dana G. "How Exercise Strengthens Your Brain." *The New York Times*, April 2, 2024. https://www.nytimes.com/2024/04/02/well/mind/exercise-mental-health-cognition.html.

Starkman, Evan. "What Is Revenge Bedtime Procrastination?" WebMD, August 4, 2022. https://www.webmd.com/sleep-disorders/revenge-bedtime-procrastination.

Steinberg, Hanna, Elizabeth A. Sykes, Tim Moss, Susan Lowery, Nick LeBoutillier, and Alison Dewey. "Exercise Enhances Creativity Independently of Mood." *British Journal of Sports Medicine* 31, 3 (1997): 240–45. https://doi.org/10.1136/bjsm.31.3.240.

Stone, Rebecca A., Jacqueline Blissett, Emma Haycraft, and Claire Farrow. "Predicting Preschool Children's Emotional Eating: The Role of Parents' Emotional Eating, Feeding Practices and Child Temperament." *Maternal & Child Nutrition* 18, no. 3 (2022): e13341. https://doi.org/10.1111/mcn.13341.

Strain, Tessa, Seth Flaxman, Regina Guthold, et al. "National, Regional, and Global Trends in Insufficient Physical Activity Among Adults from 2000 to 2022: A Pooled Analysis of 507 Population-Based Surveys with 5.7 Million Participants." *The Lancet Global Health* 12, no. 8 (2024): e1232–e1243. https://doi.org/10.1016/S2214-109X(24)00150-5.

Ströhle, Andreas. "Physical Activity, Exercise, Depression and Anxiety Disorders." *Journal of Neural Transmission* 116, no. 6 (2009): 777–84.

Tai, Xin You, Cheng Chen, Sanjay Manohar, and Masud Husain. "Impact of Sleep Duration on Executive Function and Brain Structure." *Communications Biology* 5, no. 1 (2022): 201. https://doi.org/10.1038/s42003-022-03123-3.

Teixeira, Kely R. C., Camila P. dos Santos, Luciana A. de Medeiros, et al. "Night Workers Have Lower Levels of Antioxidant Defenses and Higher Levels of Oxidative Stress Damage When Compared to Day Workers." *Scientific Reports* 9, no. 1 (2019): 4455. https://doi.org/10.1038/s41598-019-40989-6.

Tsai, H. J., Terry B. Kuo, Guo-She Lee, and Cheryl C. H. Yang. "Efficacy of Paced Breathing for Insomnia: Enhances Vagal Activity and Improves Sleep Quality." *Psychophysiology* 52, no. 3 (2015): 388–96. https://doi.org/10.1111/psyp.12333.

Walker, Matt. Center for Human Sleep Science, 2005. https://www.humansleepscience.com.

Wilson, M.-M. G., and John E. Morley. "Impaired Cognitive Function and Mental Performance in Mild Dehydration." *European Journal of Clinical Nutrition* 57, no. 2 (2003): S24–S29. https://doi.org/10.1038/sj.ejcn.1601898.

Witters, Dan, and Sangeeta Agrawal. "Poor Sleep Linked to $44 Billion in Lost Productivity." Gallup, March 18, 2022. https://news.gallup.com/poll/390797/poor-sleep-linked-billion-lost-productivity.aspx.

Yau, Yvonne H. C., and Marc N. Potenza. "Stress and Eating Behaviors." *Minerva Endocrinologica* 38, no. 3 (2013): 255–67. https://pmc.ncbi.nlm.nih.gov/articles/PMC4214609.

Zhang, Yifan, RuoFan Fu, Li Sun, YuJing Gong, and Donghui Tang. "How Does Exercise Improve Implicit Emotion Regulation Ability: Preliminary Evidence of Mind-Body Exercise Intervention Combined with Aerobic Jogging and Mindfulness-Based Yoga." *Frontiers in Psychology* 10 (2019): 1888. https://doi.org/10.3389/fpsyg.2019.01888.

## 13. HOW CHILDREN LEARN TO REGULATE EMOTIONS

Brackett, Marc A. "Giving Educators Permission to Feel." *ASCD Educational Leadership* 81, no. 6 (2024): 34. https://www.ascd.org/el/articles/giving-educators-permission-to-feel.

Brackett, Marc A., Craig S. Bailey, Jessica D. Hoffman, and Dena N. Simmons. "RULER: A Theory-Driven, Systemic Approach to Social, Emotional, and Academic Learning." *Educational Psychologist* 54, no. 3 (2019): 144–61. https://doi.org/10.1080/00461520.2019.1614447.

Castillo-Gualda, Ruth, Alvaro Moraleda, and Marc A. Brackett. "Preventative Initiatives to Promote Psychological Adjustment Among Primary Students: Findings of RULER Approach in Spanish Public Schools." *International Journal of Educational Psychology* 12, no. 2 (2023): 206–32. https://dx.doi.org/10.17583/ijep.10970.

Cipriano, Christina, Michael J. Strambler, Lauren H. Naples, et al. "The State of Evidence for Social and Emotional Learning: A Contemporary Meta-Analysis of Universal School-Based SEL Interventions." *Child Development* 94, no. 5 (2023): 1181–204. https://doi.org/10.1111/cdev.13968.

Divecha, Diana, and Marc A. Brackett. "Rethinking School-Based Bullying Prevention Through the Lens of Social and Emotional Learning: A Bioecological Perspective." *International Journal of Bullying Prevention* 2 (2020): 93–113. https://doi.org/10.1007/s42380-019-00019-5.

Durlak, Joseph A., Roger P. Weissberg, Allison B. Dymnicki, Rebecca D. Taylor, and Kriston B. Schellinger. "The Impact of Enhancing Students' Social and

Emotional Learning: A Meta-Analysis of School-Based Universal Interventions." *Child Development* 82, no. 1 (2011): 405–32. https://dx.doi.org/10.1111/j.1467-8624.2010.01564.x.

Elbertson, Nicole A., Marc A. Brackett, Tangular A. Irby, and Krista L. Smith. "Ensuring All Children Succeed with Social-Emotional Learning." In *The Economics of Equity in K–12 Education*, edited by Goldy Brown III and Christos A. Makridis. Rowan & Littlefield, 2023.

Goleman, Daniel. *Emotional Intelligence: Why It Can Matter More Than IQ*. Bantam Books, 2005.

Hoffmann, Jessica D., Marc A. Brackett, Craig S. Bailey, and Cynthia J. Willner. "Teaching Emotion Regulation in Schools: Practical and Actionable Steps for Educators." *Emotion* 20, no. 1 (2020): 105–9. https://doi.org/10.1037/emo0000649.

Jotkoff, Eric. "NEA Survey: Massive Staff Shortages in Schools Leading to Educator Burnout; Alarming Number of Educators Indicating They Plan to Leave the Profession." Press release, National Education Association, February 1, 2022. www.nea.org/about-nea/media-center/press-releases/nea-survey-massive-staff-shortages-schools-leading-educator-burnout-alarming-number-educators.

Salovey, Peter, and John D. Mayer. "Emotional Intelligence." *Imagination, Cognition and Personality* 9, no. 3 (1990): 185–211. https://doi.org/10.2190/DUGG-P24E-52WK-6CDG.

Schwartz, Heather L., Michelle Bongard, Erin D. Bogan, Alaina E. Boyle, Duncan C. Meyers, and Robert J. Jagers. *Social and Emotional Learning in Schools Nationally and in Collaborating Districts Initiative: Selected Findings from the American Teacher Panel and American School Leader Panel Surveys*. RAND Corporation, 2022. https://casel.org/sel-in-schools-nationally-and-in-the-cdi/?view=true.

## 14. BECOMING THE BEST VERSION OF YOURSELF

Beetz, Andrea, Kerstin Uvnäs-Moberg, Henri Julius, and Kurt Kotrschal. "Psychosocial and Psychophysiological Effects of Human-Animal Interactions: The Possible Role of Oxytocin." *Frontiers in Psychology* 3 (2012): 26183. https://doi.org/10.3389/fpsyg.2012.00234.

Carrillo, Alba, María Rubio-Aparicio, Guadalupe Molinari, Ángel Enrique, Julio Sanchez-Meca, and Rosa M. Baños. "Effects of the Best Possible Self Intervention: A Systematic Review and Meta-Analysis." *PLoS One* 14, no. 9 (2019): e0222386. https://doi.org/10.1371/journal.pone.0222386.

Gordon, K. C., Farrah M. Hughes, N. D. Tomcik, L. J. Dixon, and Samantha C.

Litzinger. "Widening Spheres of Impact: The Role of Forgiveness in Marital and Family Functioning." *Journal of Family Psychology* 23, no. 1 (2009): 1–13. https://doi.org/10.1037/a0014354.

Gross, James J. "The Emerging Field of Emotion Regulation: An Integrative Review." *Review of General Psychology* 2, no. 3 (1998): 271–99. https://doi.org/10.1037/1089-2680.2.3.271.

Higgins, E. Tory. "Self-Discrepancy: A Theory Relating Self and Affect." *Psychological Review* 94, no. 3 (1987): 319–40. https://doi.org/10.1037/0033-295X.94.3.319.

Loveday, Paula M., Geoff P. Lovell, and Christian M. Jones. "The Best Possible Selves Intervention: A Review of the Literature to Evaluate Efficacy and Guide Future Research." *Journal of Happiness Studies* 19 (2018): 607–28. https://doi.org/10.1007/s10902-016-9824-z.

Malouff, John M., and Nicola S. Schutte. "Can Psychological Interventions Increase Optimism? A Meta-Analysis." *Journal of Positive Psychology* 12, no. 6 (2017): 594–604. https://doi.org/10.1080/17439760.2016.1221122.

Markus, Hazel, and Paula Nurius. "Possible Selves." *American Psychologist* 41, no. 9 (1986): 954–69.

Meevissen, Yvo M. C., Madelon L. Peters, and Hugo J. E. M. Alberts. "Become More Optimistic by Imagining a Best Possible Self: Effects of a Two-Week Intervention." *Journal of Behavior Therapy and Experimental Psychiatry* 42, no. 3 (2011): 371–78. https://doi.org/10.1016/j.jbtep.2011.02.012.

Neff, Kristin D. "The Role of Self-Compassion in Development: A Healthier Way to Relate to Oneself." *Human Development* 52, no. 4 (2009): 211–14. https://doi.org/10.1159/000215071.

Neff, Kristin D. "Self-Compassion, Self-Esteem, and Well-Being." *Social and Personality Psychology Compass* 5, no. 1 (2011): 1–12. https://doi.org/10.1111/j.1751-9004.2010.00330.x.

Oettingen, Gabriele, and Klaus Michael Reininger. "The Power of Prospection: Mental Contrasting and Behavior Change." *Social and Personality Psychology Compass* 10, no. 11 (2016): 591–604. https://doi.org/10.1111/spc3.12271.

Seligman, Martin E., and Mihaly Csikszentmihalyi. "Positive Psychology: An Introduction." *American Psychologist* 55, no. 1 (2000): 5–14. https://doi.org/10.1037/0003-066X.55.1.5.

Seybold, Kevin S., Peter C. Hill, Joseph K. Neumann, and David S. Chi. "Physiological and Psychological Correlates of Forgiveness." *Journal of Psychology and Christianity* 20, no. 3 (2001): 250–59.

Sheldon, Kennon M., and Sonja Lyubomirsky. "How to Increase and Sustain Positive Emotion: The Effects of Expressing Gratitude and Visualizing Best

Possible Selves." *Journal of Positive Psychology* 1, no. 2 (2006): 73–82. https://doi.org/10.1080/17439760500510676.

White, Rachel E., Emily O. Prager, Catherine Schaefer, Ethan Kross, Angela L. Duckworth, and Stephanie M. Carlson. "The 'Batman Effect': Improving Perseverance in Young Children." *Child Development* 88, no. 5 (2017): 1563–71. https://doi.org/10.1111/cdev.12695.

## YOUR PRACTICAL GUIDE TO BUILDING EMOTION REGULATION SKILLS

Arch, Joanna J., and Michelle G. Craske. "Mechanisms of Mindfulness: Emotion Regulation Following a Focused Breathing Induction." *Behaviour Research and Therapy* 44, no. 12 (2006): 1849–58. https://doi.org/10.1016/j.brat.2005.12.007.

Fishbach, Ayelet. *Get It Done: Surprising Lessons from the Science of Motivation*. Pan Macmillan, 2023.

Lally, Phillipa, Cornelia H. M. van Jaarsveld, Henry W. W. Potts, and Jane Wardle. "How Are Habits Formed: Modelling Habit Formation in the Real World." *European Journal of Social Psychology* 40, no. 6 (2010): 998–1009. https://doi.org/10.1002/ejsp.674.

Torre, Jared B., and Matthew D. Lieberman. "Putting Feelings into Words: Affect Labeling as Implicit Emotion Regulation." *Emotion Review* 10, no. 2 (2018): 116–24. https://doi.org/10.1177/1754073917742706.

# ABOUT THE AUTHOR

**Marc Brackett, PhD,** is the founding director of the Yale Center for Emotional Intelligence and a professor in the Child Study Center at Yale University. He is the author of the bestselling book *Permission to Feel* (now translated into twenty-seven languages), which has transformed how individuals, schools, and organizations approach emotional intelligence. Marc is the lead developer of RULER, an evidence-based framework for cultivating emotional intelligence, currently adopted by more than five thousand schools worldwide. He is an author on more than two hundred scholarly articles, with his research featured in *The New York Times*, *Good Morning America*, *Today*, and the *Huberman Lab* podcast. A sought-after keynote speaker, he has headlined more than seven hundred conferences and advises Fortune 500 companies on integrating emotional intelligence into workplace culture. Together with Pinterest cofounder Ben Silbermann, Marc launched the award-winning How We Feel app, a powerful tool helping millions of people improve their well-being. He is also the producer of the acclaimed documentary *America Unfiltered: Portraits and Voices of a Nation*. Marc hosts *Dealing with Feeling*, a YouTube web series and podcast that brings groundbreaking insights on emotional intelligence to a global audience. He lives in Connecticut and New York City.